"This book will help you to consider t̲ ̲
and entrepreneurship—for you and your church. By tracing their origins, Andrew Root invites readers to examine the ends and aims of both innovation and entrepreneurship. Rather than helping the church and its congregants to thrive, unreflective practices of innovation and entrepreneurship can shift values and loyalties, and along the way contribute to anxiety, depression, and an overinflation of the self which works against genuine formation of the self in Christ. *The Church after Innovation* provides significant insights and questions regarding some of the most pressing challenges of our time."

—**Angela Williams Gorrell**, Truett Theological Seminary, Baylor University

"There's something satisfying about a story that is this big, bold, and revealing about how our cultural presumptions came to be—especially when so beautifully told. Root's grand narrative offers the significant benefit of showing in fine-grain detail why Christians who do not account for the shaping effects of our economic practices evacuate the content of the Christian confession. When Christians fall in love with ideas of leadership, innovation, and entrepreneurship, we can be sure they have ignored for too long the secular economic context in which they live and breathe. A timely wake-up call."

—**Brian Brock**, University of Aberdeen

"This perceptive and engaging book is a godsend for leaders and pastors seeking to cultivate the life of the church in a contemporary Western context. In a market saturated with quick-fix, innovate-or-die polemics on church growth, Root weaves a more nuanced philosophical and cultural critique of the captivity of innovation in capitalist culture with the theological insights to liberate the creativity we actually need. The tongue-in-cheek real-life stories of people like us struggling with this task humorously but effectively emphasize the real-world need for such a view of innovation and change. This book offers a richer path to help realize a transcendent creativity of epiphany (over innovation) that values people, nurtures personhood, and promotes flourishing for the church in a secular age."

—**Nick Shepherd**, FRSA, Archbishops' Council of the Church of England

"With penetrating analysis and prophetic force, Root exposes how the false idols of capitalism are being smuggled into the church through the Trojan horses of innovation and entrepreneurialism. Fashionable trends touting church 'growth' are fueling self-absorption and drawing us away from the cross of Christ. This is a bold, necessary, and urgent book."

—**Richard Beck**, Abilene Christian University; author of *Hunting Magic Eels: Recovering an Enchanted Faith in a Skeptical Age*

"Have you ever read a book and thought, 'This is on point, and I wish I wrote it'? That's what happened to me when I finished *The Church after Innovation*. Ministers hear so many leadership mantras today: Innovate! Be efficient! Get creative! Time to pivot! Find your voice! Be authentic! In this book, Root reveals these mantras and the engine that generates them to be the problem. They are not the jewelry but the chains that keep the church captive to a soul-sucking culture. Seminaries need to assign this book. Ministers need to read this book. I'm grateful to Root for so powerfully articulating the biggest problem facing the church—namely, our supposed need to innovate."

—**Tripp Fuller**, founder and host of the *Homebrewed Christianity* podcast

"Peppered with real-life examples, *The Church after Innovation* opens up innumerable pathways of faithful thought and action for our exhausting times. Root is especially adept at exposing and probing the cultural contradictions of neoliberal capitalism, exploring how they have shaped (and warped) the mission of the church and our very selves. Come for that critique and stay for fascinating dives into management theory, the promise of nothingness, the mystics behind Martin Luther, and so much more. This important book is worthy of reading and rereading."

—**Rodney Clapp**, author of *Naming Neoliberalism: Exposing the Spirit of Our Age*

THE
CHURCH
AFTER
INNOVATION

Questioning Our Obsession with
Work, Creativity,
and Entrepreneurship

Andrew Root

Baker Academic

a division of Baker Publishing Group
Grand Rapids, Michigan

Published by Baker Academic
a division of Baker Publishing Group
PO Box 6287, Grand Rapids, MI 49516-6287
www.bakeracademic.com

Printed in the United States of America

Library of Congress Cataloging-in-Publication Data
Names: Root, Andrew, 1974– author.
Title: The church after innovation : questioning our obsession with work, creativity, and
    entrepreneurship / Andrew Root.
Description: Grand Rapids, Michigan : Baker Academic, a division of Baker Publishing Group,
    [2022] | Series: Ministry in a secular age ; 5 | Includes bibliographical references and index.
Identifiers: LCCN 2022009309 | ISBN 9781540964823 (paperback) | ISBN 9781540966155
    (casebound) | ISBN 9781493438358 (ebook) | ISBN 9781493438365 (pdf)
Subjects: LCSH: Church renewal.
Classification: LCC BV600.3 .R6588 2022 | DDC 262.001/7—dc23/eng/20220329
LC record available at https://lccn.loc.gov/2022009309

Baker Publishing Group publications use paper produced from sustainable forestry practices and post-consumer waste whenever possible.

22   23   24   25   26   27   28   7   6   5   4   3   2   1

To Nancy Lee Gauche
with gratitude
for the years of our work together

CONTENTS

Preface   ix

1. Only the Creative Survive: How Mission Became Married to Innovation   1

2. We're All Sandwich Artists Now: Work and Backwash, Reversing a Historical Flow   21

3. Hungry, Hungry Markets: Workers in Contradiction, Children in Consumption   37

4. Let's Get Extra: Exploring the Secular Contradiction of Capitalism   61

5. Leave It to Management: Managing for Permanent Innovation   89

6. The Viennese Worm That Exposes the True Self: When Work Becomes about Flexible Projects   111

7. Justification by Creative Works Alone: When Creativity Becomes King, the Self Becomes a Star   137

8. Why You're Not That Special but Feel the Need to Be: Singularity and the Self   159

9. Standing Naked against Money   187

10. The Three Amigos of the Mystical Path: How the Self Is Freed from Singularity   203

11. Aesthetic Epiphanies, Mad Poets, and a Humble Example of What This All Looks Like   225

Index   238

PREFACE

(Don't Skip! Read Before Using)

In our family's best moments, our dinner table is a philosophical workshop. We once held a long debate about what makes something a chip. Owen was claiming that gluten-free chips were not *real* chips. We wondered what elements or components make something the thing it is. We all like to think about where things come from. Once, as we were eating birthday cake, Maisy, at thirteen, wondered about the origin of the phrase "You can't have your cake and eat it too." She mentioned that it was nonsensical. She had her cake and she was eating too. She offered to us that it would be better if the phrase were "You can't have your cake and eat it twice," which is basically what the phrase means. During that dinner we talked for nearly an hour about cake and possession and the loss of something even when having it. We were all, to different degrees, mesmerized by where things come from.

This book is born from that same inclination. If there is a popular or important new emphasis in Protestantism, it's innovation. Everyone seems to be talking about innovation. Innovation is popping up everywhere—congregations, denominations, colleges, foundations, camps, parachurch ministries. Institutions and leaders across the church have innovation fever. And why not? Innovation seems exciting, a way to infuse verve back into waning institutions, a way to embrace creativity and to be proactive. After all, innovation and entrepreneurship, along with creativity, are superstars of business, particularly in Silicon Valley.

Before the church baptizes innovation as the answer to its problems (or
design ideation as the way to uncover new church practice), we should ask
where innovation and entrepreneurship come from. Nothing comes from
nowhere. All perspectives, ideas, and practices have deep and rich moral codes
hidden within; they all have a history. This book seeks to excavate innovation and entrepreneurship so that those advocating or using innovation and
entrepreneurship in the church can know where these ideas come from and
what they are tied to. The reader should beware that this book is only a first
step. In this project I wear my cultural philosophy hat more securely than
my theologian's hat. This book is interpretive—where did innovation come
from and what moral visions of the self does it deliver? I can't really solve all
the problems I raise. *This is only a beginning step.* Other projects and people
will need to pick up where I leave off. This project fronts some questions for
engagement if innovation is to avoid creating more problems than it promises
to solve for the church.

I am deeply committed to the Isaiah Berlin and Charles Taylor school of
cultural philosophy that reminds us that our ways of being, and particularly
the ideas that shape us, have long historical tails. My goal in this book is to
point out the tail of innovation, entrepreneurship, work, the self, and the
church. Cornel West, in his superb book *The American Evasion of Philosophy*, expresses just what I hope to accomplish in this book, giving flesh to
how such thinking works. Referring to his own book, West says, "In regard to
method, this work is a social history of ideas. It conceives of the intellectual
sphere of history as distinct, unique, and personal sets of cultural practices
intimately connected with concomitant developments in the larger society and
culture."[1] This is exactly how I'm thinking of this project. Innovation and
entrepreneurship—for good and ill—are inextricably connected to capitalism. You can't engage with them without coming up against the claims and
commitments of late capitalism. This project examines the economic shape
of our lives, seeing how the economic shape of our lives is bound in a secular
age, pointing out how innovation and entrepreneurship play their part in how
we work. Perhaps it's better, if we are to get our feet on the ground, to say
that innovation and entrepreneurship are directly connected to the way we
work in a competitive, and at times dehumanizing, economy.

1. Cornel West, *The American Evasion of Philosophy: A Genealogy of Pragmatism* (Mad-
ison: University of Wisconsin Press, 1989), 6.

This project seeks to explore work in late modernity, tracing out its secular forms to examine how innovation and entrepreneurship bring these goods and commitments back into the church. I'll show that the flow has reversed. Where once Protestantism and its commitments flowed directly into work, shaping work, now the ways we work in late modernity (driving toward permanent innovation) have come flowing back into the church, shaping what counts as ministry.

But so what? This book is not an exercise in protectionism. My goal is not to protect ministry from the influence of late-modern neoliberal work. I am not arguing that the church shouldn't learn from the contemporary moment and must instead return to a cloistered form. Rather, I seek to show that innovation and entrepreneurship make distinct, formative claims about what it means to be a self. They inflate the self, leading to significant theological and formational (i.e., faith-formation) issues. Innovation and entrepreneurship are dependent on workers (and consumers) being obsessed with themselves. We must face this issue. Innovation and entrepreneurship are not value neutral; they are not absent of implicit commitments to certain theological anthropologies, even views of salvation history. It's true that there are many innovative and design processes that seek to be user-centered, student-centered, and driven by empathy for the user—and this disposition might fairly be called others-focused. But even these noble desires need to be tested. The cultural history of ideas embedded in the thought of Berlin and Taylor reminds us that expressed desires differ from the actual realities that shape us. This project is an excavation. It asks whether these stated desires of design and innovation are reachable. No form of human action happens outside the many forces that impact it. Just because there is the desire to have empathy for users does not mean that other goods do not short-circuit that desire. The very fact that such advocates use the phrase "user" for person may point to some underlying anthropological commitments.

In previous projects, I've sought to explore what late modernity does to us and how to respond to it theologically. I allowed thinkers such as Charles Taylor and Hartmut Rosa to lay the interpretive footing, using other thinkers to build off their core cultural-philosophical thoughts. I'll rely on another thinker here, turning to another acclaimed German cultural theorist who is not well-known in the English-speaking world (at least not in ecclesial or theological circles): Andreas Reckwitz. Reckwitz's field-defining work includes two important books, *The Invention of Creativity* and *The Society of Singularities*, the second of which was awarded the Bavarian book prize, which led to him receiving the prestigious Gottfried Wilhelm Leibniz Prize in 2019. My project here is particularly engendered from coming in contact with Reckwitz and others' theories. As with my other projects, I've used a running story line to lead readers to what the ideal construction might look like. But in this project especially, I'm using story to illustrate the importance of these ideas as they relate to Protestantism's new infatuation with innovation.

In what follows, I'll place Reckwitz's insights in conversation with the new Protestant ecclesial obsession with innovation and entrepreneurship. We'll see how this obsession is funded by both the late-modern drive toward singularity of the self and the late-modern invention of creativity as a high (at times the highest) good. But before doing so, we need to clarify what innovation is and where it came from, seeing its birth inside of capitalism and an age of authenticity. Then we'll explore how our economic systems came to be and how capitalism fits within the immanent frame we inherit.

The argument below is cumulative. It builds on itself. There may be times that you'll feel more needs to be said or that these claims need to be justified further. I ask you to hold on; many of those possible questions will be addressed in later chapters. To address them with the depth they deserve, I need to give the background. For instance, I'll make some critical assertions about creativity in the first few chapters. This may rub some readers the wrong way. I ask you to hold on and allow the argument to unfold. (If it becomes too much, you can jump to chap. 7 and my discussion of Michel Foucault and Reckwitz. But I've left this chapter toward the back of the book because it works best to build to it.)

The major portion of this book contains a cultural-philosophical discussion. But theology is not left out. After doing this cultural-philosophical work, understanding the location of our profession of faith and the location where we're called to be faithful, we can examine a way forward theologically. Yet readers should be aware that my theological construction will only be introductory and suggestive. What is actually needed in response to the church innovation fascination is still under construction (though I've made significant assertions about what kind of church is needed in my book *Churches and the Crisis of Decline*). In this book, I'll make some further suggestions, but a full-blown answer will have to wait. I'll focus on one issue in particular—the late-modern inflation of the self or the self's obsession to be an innovative, singular self inside the permanent innovation of neoliberalism. I'll then turn to three important, but often overlooked, theological offerings that come to us from medieval mysticism. I'll explore the thought of Meister Eckhart, John Tauler, and the *Theologia Germanica*, all of which, to differing degrees, influenced Martin Luther and his theology of the cross (or the "thin tradition"). These works are able to address the significant and hidden problem of the inflating of the self that a moneyed economy imposes on people, turning people in on themselves. In the final chapter I'll turn to Friedrich Hölderlin and his poetry of epiphany (and a present practical example) to hint at a way beyond the traps of innovation.

It's my hope that this project—by carefully examining both the location of our profession of faith and the constitution of this profession—will add texture and depth to this welcome desire to steward the church into faithfulness. In the end, we'll see if innovation and entrepreneurship are the most helpful ways forward for the church (and Protestantism) in the secular age of late modernity. As you'll see, it may be a medicine that does more damage than good.

I offer this project with some fear and trembling, understanding the popularity and significance of innovation and entrepreneurship, even among many whom I deeply respect. I hope this project is seen not as a deconstructive rant but as a way of deepening our shared understandings and commitment to steward the church and faithfully respond to God's action in the world.

Alone and staring at a computer screen, you can never be sure if your intentions are communicated. Only good friends and able reviewers can free you from your own presumptions. Therefore, I'd like to thank many who invested in this project and gave me invaluable feedback. Particularly, I'd like to thank my dear friend and running partner David Lose for reading the whole manuscript and providing important feedback. Bob Hosack and Eric Salo at Baker were amazing to work with again. Eric has been such an important editor, and Bob's overall belief in my work is a treasure. I understand that I don't fall into a clear category. My works have centered on ministry and church life yet have offered intricate and complicated arguments. My works are not quite ministry books and not quite guild-based academic books. Their "between" status makes me all the more humbled and grateful for Bob's vision and belief.

My colleagues and friends Michael Chan and Michael DeLashmutt provided insightful critique to my ideas. DeLashmutt's feedback was as funny as it was penetrating. Erik Leafblad and Wes Ellis, regular readers of my projects, again offered much to strengthen my offerings. I thank David Wood for his continued support and interest. Jessicah Duckworth, with her keen eye, offered a number of important insights. Jessicah has been a valuable dialogue partner since we were next-door neighbors at Princeton Seminary. It was at the same time at Princeton that I met my most trusted dialogue partner, Blair Bertrand. It's Blair, outside of Kara, that I trust my writing to most.

And it is to Kara again that I end with my loudest thanks—mostly for our life together. Our life together is a blessing too deep, an epiphany too grandly filled with grace for words.

1

Only the Creative Survive

How Mission Became Married to Innovation

I'd never used the phrase before. It seemed like an idiom covered in the dust of the 1940s. It was an expression that might have found its way into an early Frank Sinatra chorus. To be honest I hadn't really even understood what it meant until this very moment. But it perfectly encompassed this young pastor who stood before us, reading a story as the launch to his synod's annual continuing education conference. He looked *just* like "the cat that swallowed the canary."

Every time he read the words "THE CHURCH," a clever, proud, and gratified look came across his face. He tried to hide it, but it was impossible. His satisfaction with whatever shrewd end he was after, while hidden from us, caused him to emphasize those words. He read "THE CHURCH," taking his attention from the paper to reveal his eyes to this room full of pastoral colleagues. Those eyes glowed with wily self-assuredness bordering on smugness. He read, fighting back a mischievous smile:

"THE CHURCH has seen closures at an alarming rate."

"In its heyday, in the 1990s, THE CHURCH saw boundless growth, but now decline is the norm."

"The decor of THE CHURCH, which historically matched the aesthetic of its time, is now tired and unappealing to young people of a digital age."

1

"Things in THE CHURCH have become stale. THE CHURCH is connected with an America that has passed away and few want to return to a dead institution."

"We realized if THE CHURCH didn't change, it'd be finished."

"People just no longer seem interested in THE CHURCH. There is a disconnect. People don't want what THE CHURCH is offering. THE CHURCH needs to find a new angle."

"We'd seen ourselves at THE CHURCH as part of every neighborhood . . . and now our neighbors are ignoring us. THE CHURCH needs to find a unique and appealing way to connect again with its neighborhoods, providing them what they want."

This all led up to the last line in the story. As he began to read, the proud pleasure couldn't be contained, and though it was slightly inappropriate, a little smile, like a submerged buoy, popped to the surface of his face. He seemed unable to hold it under. Behind him, on a screen, the final line appeared as he read it. Fighting back a full-on grin, he read through his pleased smirk:

It is time to innovate or die. THE CHURCH knows that it is now or never. Design a new way forward or disappear. Innovation is THE CHURCH's only hope!

And now it was time for the punch line. Now this young pastor's colleagues at this continuing education event were allowed to see behind the curtain. This article wasn't about the church at all. The next slide showed the article's title, in bold: DOES APPLEBEE'S HAVE A FUTURE?

The young pastor, with feathers stuck to the corner of his mouth, said, as if it wasn't obvious, "This article I was reading isn't about the church at all! It's about Applebee's! Just like us, they know they need to change. And the decision before them is the same decision we have before us. Can we find the creativity to design new ways of being the church? Can we innovate? Like Applebee's, if we don't, we will die. Our synod needs to reinvent. If Applebee's gets it, the church better too. So that's what this conference this year is all about."

With that, I was introduced as their speaker.

Wobbled by the introduction, I was sure I appeared to the room as the very opposite of the confident cat that ate the canary. In my mind, I looked like the man who ate his Applebee's signature twenty-dollar combo meal too fast and now had disorienting heartburn and deep-fried coconut shrimp burps.

My disorientation seemed to have two sources. First, the heartburn came from the greasy, deep-fried way the well-meaning young pastor had connected Applebee's with the bride of Christ. I suppose there are analogies between Applebee's and the church. Both have institutional structures. But just as there are some structural similarities, there had to be some significant ontological distinctions, or at the least some radically different moral horizons that made the easy connection (even replacement of one with the other) between Applebee's and the church problematic. While both are struggling institutions in our shared cultural moment, don't there need to be radically different reasons for their existence and solutions to what could save them?

But the second source of my disorientation really pushed me off balance. Innovation seemed to be the ubiquitous answer for both the struggling entity Applebee's and the ministries of the church, which is the body of the dead, risen, and ascended Jesus Christ. Everywhere I go across the American Protestant church—even more so after the pandemic—people are speaking of innovation. Seminaries (like my own), local congregations, Christian colleges and universities, parachurch ministries, camps, and even foundations all have innovation on their lips.

I began to wonder why so many Protestant leaders think that innovation is important, even for some the church's last, best hope. Where did this relatively new attention to innovation come from? How did it become so pervasive? And why does it seem so powerful and important to so many smart, faithful, good leaders across the church?

All these questions were racing into my mind as I was giving my presentation. On the fly, I needed to reposition my content, and my very self, as an asset for innovation. I wasn't told I was going to need to do that until the introduction! Yet the more I tried to do this, the more questions started to populate my head—like soapy bubbles, one question produced a dozen others. The proliferating made it hard to concentrate. As I clicked forward one slide and a video clip rolled, my mind was drawn to an anecdote a friend had just told me a week before.

My friend Russ was the associate pastor of a midsized mainline church in South Jersey, a short drive from Philadelphia. It was a good, solid church.

There was nothing flashy about it. Nothing really set it apart from other mainline churches in the area. Its only peculiarity was its steady and engaged young adult ministry. A group of college students and young professionals, either studying or working in Philadelphia, regularly participated in a Sunday night worship service, Bible study, and social hour. This too wasn't flashy. But twenty young adults consistently participated, which is no small feat for a mainline church.

Russ figured this participation got the congregation nominated and accepted for a grant project from his alma mater seminary. The whole project was directed toward young adults. Its objective was to empower—and fund!— young adults' supposed innovative and entrepreneurial spirit within congregational life. The grant was made up of groups of young adults from eleven congregations. They were taken through a three-year innovation process in which they would design something new for their churches.

The first year was electric. Each group of young adults got to know each other—which was fun. They also got exposed to innovative exemplars in business, entertainment, and art—which was inspiring. The pull of creativity, and the invitation to be creative, produced a swelling sense of anticipation and excitement for Russ's group.

But it all came crashing down in the middle of year two. As Russ's group moved into designing and creating something, they became stuck. They had dozens of good ideas that could be a real help to their church. But the better the ideas, the more anxiety they produced. Only one idea could be funded. Which idea was the right one? Worse, they were haunted by the nagging possibility that maybe there was a better innovation, a more creative response, if they just kept ideating. As they looked around, their own idea didn't seem nearly as creative as those from half the other congregations they'd gotten to know. For some reason, that felt really bad. Their ideas were good, even helpful to their church, but in their minds they didn't seem to pass the threshold of being truly creative, possessing an aesthetic to admire. Their ideas were good. But they were taught that good is the enemy of great.

Russ just couldn't crack why. Why did innovation, which excitingly opened these young adults to creativity, seem to turn existential? Why was there intensity, even anxiety, to meet some aesthetic threshold? Why did invention or reinvention become competitive? There was nothing on the line! Each congregation was getting the same amount of funding, no one was kicked out for a mediocre idea, and no extra money was given for the *best* idea. Yet the need to come up with a truly ingenious, creative, and artistic innovation seemed to wrap itself around these young adults' sense of self. Russ admitted that it did the same to him. It did something to his self and his young adults' self. This had a direct impact on their faith formation.

I survived my presentation, hiding well enough that my mind was spinning around these questions. A guest speaker at an event inhabits two platforms or stages, even if only one has a podium. Both, at least for this introvert, call for a full dose of energy. The first, of course, is the stage where you give the presentation. The second stage is the table where you eat, filled with conference participants. My strategy is to find a table that will keep the topic on TV shows, sports, or even the weather—anything other than a continuation of the Q and A from the other stage.

But when those surface-level avenues of conversation close, my strategy is always to invite the person I'm sitting with to talk about themselves. I have genuine interest in both learning about them and, importantly, distracting them from asking for a personalized part two to my lecture.

At the dinner after my presentation with this synod, I found myself sitting next to one of the synod executives. I was slightly worried I'd missed the mark with my presentation. He assured me I hit the target. He was kind and welcoming, expressing his appreciation for my presentation. I asked him about the local college football team. But we only became comfortable with each other when we discussed our favorite Netflix docudrama series: *Fear City.*

As we ate our dessert, a lull descended on our conversation, so I asked him about his job. He explained that the bulk of his work had shifted over the last five years. Painfully, nine of the congregations (including three of the largest) in the synod had decided to leave the denomination. This denomination's bylaws state that the local synod, not the congregation, owns the church's building. In order to keep its building, each departing congregation needed to reach a financial settlement with the synod. So the synod was now sitting on millions of dollars, not sure what to do with the funds. There was no celebration in this financial boon. To see these congregations depart caused only pain. Added to this grief was the concern about how best (and most faithfully) to use these funds to serve the ministry of the congregations that remained.

"It felt a little like blood money," the executive told me. There was an initial push to divide the money between the remaining churches. Or to use the funds to maintain the synod's existing buildings. There were more than a dozen small, declining churches barely making budget that desperately needed roof repairs. A new roof wouldn't slow their decline, but it would keep them open another few years.

"That seemed so short-sighted," the executive said, and I agreed. "So we finally came to the conclusion that it was mission and only mission that these funds would be spent on. No roofs!"

I admired this, and I asked him what counts as mission.

Without missing a beat, he said, "innovation," equating the two. "We're funding only innovative ideas. Innovation is how we do mission. Innovation *is* mission. This money is for reinvention, for new invention, for something new. If you've got a new idea, pitch it. If it's truly creative, there's a good chance you'll get the funds. We don't want to waste this money. We want to do something creative and truly innovative with it. As you heard before your presentation, this synod is now truly and fully missional."

I actually hadn't heard anything about mission. "Missional" was never used even once. "Innovation" was—many times. In this executive's mind, to say "innovation" was to say "mission" or "missional." I was surprised with how smoothly (and seamlessly) mission and innovation were equated in his mind. In both the imagination of this executive and in the synod as a whole, mission and innovation were assumed to be of the same whole cloth. It was almost unthought (and perhaps unthinkable) that they could be different. The mission of the congregation, the synod believed, was to be innovative. An innovative congregation was a missional congregation. Period. Mission took the concrete and (in this not unusual case) complete form of innovation.[1]

I couldn't argue against the fact that equalizing the two was advantageous. The synod was sitting on a once-in-a-generation honeypot of resources. The problem was that this cache of cash offered a total and complete one-off chance. Once it was spent, it was never coming back. It was imperative that

---

1. Examples of books and arguments that move toward this fusing of mission and innovation are L. Gregory Jones, *Christian Social Innovation: Renewing Wesleyan Witness* (Nashville: Abingdon, 2016); Patrick Keifert and Wesley Granberg-Michaelson, *How Change Comes to Your Church: A Guidebook for Church Innovations* (Grand Rapids: Eerdmans, 2019); and Scott Cormode, *The Innovative Church: How Leaders and Their Congregations Can Adapt in an Ever-Changing World* (Grand Rapids: Baker Academic, 2020). These are good books, but they don't tease out how late modernity colonizes innovation.

it be spent in the best way possible, even parlayed into more resources for more long-term stability. The executive felt the heavy burden of this pressure.

The pressure intensified because of the undeniable fact that the honeypot of excess resources was oddly, and painfully, born from rotten spoil. It felt like blood money because it was the one-time payoff that produced the final and legal separation of those congregations from the denomination. The money finalized this devastating divorce, imbued with harsh words, shouting matches, threats, and wounds that both sides figured would never heal. With the divorce final, and no hope of reconciliation, the synod needed to move forward.

The Self after a Divorce

What do you do when you're left with the pain of a divorce but an influx of cash from the settlement? What's the best way to spend the money? The cultural answer is that you innovate and therefore reinvent yourself. The synod was merely following this dominant cultural narrative that we inherit. This narrative is played out in its most bombastic color on shows like the Real Housewives franchise. Though absent the bluster of reality TV, the synod revealed that it was following something like this narrative when it equated mission and innovation.

In this story line, the divorcée, flush with cash and disappointment, seeks something *new*. You innovate your lifestyle. You surely don't squander this chance to do something creative, to even become a unique self. You go to the gym and work on your abs, update your wardrobe, take a pottery class, learn about wines, and make new, more interesting, and creative friends. If you have the airline miles, you might even try to find yourself by eating in Italy, praying in India, or falling in love with a Brazilian businessman in Indonesia. You might visit these countries to find and even invent your own truest "I."[2]

Whatever you do, you tell yourself, you can't waste your chance to do and even *be* something different—to lean into your creative self and find out what makes you uniquely you. If you can find that creative self, you'll be happy, and your cheating spouse will regret they ever left you. Your new creative

2. This reinvention plays out in Elizabeth Gilbert's bestselling memoir and film, *Eat, Pray, Love*, the epitome of the many such cultural narratives of the divorcée innovating a new self.

self will attract new friends, lovers, experiences, and your former spouse's
jealousy. Or perhaps the result will be that you pacify the pain of what's been
lost by reinventing yourself into a new self. What greater mercy for your self,
bestowed by you, than to become a new self who lets go of all those past
disappointments?[3] You can now be a self who lives beyond, who doesn't even
remember, the losses of the old, less creative world that you once inhabited.
You can even call the divorce good, or at least necessary, because it got you out
of your rut, replanting you into creativity and helping you find your unique
voice, vision, and direction. At all costs, you use the disappointment and the
funds of the settlement to make a creative switch, to innovate your way of
being in the world in your mission of being a happier self, having unique and
creative experiences.[4]

Money for the Creative

Money buys the opportunity to be creative and seek innovation. Of course,
sensibly spent money can buy security and stability. Those things are nice and
important but also boring, our culture assumes. The wrong way to respond to
a divorce and its financial settlement is to choose security and hunker down
with your disappointment and max out your 401(k) (or to upgrade roofs).
Money can create stability, but not creativity. A new roof would give a small
church some measure of security and budget stability for years, maybe a
decade. But it would not provide the new creative thrust to shake that little
church loose from its drab commonality, pushing it into the future.

Within the logic of late modernity, it's assumed that without the creativity
of the self, there simply is no future. Or to state it more brashly and bleakly,
it's assumed that without the creativity of the self (without creative uniqueness), there's no real reason to live at all. Creativity has a powerful place in
the vision and commitments of late modernity. True, creativity is a good and
deeply theological commitment. But blended with the pursuits of the self in

---

3. See Glennon Doyle as an example of this.
4. Andreas Reckwitz adds, "The demand to be creative calls on people to realize their innate
potential by working on themselves. This universalization of creativity leads to a second social
differentiation between creative and non-creative acts and people. If creative achievement secures
social inclusion, then a deficiency therein will lead to social demotion and marginalization. The
deficient must assume the responsibility for not having made proper use of their potential."
Reckwitz, *The Invention of Creativity: Modern Society and the Culture of the New* (Malden,
MA: Polity, 2017), 222.

late-modern capitalism, it becomes something the self performs (we'll explore this further in chap. 7).[5]

In late modernity, the individual or institution that doesn't want to be creative doesn't want to live well. These individuals or institutions must change and seek creativity; they need innovation. Late modernity asserts that the best way to ride into the future, and not to be defeated by the future, is on the wave of creativity produced by the self.[6] To not want to be creative is to not want a future, to not want to be unique, to not care to be a distinct self. The ultimate aim of being a self is to seek and curate your inherited (and yet somehow at the same time, achieved) uniqueness.

The synod assumed that the money would be wasted if spent on anything other than creativity and innovation in its congregations. The synod needed to be missional, because mission was never a waste. That approach seemed theologically justifiable, but even more so, it fit the presumptions of late modernity. Mission could never be a waste because it was assumed to be a creative enterprise. Mission fused with innovation because both attended directly to the future, seeking creative ways to move into something new. The synod felt deep down that it would be a waste to not spend the money on a creative initiative, because creativity (never just cash) secures a future.

Because innovation could be equated with mission, innovation was the opposite of waste, even a safeguard against it. In the synod's mind, seeking something novel and discarding things for the sake of new invention was considered the antithesis of waste. In the logic of mission-as-innovation, it's assumed to be a waste to maintain what was. This odd logic is nevertheless deeply embedded within us all in late modernity. It's odd because innovation and invention almost always produce large amounts of waste. You innovate by successive failure. For example, Thomas Edison, the crowned genius inventor of the modern age (until Steve Jobs usurped him), whom business books love to reference,[7]

---

5. Willie James Jennings, in *After Whiteness: An Education in Belonging* (Grand Rapids: Eerdmans, 2020), chap. 2, calls attention to a genealogy of creativity that was used to colonize and to create whiteness.

6. Reckwitz states, "Throughout all its component parts, the creativity dispositive makes creativity a universal focus. Every individual and every social practice can and must assume the positions of the creative producer and recipient. The ideal of a creative form of living dictates the comprehensive participation in the practices of the creativity dispositive." Reckwitz, *Invention of Creativity*, 220.

7. One example book says, "As Thomas A. Edison reportedly said, 'to have a great idea, have a lot of them.'" Linda A. Hill, Greg Brandeau, Emily Truelove, and Kent Lineback, *Collective Genius: The Art and Practice of Leading Innovation* (Cambridge, MA: Harvard Business

had a strategy for innovation built on waste.[8] Edison innovated by making small incremental changes—piling up glass bulbs into a mountain—until bang, one of those little changes, and the waste that necessitated it, brought the big innovation. Edison believed you just keep making small tweaks, discarding old versions, wasting resources, swinging for the fences, as you search for your home-run invention. It's no surprise that Edison yo-yoed between opulent fortune and financial failure his whole life. This drive to invent, as business books reveal in their lauding of Edison, makes Edison a genius of the late-modern creative aesthetic. Edison was willing to risk it all for the thrill (and fame!) of his innovation.

The synod didn't want to waste its funds, but it also knew that it couldn't hold its money as a miser would. It wanted badly to seed its congregations. It believed that the only soil where this seed-money could grow (grow being an interesting word that we'll return to in chap. 10) was ground tilled by expressive creativity. Creativity bound in the self—in late-modern capitalism—grows money into more money. Edison and J. P. Morgan knew this, creating a partnership in which Edison provided the creativity and Morgan the money. This partnership led to a heated rivalry over who was the more essential component. Most of us would pick Edison, because we laud creativity. We know creativity has the great advantage of bringing growth by making resources appear to have some greater purpose than just being a resource. Innovation even says this growth is itself creative.

Creativity is the engine that grows a commodity. That growth can produce the resources for a future of more creativity. More creativity, turned into more resources, can produce a stable, even inspiring, bridge into the future. And not just a bland future filled with base resources, but a future where you're a more interesting self, made so by your own attention to creativity. Creativity gives you a future rich in both material goods and meaning. It provides resources for the future and forms you into an interesting and unique self in

---

Review, 2014), 138. Tim Brown adds, "Thomas Edison led the way with the opening of the first modern industrial research lab—the so-called invention factory—in 1876, and research and development has been part of manufacturing companies ever since. Though they may not be quite as ambitious as 'the Wizard of Menlo Park'—Edison famously promised a minor invention every ten days or so and a 'big trick' every six months—most manufacturing companies assume that the way to ensure a stream of products tomorrow is to invest in technological research today." Brown, *Change by Design: How Design Thinking Transforms Organizations and Inspires Innovation* (New York: Harper Business, 2009), 180.

8. See Edmund Morris, *Edison* (New York: Random House, 2019).

this future. Inside these deep assumptions about creativity, innovation can be lauded and then fused with mission without much reflection.

Stale money, used to procure security and stability, is not the same as innovation. It's actually the opposite of being innovative. Innovation is always a risk for the sake of creativity.[9] It's a risk that wagers that the expense in and for creativity will produce more dynamic, sustaining resources and more interesting (unique) institutions and individuals. The creative institution, company, or congregation risks security and stability for a unique design born from creativity itself that can produce a future of resources.

After all, who wants to be IBM when you can be Apple?[10] Apple uses its money for creativity. Creativity grows money, giving Apple more resources to chance more creativity. More creativity grows more money, but all for the sake of more creativity—or wait, is it all for the sake of more money? It doesn't really matter as long as the commitment isn't broken. The creative Steve Wozniak and money-growth-obsessed Mike Markkula worked together long enough to make Apple into a juggernaut because they agreed on this creativity-for-growth equation. It doesn't matter if Steve Wozniak thought the equation's final answer was more creativity, or if Markkula thought creativity was intended for more money (or higher stock prices). The equation just keeps working, producing more creativity and more money for more creativity and more money. The system even works best when a company's or institution's leaders disagree on the purpose of creativity. The money folks drive harder when they assume money is most important. The creative folks give more when they assume creativity is the highest good. It's best when programmers and designers, for instance, believe in creativity for the sake of more creativity and when CFOs and accountants see creativity as a means to fiscal value. This tension can spur on a company, but it can also cause one of the leaders to leave the company in anger, asserting that the organization no longer cares about creativity or is fiscally irresponsible, exposing its shareholders to reckless risk.

9. "In a time of rapid change, the ability to innovate quickly and effectively, again and again, is perhaps the only enduring competitive advantage. Those firms that can innovate constantly will thrive. Those that do not or cannot will be left behind." Hill, Brandeau, Truelove, and Lineback, *Collective Genius*, 9.

10. Apple has become the richest company (worth over $2 trillion) because it has been the most innovative and creative. Apple is a tech company for singularity, IBM for a rationalized modernity. Apple grabbed the market by pushing creativity and self-uniqueness. Its technology is the tool used to create innovative selves.

Ultimately, Apple is seen as innovative and IBM not because Apple is creative. It procures its growth by creativity, which produces more creativity without end. Innovation is valuable, as we'll see in coming chapters, because it has within itself an inherent sense that it's cold fusion, a form of growth without limit. When creativity is the energy source that fuels an organization, congregation, or self, its emissions are more creativity. Creativity is assumed to be a self-propellant that produces more creativity in an endless loop (forget all the piles of glass bulbs and all those chemicals needed for processors).

Unlike IBM, Apple is first a creative firm, more than it is rational or technical. It's as much a design and marketing firm as a technology company (really it has redefined a tech company to be equivalent to a creative firm). Late modernity touts that the future belongs to the creative who is singularly unique. From within late modernity, only creativity seems to be able to deliver a future. And only the unique seem to survive.

The synod could use the money to sustain its congregations. But that would only make the synod a welfare state, disincentivizing each congregation from using its creativity to either sink or swim. In the synod's mind, its congregations were *not* ultimately facing a financial challenge. Rather, the synod tacitly assumed that the congregations were facing a deficit of creativity, which only inadvertently created the financial challenge (and mission became creativity encased in theological rhetoric).

The synod believed its congregations didn't really need the money, but instead should use it to awaken (or expose the lack of) creativity. Creativity could save. The synod leadership couldn't stomach (it felt wrong and wasteful) throwing money at uncreative congregations (yet, if you could show your creative/innovative stripes, pointing to a missional attention, the money was yours!). When the synod looked into the future, it believed it needed congregations that were creative and that sustained themselves through creativity.[11] These kinds of congregations had a mission, a clear direction on how to move by creative uniqueness into a dawning future. Their creative uniqueness would produce resources to sustain the congregation into the future. This combination of clear direction (mission) with surging energy to be creative, even planting a flag in uniqueness, gave some congregations, in opposition

11. There are many little congregations that are indeed creative, but cannot, even in that creativity, sustain themselves financially. Inside this logic, they are somehow not creative because this creativity is bound in the ideals of the growth economies of neoliberalism. Much more on this below.

to others, the label of "innovative." Those that were creative and unique, and able to use this creativity and uniqueness to procure a future, would receive the money. They were an investment in innovation.

Innovation was the way to use this money well. It was the best way to live after the divorce proceedings. Supporting creativity was the most advantageous way to be for the future. And in turn, it was the best way to broadcast to all the haters that the synod and the denomination itself were still interesting and vibrant. Innovation as the manifestation and mobilization of creativity was the way for the synod to get its groove back.

An individual or institution whose creativity surpasses a certain threshold reaches the status of being singularly unique. You have reached the summit of creativity and achieved a high good in late modernity when your self or your institution is so creative that it is one of a kind. There is little better in late modernity than to be singularly and undeniably unique.

Authenticity and Its Uniqueness

Late modernity highly values uniqueness because it is bound in authenticity. We live in an age of authenticity, as Charles Taylor describes it and as I've discussed in other places.[12] Our age drives toward being authentic. Every age makes assertions about the right way to live a human life and therefore about the appropriate shape of its institutions. Our age says that a well-lived life is an authentic life. A life becomes authentic when the individual (or institution) who is living in the age of authenticity embraces their own uniqueness. Authenticity and uniqueness are *not* the same, but the overlap is extensive. They necessarily and mutually feed off each other.

Uniqueness, for instance, can be interpreted only as a compliment, never an insult, because it's embedded in an age of authenticity. If a neighbor or coworker were to look at your outfit and say, "Well, aren't you a unique one," most of us would take this as a compliment and beam with pride. Even if the comment had a passive-aggressive edge, we are mainly culturally wired to take it as an affirmation. But to say "Well, aren't you a unique one" to someone in the age before the dawn of authenticity would be an insult. Unless you were a bohemian painter in Paris or a Romantic poet in

---

12. See Charles Taylor, *The Ethics of Authenticity* (Cambridge, MA: Harvard University Press, 1991); and Andrew Root, *Faith Formation in a Secular Age* (Grand Rapids: Baker Academic, 2017).

Weimar, you'd assume you were being ridiculed by the comment. Before the age of authenticity (and still now in places that don't embrace the age of authenticity), to be called "unique" was to be called odd and weird (which, unlike today, had only bad connotations).[13] This means that uniqueness, while maybe in the smallest measure interesting, was, more so, reason for exclusion and ridicule.

A phenomenological genealogy of bullying would reveal this (though I don't know if one has ever been done). I believe it would show that uniqueness, or standing out, once was reason for derision. You wanted to fit in by being unnoticed, conforming to the fashion and practices of your school or neighborhood. However, now being ignored is its own heavy form of scorn. To not be recognized for your own uniqueness is to encounter a form of oppression.[14]

In late modernity, almost universally, to say "This is a unique coffee shop" or "This church is so unique" or "You're a very unique person" is to say that this coffee shop, church, or individual is attractive and therefore good. This coffee shop, church, or individual has a sure future because the shop, church, or individual is so creative that it has made itself into a singular being or place. This creativity becomes truly unique, hitting the threshold of singular uniqueness, when it answers only to its own creative impulses. Its uniqueness is found within its own self. It is unique by following its own singular, creative, interior impulse to be itself (again, uniqueness is both somehow an inherent and yet achieved reality for the self).

In late modernity, the unique individual or group is the creative who follows their own impulses as an ethic (the right way of being and doing). Taylor has said that the age of authenticity is born from an ethic of authenticity. This ethic goes something like this: no human being should tell another human being what it means for that unique human being to be human.[15] The ethic asserts that no one should ever tread on someone

13. Keith Sawyer adds, "In the United States, we tend to equate creativity with novelty and originality. But the high value that we place on novelty isn't shared universally in all cultures." Sawyer, *Explaining Creativity: The Science of Human Innovation* (New York: Oxford University Press, 2012), 27.

14. I don't say this flippantly in any way. Recognition since the days of Hegel has been very important. I've written about this in *The End of Youth Ministry* (Grand Rapids: Baker Academic, 2020), chap. 7. But for much more on the importance of recognition in late modernity, see Axel Honneth, *The Struggle for Recognition: The Moral Grammar of Social Conflicts* (Cambridge, MA: MIT Press, 1995).

15. See Taylor, *Ethics of Authenticity*, 1–25.

else's creative impulse, because everyone should be *free* to seek their own uniqueness.[16]

Overall, the uniqueness reveals that the coffee shop, church, or individual is following only what speaks to it, that the coffee shop, church, or person is taking a heroic step to determine itself, living out of a creative center within itself. You're authentic when you're uniquely and singularly doing you, when you are living and acting as you wish, creatively presenting your unique self to the world. To be authentic is to be one of a kind. This is why my friend Russ's group felt stuck, unable to move forward with their idea. It just didn't seem to be truly unique; it didn't unveil in its aesthetic that they were authentic selves. The ideas they had for their church were helpful, but not unique enough, especially compared to the other groups. The goal of the grant, to its credit, had a much larger aim—to mobilize young adults for God's work. But this aim, to Russ's surprise, was so quickly and easily supplanted. They couldn't let go of their anxious comparison, even when the grant team and Russ told them it didn't matter that their ideas weren't creative enough. The drive to be a creatively unique individual or group held a heavy moral and ethical weight that they couldn't quite name.

Where Authenticity and Uniqueness Diverge

Authenticity and uniqueness mutually reinforce each other—and overlap. But we need to explore also how authenticity and uniqueness are different, each imposing different claims on us. This difference explains why authenticity and the freedom to be unique (from within your own creative center) have failed to produce anything like a utopian society of free-flowing affirmation. If we had achieved this, the tweets populating Twitter would *only* consist of positive affirmations, instead of the dumpster fire of hate that fills it now. As part of our cultural imaginary, authenticity and uniqueness are deeply related. Uniqueness is assumed to be a compliment (a statement of something good) because of its location inside our age of authenticity. But uniqueness nevertheless has elements to it that produce tensions in our late-modern age of authenticity.

16. I emphasized *free* here only to point out that this ethic has so much to do with views and senses of liberty. It might be better to say that it undercuts and confuses people about what liberty really is. For instance, inside the ethic of authenticity and the drive to obey your own impulses, public health mandates to wear a mask become perceived as a violent act that destroys an individual's authentic way of being.

My commitment to or even support of authenticity is in large part hands-off. I'm even ethically supporting authenticity when taking steps to be hands-off. I'm hands-off (even as a parent of an eleven-year-old) by allowing another to seek their own authenticity. I affirm this pursuit of authenticity by giving this other the space (from judgment or cultural expectation) to wield their creativity and be unique. And I allow our age to be authentic when I live and let live, when I refuse to tell another self (even a coffee shop or church) how to live their own life. I support the age of authenticity when I let the coffee shop, church, or individual self do their own thing, refusing to judge or deride them for their pursuit of creativity. In an age of authenticity, refusing to tell another human being how to live their life is ethical.

I support an authentic society when I stand up against those who are too hands-on (whether for political or religious reasons) in telling others how they should live their lives. I can even become quite forceful, even verbally and violently enraged in my commitments to the hands-off-ness of authenticity, when I perceive someone else imposing their own views or will on another individual's uniqueness and creative freedom to do their own self.

I must remain hands-off, allowing any self to live from their own creative center. An age deeply ingrained in authenticity will, not surprisingly, honor and laud uniqueness. But here's where uniqueness ultimately asks something different of us than authenticity asks (which leads to a conundrum): uniqueness cannot actually be honored (and even affirmed) in a hands-off manner. While authenticity asks me to live and let live, to be hands-off, uniqueness seeks and demands (even if it hates) my direct judgment. Authenticity tells me no judgment is allowed, but uniqueness can be substantiated both culturally and existentially only by the fire of judgment.[17]

The unique individual or coffee shop is, and can only be, unique in relation (even competition) with others. No wonder Russ's group felt paralyzed by their merely "good" ideas. No wonder, even over and against the wishes of the grant, the young adults (even Russ) felt a stab of competition in the

17. This collision seems to pop up everywhere in our time. Those seeking to be unique demand the hands-off-ness of authenticity ("What does it matter to you who I sleep with?") and yet can't accept this hands-off-ness. At some point they demand recognition, even accepting negative judgment for its charge to ignite a more ambitious articulation of uniqueness. Our society is divided not only because authenticity is the ethic we live by (this could be good) but because inside of authenticity is this existential drive for uniqueness that needs to live with deep judgment of both friends who affirm and enemies who deride. Both give the juice to continue my pursuits of singular uniqueness as a self.

process of innovation. This invitation into creativity moves quickly from the free space of authenticity to the drive for uniqueness. And uniqueness, which innovation in some measure seeks, is laced with heavy forms of judgment. The young adults felt that if they couldn't come up with a singularly unique idea that was deeply innovative, their very selves would be less creative, less unique, than others. Uniqueness is a fundamentally ranked category.

For instance, a young woman is considered unique because her creative originality outstrips that of others. To be a unique coffee shop means there must be a hundred that are not unique (like all those Starbucks). To call this coffee shop or individual unique, I must judge her as so in opposition to all the others. To testify to uniqueness, I must do something authenticity is uncomfortable with: use direct and bold judgment. Both authenticity and uniqueness mutually glorify, and feed on, creativity—and therefore both uphold the importance (and dream) of being singular. Both affirm that this singular creativity has its source in the impulses, drives, and desires of the inner self (they laud subjectivity). But authenticity calls me to be hands-off and to never judge, to live and let live, while uniqueness calls me to always, as my very lifestyle, judge and evaluate everything and everyone. It takes little to see this ranking and judging everywhere in our culture. If I'm good enough at this judging evaluation (doing it uniquely enough), I can even make this evaluative judgment the very conduit for my own unique creativity (hence, countless ranting YouTube stars giving their judgments on everything from face lotions to senators). In late modernity, you must somehow never judge while always judging. Other than the stars of *Queer Eye*, very few can elegantly pull this off (we'll return to this in chap. 8).

Back to Innovation and Mission

This discussion about authenticity and uniqueness provides some insight into why the synod executive so quickly equated mission and innovation, and why the language of innovation has become ubiquitous across American Protestantism. Mission and innovation are so easily equated because they both *appear* to do two things at once. First, both appear to produce *more* (more direction, identity, members, market share, energy, and overall growth) out of the initial investment. This felt good and smart to the synod. In a world organized by fiscal capitalism (run mainly by financial markets and the rise and fall of stocks and dividends, as opposed to the labor output of supply and demand of manufactured products), there's nothing more astute than to turn a one-time payoff into an exponentially recurring return. Innovation allows your money (or energy, creativity, etc.) to work for you. It allows the mission to continue, for you to be continually missional. To turn a one-time investment into continued returns is a successful mission, which requires real innovation.[18]

Second, mission and innovation can be equated because something other than future returns is promised. Mission and innovation both seem to be forms of keeping your eye on the future while nevertheless producing new ways of inhabiting the now. Innovation as mission delivers the relevance of authenticity and common cultural drive for uniqueness. Mission and innovation (innovation as the shape of mission) produce (for an institution or individual) a kind of lifestyle, a way of living creatively and uniquely that produces meaning by creativity and the drive for uniqueness. Mission as innovation is fit for both growing future resources and producing a sense of meaning in the now, because both embrace the late-modern hypergoods of creativity and uniqueness.

––––––––––

The next morning, as we gathered for the second session of the conference, it appeared that the whole Applebee's thing wasn't digested well by all the pastors in the synod. The same executive I ate with the night before stood to introduce me. But before he did, he reminded everyone that the synod was after innovation that was faithful and unashamedly Christian innovation. They were only talking about innovation because it was for the sake of the gospel. This innovation was seeking a direct connection to God's own innovating work in the world. The point wasn't to cash in on growth, he said. I figured he said this to remind himself as much as the others in the room. Rather, he continued, the synod supported innovation for the kingdom of God. It was innovation as mission, to join in God's own mission in the world.

I nodded my head in affirmation.

I was then reintroduced.

18. The heart of the missional church movement is *missio Dei*. I personally am quite committed to it. But even within the missional church conversation there has been some slippage. Though mission is bound in the act and being of God, there seems to be this ever-present temptation to move it from a revelatory, even transcendent, reality to a management reality. Particularly in practical forms of the missional church conversation, mission is often connected with a new—more theologically legitimate—modern sense of growth. It may be no longer in a crass church-growth way, but nevertheless the innovation impulse can fall into these traps.

After my presentation, I found myself at the lunch table of a group of mid-to-late-career pastors. Many had been in the synod for decades, each one of them for longer than the executive. I was listening intently for an opening, hoping someone would mention some TV show I could turn the discussion toward. But it never came. Instead, a fit man with a well-kept white beard that started just above his light brown turtleneck said with an edge in his voice, "Well, I think you're handling all this innovation garbage quite well."

I froze, not knowing what to say. It was a compliment, I guess, but one that put me in an odd spot.

Frozen in that moment, I realized I was at the table of contrarians. I quickly recognized that these were the pastors who wanted the money divided. A few of them could have really used a roof repair. But as they spoke, they didn't justify their opposition in such self-serving ways. Rather, they talked of liturgy, creeds, and sacraments. Innovation was wrong because it wasn't deep, because it ignored the tradition, because it was a fad, just a hipster spin on church growth.

I had my own concerns with the easy equation of mission and innovation, but these innovation-allergic old-schoolers made me long for the executive's energy and direction. I had my apprehensions about innovation—I sensed there were hidden goods within it that needed to be reflected on. But this stale, thin opposition, framed as the defense of tradition and intellectual depth, seemed the height of banality to me. I realized, as I politely but quickly finished my lunch and made my exit, that the executive and the pastors for change in the synod would need to do some deeper thinking than they had. I was mainly on their side, but I was convinced that just adding "faithful" or "missional" to innovation, or claiming it was God's work, wasn't enough. All that was maybe true (maybe!), but we needed to think much deeper about it all.

For instance, to say that innovation is faithful demands an articulation of both what you're faithful to or who you have faith in. And, just as importantly, faithfulness demands a clear understanding of the location in which you profess faith and live out this faithfulness. I was now convinced that the thought leaders who were pushing the church to embrace innovation as mission had not helped the synod executive recognize the content, object, and location where such innovation would take place. They assumed that innovation was a practice free of the moral horizons of late modernity. To them, innovation and social entrepreneurship could be picked up and used without recognizing that they were tools or texts born inside the presumptions of the immanent frame of late modernity.

If innovation is to be faithful, to be a profession of faith, if innovation is to be at least a continuation of Luther's "Here I stand, I can do no other" (the heart of Protestantism's cleaving to faith), then more work needs to be done to understand where this *here* is that we stand, and how standing *here*, in late modernity's secular age, we embrace an ecclesiology that is truly faithful. It may be that innovation is indeed faithful, but we will know that only if we examine in depth what we've started above.

Those like the executive see innovation as an ecclesial good. Period. Yet when you look at the use of innovation in the history of the Western church, it is almost always derogatory. Only in our contemporary moment has innovation become an overwhelmingly positive term. Before modernity (pre-eighteenth century), it was used negatively. Throughout modernity (eighteenth through twentieth centuries), it was mostly neutral. In late modernity (late twentieth and early twenty-first century), it has been used almost exclusively in positive, even laudatory, fashion.[19] To be innovative, creative, and inventive is the highest praise we can give to an individual, institution, or product. To be an innovative theologian pre-eighteenth century was to be a heretic who should be avoided.[20] To be an innovative theologian in the twenty-first century is to be exciting and well worth the read. This interesting development may tell us something important. Our task in the chapters to come is to answer why innovation in the church has shifted from being morally suspect to morally admirable.

19. For more on this idea, see Robert Pogue Harrison, *Juvenescence: A Cultural History of Our Age* (Chicago: University of Chicago Press, 2014).

20. In their excellent book, Lee Vinsel and Andrew Russell say, "In fact, during the Middle Ages, innovation—from the Latin word *innovare*, meaning 'to make new'—was a distinctly bad thing. Church dogma was society's guide, and innovation, or the act of introducing new, heterodox ideas, was heresy that got lots of people killed." Vinsel and Russell, *The Innovation Delusion: How Our Obsession with the New Has Disrupted the Work That Matters Most* (New York: Currency, 2020), 20.

2

We're All Sandwich Artists Now

Work and Backwash, Reversing a Historical Flow

I was raised on *Seinfeld*. I know that dates me. But what really dates me is that my college roommates and I recorded hours of the show, not on DVR—which is itself old—but with a VCR, which is ancient. We watched those tapes every night when we should have been studying. I guess I'd say to younger readers that *Seinfeld* was *The Office* of today—an easy, relaxing escape, a kind of mind-soothing warm bath. Our dusty, clunky VHS tapes were our inconvenient Peacock.

Jerry and his friends taught us to create secret names for those we had awkward social interactions with. The name bound the person to their action: the Close Talker, Denim Vest, the Two-Face, Low Talker, and Man Hands. It's a particularly appealing, if juvenile, social practice for introverts who always feel like they're observing the social moment more than living in it. It's even more appealing if, like me, you're an introvert who's terrible with names. But you really know Seinfeld's juvenile humor has entered your system when you use these secret names with just yourself.

After that young pastor's exercise before my first presentation, I started calling him Applebee's Boy. Mind you, I only did this in my own head. But still I did it. And enjoyed it.

Applebee's Boy and I said hello as we crossed paths at the conference center. He was even kind enough to help set up my computer before my next two presentations. We started to build some rapport without much of a conversation. (Gold for an introvert!) Applebee's Boy might have been capable of swallowing a canary whole, grinning with pleasure and feathery belches, but he also struck me as a guy who liked to talk about TV. So I sat at the open seat next to him at the final meal of the conference.

But Applebee's Boy *never* took the TV bait. Not even a nibble. He was too earnest.

"Hey, thanks for your presentations. I enjoyed them," he said.

"Thanks. I appreciate that. Have you been streaming anything good lately?" I said.

He said, "I think your presentations were needed. The churches in this synod really need to innovate or they'll *all die*. If we hope to have a future, if there is any way beyond this decline, it's innovation or bust."

"Have you seen *Search Party* on HBO?" I said.

"Plus, who doesn't want to be creative? It's so exciting! I just don't get these pastors who don't want to do something new."

I knew just who he meant: Bearded Brown Turtleneck from my uncomfortable lunch at the contrarian table.

"Have you tried *Yellowstone*? It's good," I said.

He said, "Your presentations about our secular age made me think of how close death is for our synod and maybe all Protestant churches. Don't you agree?"

I dug deep and said, "Did you watch *Game of Thrones*? What did you think of the finale?"

He said, "I just don't get it. These pastors . . . This is a great way to work. Who wants a job where you can't be creative? I don't get that. At least people at my church understand that. They work for businesses where you have to create and be creative. How can the church possibly hope to reach and retain people who work like that in churches that refuse to do so?"

I kicked myself. I should have asked him about the UK *Office* or *Silicon Valley*.

When Work Changes

Applebee's Boy had a point. But it wasn't his earnestness for creativity that caught my attention, but the way he connected innovation and creativity with work. I had the sense that he was right. In the West, the occupational and vocational shape of our lives has shifted hard in this direction. Just look at the job titles given by some retail companies. Lululemon calls its retail staff "educators," Kate Spade calls them "muses," and Best Buy has a Geek Squad. Other companies have "brand ambassadors" instead of checkout clerks, and back when Seinfeld was airing new episodes, Subway renamed its employees "sandwich artists." The point of these titles is that even when your work isn't *really* creative and innovative, you're supposed to think about it as such.

Applebee's Boy was right: work had turned hard in the direction of a constant longing, even necessity, for creativity. The structural carrier of this new attention to innovation and creativity was the shifting place of work in late modernity. Seeing this connection between work and creativity, it made more sense why innovation was popping up everywhere across Protestantism. Protestantism is not more creative than other Christian traditions (actually it's been *less* concerned for an aesthetic than other traditions). But compared to these others, work has been central in the Protestant imagination. Protestant congregational life has always been directly shaped by the work life of its people. In our time, innovation and creativity seem ubiquitous across Protestantism. As innovation and creativity have found their way into the center of work life, so too have they nuzzled into the Protestant congregational imagination. Of course, innovation as creativity appears in other traditions. It pops up in Catholicism and Eastern Orthodoxy, but not nearly as much as in the late-modern Protestant societies that have welcomed the age of authenticity. As authenticity and uniqueness have bled deeply into the fabric of work life, taking the shape of innovation and the need for constant creativity, so the dye has reached the practical shape of Protestant congregational life.

But the spread of innovation and creativity from work life to Protestant congregational life doesn't mean that Protestantism has a monopoly on creativity. Actually it's quite the opposite. Of the three great Christian traditions, Protestantism seems the least aesthetic, particularly in its worship spaces and liturgies. Compared to Catholicism and Eastern Orthodoxy, Protestantism is much less infused with artistic creativity than these two other traditions. A Puritan prayer house is beautiful in its own right, but it's not exactly dripping in art compared to the cathedrals and chapels of Tuscany or the Eastern Byzantine buildings with their mosaics and icons. And we have to remember that it was the purse of the Catholic Florentine Medici family that funded the Renaissance, the greatest burst of artistic creativity and innovation the West has ever known.

Yet even this burst of creativity, though it changed Europe, was not located in work itself. The Medici cannot be mistaken for anything other than cutthroat businessmen with deep ambitions to make their own name and the name of Florence great. The Medici could have put their weight behind the transformation of labor, creating unions and minimum wages (Lorenzo the Magnificent may have had some of this in mind, but it never happened). The Medici could have sought to transform work through their banking monopoly, but instead they sought to make Florence a great city, not through the reforms of labor but through the proliferation of beauty. Beauty, they imagined, would make Florence great and the Medici revered, but it would also in turn connect the people to God, not just connect them to more meaningful work.[1] Beautiful paintings and sculptors reflected God's own nature as majestically beautiful. A piece of art was not to be worshiped in itself. But to experience the rays of beauty warming your face as you encountered the architecture of a Florentine building, the frescos in the chapels, and sculptures in the piazza was to remind you directly of (even push you into) the bright sun of God's own infinite beauty.[2]

The referent of the creative endeavor (i.e., the purpose of art), even for the power-hungry Medici, was not bound in the uniqueness of the self of the artist but the reflection of God's own beauty in the painting, sculpture, or architecture (see particularly Lorenzo de' Medici's patronage of Sandro Botticelli for an example). Art was never intended to reflect the creativity of the artist but to unveil a glimpse of God's own beauty. Creativity was not really done for the name of the artist or inventor.[3]

---

1. If downgrading meaningful work bugs you, you might have some Protestant imagination running through you! Admittedly, though, Catholic reform movements from the days of the Medici (see Girolamo Savonarola) to the liberation theology movement in South America have pointed to labor and work (particularly to the oppression of laborers and the poor). So it might be better to say that if that statement bugs you, you have some Western Christian reforming impulses in you. This reforming impulse, which has been endemic in Catholicism, came to its great schismatic climax in Protestantism. And Reformed Protestantism especially has engaged work life from its beginnings.

2. Niklas Luhmann, in his field-defining text, *Art as a Social System* (Stanford, CA: Stanford University Press, 2000), explains, "Apparently, the development of art was motivated less by the private interests of the upper classes than by the presentation of public-communal affairs of a political or religious nature; art, in other words, developed with an eye toward certain functions" (137).

3. Luhmann adds, "There was never a direct transition from a magical understanding of art to artistic autonomy. Artworks of the Middle Ages (more accurately, works that we would identify as art) were meant to highlight certain religious or other social meanings; they emphasized such meanings and ensured that they could be experienced repeatedly. Within a well-ordered

In Florence, if any human name was to be connected with a creative endeavor, it was the name of the patron. The Medici who commissioned the work, not the artist, was to receive fame and glory. It's only as modern people that we've become intrigued by the personalities of the artists of the Renaissance. Only in modernity has the name of the artist eclipsed the name of the patron.[4] Nowadays everyone knows the names Rafael and Michelangelo. As modern people, we're drawn to tales of these artists' manic outbursts of creative genius. But in the fifteenth century, any creative innovation was undertaken for the name of the patron, who praised God.

The Renaissance's greatest creative genius, maybe the greatest creative innovator the world has ever known, Leonardo da Vinci, died in France, though he was a citizen of Florence. The French king Francis I brought Leonardo to France not for the sake of Leonardo's creative name taken into a new land. Leonardo's arrival in France was nothing like the Beatles' arrival at the JFK airport; it wasn't Leonardo mania conquering a new market. Rather, Francis I brought Leonardo to France for the sake of Francis's own name.[5]

Poor Leonardo died in France. His unfinished paintings (*all* Leonardo's paintings are unfinished—the dude was a genius who couldn't complete a thing!) were not returned to his family's village outside Florence upon his death. They weren't assumed to belong to Leonardo. They instead became the property of the king of France. No one thought twice about this, because Leonardo was not a servant to creativity or his own uniqueness but a vassal of the king. His creativity was *for* the king. Therefore, Leonardo's paintings were Francis's property. To this day, the *Mona Lisa* hangs not in the Uffizi in Florence but in the Louvre in Paris. Leonardo's great smirking lady is the property of France.

The great explosion of creativity in the Renaissance had little direct impact on the shape of work. Creativity had little to do with work, other than for the hundreds of artists who found patronages in Florence and across Italy.

---

cosmos, created for the sake of the Good and the Beautiful, art took on memorial and educational functions. Its task was transmission, not innovation, and the only freedom it claimed (a freedom nonetheless) was ornamentation (we assume that *ornamentumlornatum* was understood in the sense of the rhetorical tradition, as expressing the perfection of the creation, rather than as mere adornment). Not until the late Middle Ages can one speak of a situation in which art follows internal criteria." *Art as a Social System*, 159.

4. For more on Florence and patronage in relation to art, see Luhmann, *Art as a Social System*, 160–62.

5. For an insightful biography on Leonardo, see Serge Bramly, *Leonardo: The Artist and the Man* (New York: Penguin, 1998).

Of course, the Renaissance affected the economy in many ways, some good and some bad, but it didn't really change work or make it something different before God. Downstream, the Renaissance would make its mark on work, but far downriver. The Renaissance would irrigate once-dry lands with humanism, which would fertilize the soil for the coming Reformation. And the Reformation, and the Protestant theologians born from it, would profoundly and thoroughly change work forever. Let's see how.

Reforms Meet Work

Renaissance humanism mixed with Augustinian theology and the existential crisis of a young monk named Martin Luther brought the self into view like never before.[6] The self stood before God in need of justification. The self was now responsible for itself; it bore its own sin but also participated in its own freedom. Soon the self could read the sacred text for itself, nurturing itself, even praying the confession for itself, receiving that freedom to be a forgiven self before a merciful God who justifies. The Reformation broke the firm clerical hold on the confession of sin and reflection on the sacred Scriptures. This meant that the heart (as an inner feeling of your own self-consciousness), as opposed to the Mass within beautiful cathedrals, was now the place where God did God's work.[7] The heart moved in the world; it put hand to plow and scrubbed floors.

A huge shift was now underway. In a sense, Protestantism kept an opulent space for an encounter with God: the heart. This ornate space, still necessary, shifted from a lavish building to an elaborate self-consciousness (the heart). No longer did it matter that cathedrals were draped in art, bearing the marks of aesthetic beauty. The heart of the inner life of the self became all-important. The altars needed to be stripped of magnificence and the frescos painted over so that the self could be made the intricate space for meeting God. Like never before, the inner self needed to be examined. The inner self could be examined through feelings, although this wasn't the fundamental way

6. See Charles Taylor, *Sources of the Self: The Making of the Modern Identity* (Cambridge, MA: Harvard University Press, 1989), part 2.

7. See Michael Allen Gillespie, *The Theological Origins of Modernity* (Chicago: University of Chicago Press, 2008); Larry Siedentop, *Inventing the Individual: The Origins of Western Liberalism* (New York: Penguin, 2014); and Raymond Martin and John Barresi, *The Rise and Fall of Soul and Self: An Intellectual History of Personal Identity* (New York: Columbia University Press, 2006).

of taking the temperature of the self until the very end of the Victorian age in the late nineteenth century. In the Victorian age, we began to assume that the self had feelings coming from origins, particularly in childhood, hidden to the self. I'll tell this story in more detail below, using the insightful thought of Eva Illouz's sociology of emotion. The contention that we have hidden emotions that negatively affect how we act in the world (psychology being the science that examines these emotions with hidden causes) played a huge role in shaping work life in the twentieth century and, in turn, in unleashing the creative/innovative impulse into the economy.

For now we need to see that in the early periods after the Reformation, the way to determine the state of the self was through behavior, and indeed how you felt (e.g., guilty or assured) about those behaviors. How you felt about what you did determined the state of your soul. True, justification had *nothing* to do with your behaviors or actions. No works could save. But having been justified, this self needed to live (behave) as a priest. It made no difference what your actual occupation was. You were now justified, and like a priest, you had a vocation to serve God with your whole heart, whether you spent your hours lifting the chalice or cleaning out chamber pots. This is "the priesthood of all believers."[8]

Because we live after the democratic revolutions of the eighteenth and nineteenth centuries, after the end of global colonial rule in the twentieth century, and because we still have a social imagination that has not completely been exorcised of the Cold War face-off between free democratic society and restrictive communism, we tend to interpret the priesthood of all believers similarly to the French Revolution's motto of "liberty, equality, fraternity." In other words, the priesthood of all believers, we contend, is Protestant shorthand for liberty, equality, and fraternity. We believe it's about freedom without hierarchy.

But that's not quite right. After the Reformation, the priesthood of all believers was *not* imagined as a release from the high bar of religious commitment

---

8. The priesthood of all believers has much deeper theological foundations than this. It is much more nuanced and directed toward forgiveness. But as Charles Taylor describes in *A Secular Age* (Cambridge, MA: Belknap, 2007), it had the effect of raising the bar of commitment (particularly in the Calvinist countries). This had more direct impact on the Reformed nations than the Lutheran. My point is that it raised the bar of everyone in every vocation to work as if a holy vow was on them. Luther accomplished this more so in his doctrine of vocation than in the priesthood of all believers. But across Protestantism the priesthood of all believers came to mean living as a priest in your work.

to enjoy freedom and escape hierarchy (which was the goal of the Enlightenment, not the Reformation). Rather, the priesthood of all believers was an exponential raising of the bar. In the priesthood of all believers, we were indeed free from the tyranny of ecclesial despots who held back grace for their own gain. But, more so, the priesthood of all believers meant that each one of us, in our own hearts, inside our own vocational work, must live fully and completely devoted. We must *all* now live as priests who take the most sacred of oaths (which we do in the confirmation of our baptism). This high, sacred oath that the most ordinary of us takes is to have our hearts fully and completely devoted to God. All our behavior must meet the high bar of the priest. Early Protestantism imagined nations, or at least congregations, of priests. It didn't matter if you were pastoring a small village congregation or cooking meals for travelers at the inn; you needed to behave as a faithful and devoted priest. Your work was now sacred. This was quite a radical shift!

With this shift, what mattered in your behavior wasn't, as Charles Taylor has said, *what* you did but *how* you did it.[9] What mattered wasn't *what* the self did in the cathedral but *how* devotedly the self acted in the world. *How* the self acted in the world—in one's work—revealed if that inner house of God, known as the self (or heart), was in a place of order or chaos. Particularly in the Reformed traditions (and Puritanism specifically), order replaced beauty as the focus. What was beautiful was orderly.

God encountered us now in the self. *How* we did our work revealed the state of our soul. This shift to the self and the making of all priests undid the clerical hierarchy of work. For Luther, and Calvin following him, all work had deep value. *All* jobs were done before God, because God was the Word loose in the world, unbound by the cultic acts of the Mass. All work was done before God, because the place God encounters us was no longer in the Mass but in the devoted heart. The heart was faithfully tuned to God when it worked both with devotion to God and to the task at hand. It was no longer just the priest or bishop (the *what* of ecclesial work) that was done directly before and for God. Luther asserted that farming, changing diapers, and even swinging the axe of the executioner could be a holy vocation. We lived out our justification—we reflected that we were faithful to God—not primarily in *what* we did in the cathedral but in *how* we worked. Devotion was bound in the duty to work. Welcome to the Protestant work ethic!

9. See Taylor, *Sources of the Self*, part 3.

Whether in Luther's sense that vocation was the way we lived out our freedom as justified or in Calvin's sense that how we worked was the third use of the law making hard work a fruit of our predestination, what clearly mattered was *how* we worked. The Sunday gathering, for Protestants, was a gathering of workers. Whether a merchant selling buttons, a farmer tilling the soil, or a mother nursing a child, you had a vocation (a form of work) that you were now to do faithfully before God with your whole heart.

The Creative Aesthetic Strikes Back

By focusing on the self, order, and duty, Protestantism takes a sharp turn away from art, the aesthetic, and even creativity as resting at the center of religious practice. This sharp turn makes it all the more surprising that creativity would return, particularly to Protestant congregational life, in late modernity. This return of creativity strongly hints that creativity and innovation are, more than we assume, tangled like vines around the commitments and conditions of late modernity. For aesthetic creativity to return to Protestantism, it would have to do so with some coherence on a well-worn and familiar, but also radically shifted, path.

Work carries creativity and the drive for the aesthetic back into the Protestant church that had once abandoned it. As Applebee's Boy said, the church must embrace creativity as innovation because creativity as innovation is the context in which people work today. To be concerned with how people work, and to connect work with faith, is the legacy of the Reformation and the primary reason we see more innovation talk in Protestant traditions than in Catholicism or Orthodoxy. Protestantism abandoned the cultic aesthetic of the Mass for the sake of making all work sacred, to connect the confession of faith with vocational and occupational behaviors in the world. The aesthetic returns to Protestantism in late modernity for the same reason: it returns to help congregations engage with people who work in the world (it's not illogical to equate innovation and mission, even if it is problematic).

This time around, though, the aesthetic returns to Protestantism without any referent to the divine. The aesthetic of the Mass was abandoned because it imposed on God's freedom. The Reformers saw the Mass as a kind of twisted magic that believed it could possess God through its pomp and ritual (particularly its practice of the Eucharist). The creative aesthetic was locked inside this ecclesial form. It had to be abandoned so that work outside the Mass could matter.

But now the opposite has occurred. A creative aesthetic returns to Protestantism from the competition of the market as the need for constant innovation. Protestantism put an end to the cultic aesthetic so that work could matter. Now in late modernity, because work still matters to Protestantism, work brings back the necessity for an aesthetic creativity.[10] Yet this time the aesthetic creativity is not animated by a transcendent (even magical) force.[11] Rather, what animates the drive for creativity and innovation in late modernity is the competition of markets and the loss of market share. Companies need to creatively innovate to avoid losing market share and therefore decline. Protestant churches need to embrace innovation to not lose members or relevance and therefore escape their decline.

From Industrial to Postindustrial

It took some time, and a handful of cultural transitions, for work to return the importance of creativity to Protestant congregations. When the industrial revolution arrived in Protestant countries, it seemed that the aesthetic would be buried forever.[12] With the arrival of the machine, work was changed be-

10. This is not to argue that Protestant nations and persons weren't artistic. The great artists of the late eighteenth and nineteenth century were often Protestant. One thinks particularly of Vincent Van Gogh. What's interesting is that Van Gogh desired to be a pastor, but he failed, finding it hard to use his great artistic skill in parish life. When he transitioned to painter, the subjects of his most important paintings were very Protestant in the sense of honoring ordinary life. His *Peasant Character Studies* are some of the most beautiful of his early paintings. They depict ordinary people working in villages. Van Gogh paints them like a Renaissance painter would the Madonna, which shows that his Reformed imagination knew that their ordinary life was sacred before God.

11. It would take us too far afield to get into it deeply, but it's important here to point out that it's inside this kind of logic that Protestantism offers a different tone to its understanding of transcendence. The movements away from the Mass and out into the world, the transitions from the cathedral to the self, don't abandon transcendence (as some radical Protestant theologians sometimes propose) but embrace a form of transcendence that is bound more directly within the ordinary.

12. Of course, even in Protestant nations like the Netherlands, England, and Scotland, art, creativity, and the importance of an aesthetic never disappeared. But it did get locked inside class structure. The truly aesthetic in the eighteenth and nineteenth centuries were not common workers but the elite. The landed class and new money industrialists entered enclaves of aesthetic appreciation. They attended orchestras and operas, shopped for nice clothes, and adorned their homes with beautiful dishes. They always lived under the guilt of the Protestant call for austerity but also under the invitation to nurture the inner space of the self. It really wasn't until the late

yond what any sixteenth- or seventeenth-century Protestant leader could have imagined. The arrival of the machine gave work a much different purpose. Whether intentional or not, the industrial revolution challenged the Protestant assumption that the self can flourish in any kind of work. It was much harder to be a priest on the factory floor. The machine seemed to gobble up worker-priests like candy, and spit them out as if that candy were black licorice. It was much harder to be a priest when the markets of the industrial revolution didn't see you as a human person but as a commodity called "labor." Protestantism failed to adequately meet this challenge, though not without trying (we shouldn't overlook child labor laws and capped hourly workdays). There were a plethora of workers' movements, socialist initiatives, and other efforts led by Protestant ministers in the nineteenth and twentieth centuries.

The machine and factory, having its height in Henry Ford's assembly line, was no doubt inventive and creative. Fordism was indeed an innovation. But it was far from—even the opposite of—imposing a creative ethos on all workers. The best industrial workers were just cogs in machines, doing the same operation over and over again without any concern for creativity, uniqueness, or an authentic expression of the self. Protestantism, at its origins, wrapped work in priestly attention. An industrial economy, perfected by Ford, drowned this priestly quality of work both at the level of the worker, who was made into a commodity, and at the level of the industrialist, who cared much less about humbly witnessing to his predestination as shop owner than about the huge amounts of profits that could be garnered by his corporation.

After the industrial revolution, and into our own time, this priestly quality to work has had a hard time returning to the surface. Again, not without trying. Lilly Endowment, for instance, has funded hundreds of projects on vocation, and handfuls of books have discussed vocation (work) as a spiritual practice.[13] But even with all this attention, the priestly quality of work remains submerged; it has not made its way back to the surface. Luther's

---

nineteenth and into the twentieth century that working-class folk culture was honored for its artistic value. Yet neither high-culture aesthetic nor folk-culture artistic forms had a direct or immediate connection to ecclesial life. That direct connection had been severed.

13. Examples of books are Mark R. Schwehn and Dorothy C. Bass, eds., *Leading Lives That Matter: What We Should Do and Who We Should Be*, 2nd ed. (Grand Rapids: Eerdmans, 2020); William C. Placher, ed., *Callings: Twenty Centuries of Christian Wisdom on Vocation* (Grand Rapids: Eerdmans, 2005); and Kathleen A. Cahalan, *The Stories We Live: Finding God's Calling All around Us* (Grand Rapids: Eerdmans, 2017). For an examination of the fruits of Lilly's funding of vocation, see David S. Cunningham, "A Plentiful Harvest: The Fruits of Lilly-Sponsored Programs on Vocation," Resources for American Christianity, accessed February 21, 2022,

own views on vocation are interesting, even inspiring, but of little help in postindustrial societies. Even in our time, the priestly dimension of work seems to be swimming against a stiff current. This current pushes all work strongly toward immanence rather than transcendence. This current keeps the priestly dimension of work locked in the category of a "nice idea" that workers themselves find hard to actualize in their tasks as brand ambassadors, yoga pant educators, and tech geeks.[14]

The industrial revolution proved to be anti-Protestant in the way it flattened work, making the self into a commodity that feeds machines to win market share. Fordism was unconcerned that the inner self of the worker was an intricate, opulent sanctuary for God's presence. Workers were not selves but commodities on par with the products they made. Yet, to risk overstatement, it was also not coincidental that the Protestant nations led the way in industrializing. The aversion to the aestheticism of the cathedral and its Mass, which fed the Reformation, conditioned the Protestant nations to accept forms of work that were absent aesthetic craftsmanship.

It would take a postindustrial and information economy for creativity as innovation to enter all parts of work for the first time in broad scale. I'll show how this took place in the next chapter, but for now it's important to say that in our postindustrial society of an information economy, work became linked with creativity. Whereas the flow in Protestantism once moved from the church to work, now it's been reversed, as Applebee's Boy testified. The flow of work as creativity has, for good or ill, washed back into the church. This backwash allows the synod, without reflection, to claim that mission is innovation. It seems obvious that mission is innovation because there is a canal, dug in the earliest days of Protestantism, that connects the church with work. But what hasn't been explored, and therefore has allowed for the unreflective equating of mission as innovation and Applebee's with the church, is that the flow has reversed directions. The water the synod bathes in comes carrying late-modern commitments around growth, stabilization, the self, the good, and even what counts as meaningful. It is no longer the church's theological imagination of work that washes into society. Instead, it is society's view of work that is washing back into the church, shaping its ministry and leading pastors and

available at https://web.archive.org/web/20141029223036/http://resourcingchristianity.org/sites/default/files/transcripts/research_article/DavidCunningham_A_Plentiful_Harvest_Essay.pdf.
    14. Matthew Kaemingk and Cory Willson discuss something similar in *Work and Worship: Reconnecting Our Labor and Liturgy* (Grand Rapids: Baker Academic, 2020), chap. 1.

denominational officials to make passionate pleas to shape congregations and whole synods around an aesthetic of creative innovation.

The Backwash to the Secular

This backwash of work into the church isn't necessarily to be grieved, but it is important to be aware of. There is nothing necessarily wrong with the late-modern conception of work washing back into the church. The church (particularly in Protestant forms) should never fear the world. After all, it's only in relation to the world that the church is faithful. There is no reason for the church to build a high seawall to keep all societal tides from washing in. Such a seawall is not only unfaithful but impossible.

Even with this important disclaimer, though, we shouldn't short-circuit the need for reflection. We need to recognize that late modernity's sense of work as creative innovation carries creativity as innovation back into the church—this might be good. But we should also be acutely aware (more aware than Applebee's Boy and his synod are) that if we are not very careful and attentive, what comes with it are the norms and goods of late modernity. This form of creativity returns to the church, now from the bay of late modernity, completely secularized. This creativity has no need for a living God. It is a creativity that is severed from the beauty of God—which is what makes it so advantageous for making money and winning market share.

The aesthetic of creativity as innovation comes washing back into the church stripped of divine action and even transcendence. Throughout modernity, the link between creativity as a ray of beauty and its source in the totality of God's own beauty has been, slowly but surely, broken completely. The creativity as innovation that populates the corporate world of later modernity sees, and wishes for, no connection to God. As Keith Sawyer shows in his book *Explaining Creativity*, creativity before the nineteenth century and the Romantic response to the Enlightenment was a trait of the gods or God.[15] Rarely were human beings assumed to be uniquely and singularly creative. The only singularly creative being was God. Creativity had its source and end in God's own being. For any human being, even Leonardo (who doubted the existence of the biblical God), to be creative would entail them receiving

15. Keith Sawyer says, "Until the modern era, creativity was attributed to a superhuman force; all novel ideas originated with the gods." Sawyer, *Explaining Creativity: The Science of Human Innovation* (New York: Oxford University Press, 2012), 19.

something from a transcendent source. Creativity was not produced by the self (you need Protestantism to get to this),[16] but creativity came as a kind of revelation from outside yourself. Its source or cause was transcendent. The word "creative" wasn't really used as an adjective or descriptor for a person, and it was assumed to be an insult. Few used "creative" to describe a person because creativity was God's alone. To do a creative thing, even repeatedly like Leonardo, meant you were linked in some way, even mystically, to the divine.

In our secular age of late modernity, creativity and innovation have no direct link to the divine, and they wish for none.[17] The creativity and innovation that wash back into Protestantism from the bay of late-modern work life return carrying the minerals and pollutants of the immanent frame, a framework late-modern people inherit that imposes a vision of the world and all the phenomena in it as finally and completely natural and material. The immanent frame gives us a world absent transcendence, a world in which all phenomena in it can have only a natural (not supernatural) source.[18]

Applebee's Boy and the synod can't see but *must* acknowledge and confront this challenge. If the synod wishes to embrace creativity and innovation (and it and many other Protestant ministries may be right to do so), it nevertheless must be acutely aware of how creativity as innovation comes from postindustrial, late-modern work life, bringing with it assumptions and a commitment to immanence. The synod needs to be aware of how work as creative innovation is shaped by immanence and the glorification of the entrepreneurial self. Creative innovation takes the gift of Protestantism's attention to the self and

16. Ultimately you need German Romantics inspired by Johann Hamann and his own return to Luther to get to this. Through the Romantics, like the poet Friedrich Hölderlin, we get to this unique creative self thanks to Hamann and Luther, but many of the Romantics have no need to hold on to Luther in any faithful way. The Romantics embrace the self, but their novel move is not to return to the Protestant commitments to a self but to claim that creativity itself is centered more deeply in the self as its source than in a transcendent personal reality that comes from outside the self. Keith Sawyer adds, "The word 'creativity' was invented in the late 19th century, when many people began to draw connections between the arts and the sciences. It appeared in an 1875 text *History of Dramatic English Literature*, by Adolfus William Ward. . . . It doesn't appear in French or Italian until 50 years after that, and didn't appear in standard English dictionaries until after World War II (it's not in the second edition of the New International Dictionary in 1934, but it is in the Third New International Dictionary of 1961)." *Explaining Creativity*, 19.
17. Charles Taylor discusses this in *A Secular Age*, part 5.
18. This conception is developed by Charles Taylor, *Secular Age*, 542–57. I've drawn on this idea in multiple places and for multiple purposes; see particularly Andrew Root, *Churches and the Crisis of Decline: A Hopeful, Practical Ecclesiology for a Secular Age* (Grand Rapids: Baker Academic, 2022).

radicalizes it to the point that life itself is no longer about living and working before God as a self but about being the most unique, singular self you can creatively curate.

Concluding and Moving Forward

Now we can return to Bearded Brown Turtleneck, that gruff pastor who found all the creative innovation talk to be garbage. It would be hard to find many Protestant leaders who don't agree that work (and how we live in the world) matters. Not even Bearded Brown Turtleneck, and his chorus of scoffers, would disagree with this. They weren't pushing for the aesthetic to be placed back in the hands of the ecclesial hierarchy (I don't think!). They weren't seeking a return to *what* we did over *how* we did it.

Instead, they seemed to grieve—and this grief came out as self-righteous anger—the direction of the impact. Without being able to name it, they were aware of and uncomfortable with the backwash of ideals and imagination from society into the church, instead of the flow going the other direction. This cacophonic choir of scoffers were at their worst when they were seeking to build a seawall, using the rhetoric of the importance of liturgy, ancient creeds, and the need for intellectual heft as the stones in the wall. Yet I think if they could escape their insecurity, hidden under layers of crotchety elitism and theological protectionism, we would recognize that they had a legitimate concern. They wondered how the flow had switched directions. How have church practices that once impacted and ennobled work been drowned out? They wondered, and we should with them, just how the shape of work is molding, and even imposing on, church practice and ministry in our time.

To answer these questions, we need to fill in the story of how sales associates became known as muses for the consumer-artists who are innovating the self, and how people preparing fast-food sandwiches became artists painting on the canvas of five-dollar footlongs.

3

Hungry, Hungry Markets

Workers in Contradiction, Children in Consumption

I was surprised to see Synod Executive Guy (that's what I started calling him) at this conference on the other side of the country. I shouldn't have been surprised. It made sense he would be at this national conference of leaders in his denomination. I was in the middle of taking one-on-one questions, after my presentation, when he interrupted and said hello. I was a little too exuberant to see him (though I did need to hide that I had no idea what his name was).

I said, "Hey! How are *you*?" as we awkwardly shook hands.

In my defense, my exuberance was equal parts surprise to see him in this other context *and* the desperate need to find someone to sit with at lunch. The line of individual question-askers was making me nervous that lunch would not be safe for my introversion. We agreed to meet outside the building in ten minutes.

After we grabbed our lunches and sat in a quiet, hidden corner, I remembered again why I liked Synod Executive Guy so much. His first words assured me that my uncomfortable exuberance to see him wasn't totally uncalled for. Because the first thing he said after we sat down was, "So have you seen *Inside Bill's Brain*?"

Inside Bill's Brain is a 2019, three-part docuseries on Netflix that explores the innovative initiatives the Gates Foundation and Bill Gates himself are pursuing.[1] It's an inspiring three episodes. Watching it would make anyone want to be a creative, inventing innovator. Without a doubt, Bill Gates would be one of the heads on our late-modern Mount Rushmore of entrepreneurial leaders. Gates, a middle-class kid of some privilege, became the richest person in the world (until he started giving money away). He achieved his fortune, it's assumed, by the sheer genius of creativity. Gates has done more than his part to turn all work in the direction of creative innovation.

I don't know what it says about me, but my favorite episode of the three was the first: on toilets! More specifically it's on the innovation around toilets and water-purification systems in central Africa. Scientists and doctors discovered that communities were suffering and children were dying from dysentery and cholera because wastewater was washing back into their drinking and bathing water. The backwash was literally killing them.

Commendably, the Gates Foundation set its sight on innovating a solution to this problem and therefore saving lives. In the process of this pursuit, the foundation tapped their best innovators, inventors, and designers, funding a competition between them for the best toilet. From the innovation engendered through the competition of private firms, multiple solutions were discovered (some more viable than others). All these solutions, all these toilets, not only solved a problem but bore the marks of art. The solutions and design were one. The firms needed to make a toilet that not only functioned but also was attractive so that people would use it.

These private firms, it was assumed, could do something that large governments couldn't do to solve this problem. Large national governments and international agencies might have more power. But *it's assumed* they lack the one key ingredient that private firms competing in the cutthroat pursuit for market share possess: creativity. In late modernity, creativity is assumed to be the blessed child born from the heated death struggle of cutthroat competition. And in late modernity, creativity is almost always perceived as an individual, as opposed to a communal, trait. Individuals are geniuses, and geniuses are bastions of creativity. Individual geniuses work best in zones free of regulation and restriction, as free of bureaucracy as possible. Creativity is

1. For more on the Gates Foundation and the moral conundrums of ultra-rich philanthropy, see David Callahan, *The Givers: Wealth, Power, and Philanthropy in a New Gilded Age* (New York: Vintage, 2017).

in its most natural habitat, late modernity assumes, when it works in a private firm rather than through a bureaucratic structure. A bureaucratic structure cannot be creative because it doesn't welcome competition. Creativity through the lens of late-modern work is always forged with and for the purpose of competition. In late modernity, private firms over public institutions or government agencies promise space free from regulation and restriction for creative people to be their most inventive, winning the firm market share. Episode one was clear: creativity, not bureaucracy, would solve this toilet problem.

By embracing innovation as mission, Synod Executive Guy was making a similar claim. The synod, too, recognized that bureaucracy was no solution to decline. Of course, the synod had its honeypot of funds only because of bureaucracy (the bylaws declared that the denomination owned the buildings that brought the funds). Though bureaucracy got it the money, it seemed to assume that bureaucracy was no way to spend the money. Even the denominational bureaucrats like Synod Executive Guy didn't trust bureaucrats (even if he was one). Creativity, not bureaucracy, would assure the money was spent well (this assumption has some deep problems, but it's been part of our imaginary since the mid-1980s, as we'll see).

Creativity allows innovation to fuse with mission. Mission is creativity, and creativity is the opposite of bureaucracy—or so our work lives have informed us. The shape of work in private firms had caused this assumption to wash back into church practice. It may even be a good assumption! I personally would choose creativity over bureaucracy. But we need to test it to make sure this assumption is correct. We need to test that the water washing back into church practice from work isn't filled with microbes that will give the church dysentery. Innovation may indeed be the next faithful step for Synod Executive Guy and those congregations, but first he should test to see if the norms, goods, and presumptions of the late-modern secular age and its immanent frame are hidden in this assumption.

To do this testing, we need to step back and hear the story of how work was made creative and innovation became a permanent task.

From the Woods of Vermont

New centuries never start on time. Our calendars may say one thing, but events, not dates, set the parameters for the times we live in. And, of course, what happens in one century is never cordoned off from the next. This is true for years too. For instance, I'm writing this in fall 2020, a crappy year by any measure for most everyone across the globe, thanks to COVID-19. It's become fun on social media in these last few weeks to wish the year away, illogically reassuring ourselves that when the calendar turns to 2021, this nightmare year will be finished. But events, not dates, frame our times.

With this in mind, it would be right to say that the nineteenth century in the Western world began *not* on January 1, 1800, but on November 20, 1815. Napoleon had been defeated at Waterloo in June and exiled in July, and the Treaty of Paris was signed on November 20. Besides a few small skirmishes, this treaty brought forth the longest period of peace ever seen on the continent.[2] The record still stands. We ourselves are also in the middle of long-standing European peace, with only a few people still alive who remember the last great conflict. And yet we're still decades away (2044 to be specific, though Russia's invasion of Ukraine threatens that date) before we'll match the nineteenth-century peace. The signing of the Treaty of Paris was followed by ninety-nine years of peace across Europe. These years raised the European standard of living by leaps and bounds, bringing forth the first true middle class and modern economies. It was the golden era in Europe. Industry in Britain, philosophy and music in the German nations, and art and fashion in France and the Netherlands blossomed. And America, a world away, was poised for a "bright" future as it pushed West and built new megacities for industry.[3]

But it all came crashing to the bloodiest of ends in August 1914 with the declaration that brought forth the Great War (World War I). The nineteenth century, born a decade and a half late, ended a decade and a half after the calendar turned. The twentieth century began with its feet in blood in 1914, the pools deepening through its first five decades. One nightmare seemed to produce the next. From a Great War to a Great Depression to a greater, more horrifying war led by fascist dictators with blitzkriegs and death camps.

In the middle of World War II, in 1944, in a small room in rural Vermont at Bennington College, a man who couldn't be more out of place in this rural

2. Some of those skirmishes include the Franco-Prussian War that lasted ten months from 1870 to 1871 and is the exception that proves the rule, as well as conflicts outside Europe like the Spanish-American War (1898) and the Second Boer War (1899–1902) between the British and Afrikaans in South Africa.

3. And stole lands and oppressed indigenous peoples. The golden era is relative, of course. The colonizing spirit of the eighteenth and nineteenth centuries did much harm. But this harm secured the modern economy, which is the story I'm telling here.

American setting wrote one of the most important economic sociologies ever to be penned. Karl Polanyi was an intellectual nomad. Born and raised in Hungary and having fought in WWI, the political climate after the Great War pushed him from his Hungarian homeland to Vienna. In contrast to the rest of central Europe, Vienna thrived in the 1920s and early 1930s, and with it Polanyi. But the harsh economic situation in the rest of central Europe produced a furious political climate in Germany, and it pushed into Vienna. Upon the suggestion of his younger brother, the eminently gifted scientist and philosopher Michael Polanyi, Karl immigrated to the UK. England became his new home and the backdrop for much of his economic thought.[4] Yet, unlike his brother, the elder Polanyi always found it hard to secure a permanent academic post in the UK. When an invitation came to spend a year in the US teaching and writing, even at tiny Bennington College, Polanyi grabbed hold of it.[5]

The Great Gain and Great Crash

Amid the pines of Vermont came *The Great Transformation*. In this classic text (which only found acclaim in the late 1980s, long after Polanyi's death), Polanyi lays out how the cultural and economic commitments that produced the golden era of a hundred-year peace in the West also created the conditions for the multiple-headed monster of the twentieth century. The Great War, the Great Depression, and the great fascist takeover were all seeded by four realities that produced nineteenth-century prosperity.

The nineteenth-century peace and prosperity was built on these four pillars of sand: (1) the balance of powers, (2) the self-regulating market, (3) the liberal state, and (4) the international gold standard. Number one is important

---

4. Karl Polanyi's story is somewhat similar to Isaiah Berlin's, the Oxford don. Britain benefited greatly in the early and mid-twentieth century by welcoming protégés from Eastern Europe. Both Polanyi and Berlin, in different ways, are philosophers of the history of ideas.

5. For a well-done biography on Karl Polanyi, see Gareth Dale, *Karl Polanyi: A Life on the Left* (New York: Columbia University Press, 2018). Polanyi, like his brother (but in different ways), was very sensitive and open to Christian faith. Dale offers some thoughts on this in another book called *Karl Polanyi* (London: Polity, 2010). Dale says, "Yet his attitude to Christianity per se was far from hostile. Even when writing those words (in 1911), Tolstoy was an intellectual enthusiasm, and Polanyi had come to appreciate the 'socialist flavour' of New Testament revelation. Like Tolstoy, he neither became an observant Christian, nor believed in the divinity or the resurrection of Jesus, but did perceive religion to be an indispensable social construction. Defined broadly as a total conception of the universe and man's place within it such as to warrant the belief that life itself has meaning, religion furnishes a framework essential to the individual's sense of moral purpose" (9).

but not necessarily economic, and therefore helps little in our story of the changing shape of work in late modernity. But here's a quick summary: "By the balance of power system, [Polanyi] means the system of changing alliances among the European powers, which prevented any single power from gaining a dominant position. . . . These shifting alliances helped maintain the peace through deterrence, as the high probability of retaliation by a group of opponents made armed aggression . . . too costly."[6]

Polanyi finds the final three realities most important, because all three are interconnected, allowing for both growing prosperity and catastrophic collapse. There is almost a Hegelian thesis-antithesis tug-of-war in the nineteenth-century economy (and, spoiler alert, this same tug-of-war returns in the 1980s). There's constant tension that must remain to keep one side from being pulled violently into a deep, thick mud pit.[7]

On one side of the tug-of-war is the self-regulating market, championed by the thought of two British eighteenth-century thinkers, David Ricardo and Thomas Robert Malthus.[8] Both Ricardo and Malthus, though in different ways, believed that if markets were left alone, they'd balance themselves, bringing supply and demand into equilibrium, which would produce growth. Markets would self-regulate without any direct help from the government. As a matter of fact, any tinkering or regulating of these markets by the government would, instead of helping, seize up the markets and bring mayhem.

The government needed to allow markets to be free. Therefore, the government needed to oversee liberal states. This is Polanyi's third reality. In liberal states, the government seeks to enhance freedom and rights. But there is an inherent tension here that sets up the tug-of-war. As a liberal state, the government protects the markets' freedom by enforcing a doctrine of laissez-faire, embracing the orthodoxy of free trade, and opposing all protectionism. The government's job, in such liberal states of self-regulating markets, is to remove all the fences that restrict markets. Markets need to roam and feed as they

6. Fred Block and Margaret Somers, *The Power of Market Fundamentalism: Karl Polanyi's Critique* (Cambridge, MA: Harvard University Press, 2014), 11–12.

7. Karl Polanyi discusses this tension in *The Great Transformation: The Political and Economic Origins of Our Time*, 2nd ed. (Boston: Beacon, 2001), 3–15.

8. Malthus had made dire predictions that population growth would outstrip food production in the late eighteenth century, leading to great famine. (He came to this theory by contemplating the ramifications of Rousseau's work.) Malthus's thought was responsible for the shape of economic life in the nineteenth century, and he was a great inspiration to Charles Darwin. Darwin saw the competition of populations for food stretching back into all species, propelling evolutionary adaptations.

wish. But at the same time, the liberal state should support and enhance the freedom of individuals (which is the justification for free markets in the first place). To give an example from our time, it's assumed that free self-regulating markets don't like a government-imposed minimum wage. The market should set the cost of labor. But individuals cannot be free without the means of labor to live. So the liberal state has to walk the tightrope of serving two masters: the freedom of the market and the freedom of the individual. Great effort and challenging acrobatics are required to show that freedom for the individual is freedom for the market and vice versa.

These freedoms are supposed to work together. In the liberal state, self-regulating markets must be free. Freedom is always a good. But because freedom is the high good of the liberal state, individuals too must be free to reap the rewards of the markets working in their favor, free to be rewarded for their creativity. All individuals must be protected and given the freedom of food and shelter. The good of every individual's freedom entitles each individual to a standard of living. But this entitlement to live as a free individual risks imposing on the freedom of the market to roam and feed in the direction it wishes. The liberal state, then, is torn between freedoms.

It's the fourth reality, Polanyi believes, that made it impossible for this somewhat utopian sense of self-regulating markets and the balancing of freedoms in the nineteenth century to be realized.[9] This fourth reality was the international gold standard. Throughout the nineteenth century, all European economies aligned themselves with the gold standard. The gold standard allowed markets to freely expand across national borders, allowing for assurances of trade (until it didn't!). The gold standard was cruise control for the market. By putting your national economy on the gold standard—meaning the value of your currency was correlated to your gold reserves—the market was free to automatically adjust. Actually, instead of cruise control, gold was more like artificial intelligence or at least machine learning for the market, ensuring that the market was always looking out for itself no matter what.

Polanyi goes to great lengths to show that the gold standard was a devastating poisonous pill. Like the Matrix, it was AI that turned against the whole system. The gold standard imposed what Polanyi calls a "double movement." In one movement, it allowed the markets to be free. The gold

9. Actually, Polanyi considers this to be starkly utopian, not just "somewhat" utopian. Polanyi discusses this market utopianism in *The Great Transformation*, 267–68.

standard kept the will of capricious politicians or pesky voters in growing liberal democratic states from imposing on the market's freedom for their own advantage. But the second movement came rudely crashing in. While the gold standard allowed markets their freedom, it in turn tied the hands of the liberal state. The market could turn quickly, thrusting large parts of the society of one country into starvation. Governments could do little, unable to borrow from other countries because their own currency was too weak in relation to the gold standard. They were in crisis because of the gold standard, but also unable to crawl out of this trouble because of the gold standard. The gold standard led to a crazy roller-coaster ride of inflating and deflating currency values. Ultimately, the gold standard bound governments in golden handcuffs, making them unable "to protect their citizens from the disruptions caused by market processes."[10] The gold standard assured that the market could roam freely and feed without fences, but the market soon began trampling people, and there was little that governments could do to stop it.

The nineteenth-century peace in Europe was being eroded slowly by the animosity over trade and how the gold standard was pitting one country against another. Some countries were unwilling to trade, or offered unjust trade deals, pointing to the gold standard as justification. The nations needing these deals were starving, but the logic of the free market and the handcuffs of the gold standard kept them from any deals. Bad feelings grew and, ironically, a new rigid nationalism rose from within hyper-free-market and liberal states. "Nationalism was expressed in the heightened Anglo-German global rivalry in trade and arms that began in the 1890s and which ultimately allowed the assassination of an Austrian archduke to escalate into World War I."[11]

It's always hard for a novice historian to understand what started WWI. There seems to be so many small, weird causes. It's as though a thousand paper cuts opened up an anterior artery. Polanyi's contribution shows that economic conflicts, originating in the contradictions of the free market, brought it forth. *The gold standard served markets, not the needs of the people of liberal states.* This bred animosities and resentments between these states.

10. Block and Somers, *Power of Market Fundamentalism*, 14.
11. Block and Somers, *Power of Market Fundamentalism*, 15.

Unfortunately, the lessons of what led to the Great War weren't learned. At the Treaty of Versailles (January 10, 1920), the French, English, and Americans used the gold standard to calculate the debts the Germans owed for the war. The gold standard, the liberal state, and the self-regulating market were reimposed—and harshly so. Within a decade, unemployment, rampant inflation, and starvation were strangling the West. Beyond the painful ebbs and flows of lethargy of the late nineteenth century, in the 1930s the markets were thrust into a deep and great depression. From this depression rose a furious and violent nationalism, with anger and resentment not seen on such a scale before. Hitler promised payback to all those nations that used the gold standard to devalue German currency and Germany itself. He would avenge their humiliation! He promised that Germany needed more than just a strong leader: only a true Führer had the force to oppose Versailles and shatter the handcuffs of the gold standard.

When Polanyi finished his book, WWII had not yet been won, but the Allied powers were marching to Berlin. Franklin Roosevelt's New Deal had been in place for a decade in America, reigning in the free market so it no longer would trample people but instead actually work for them. After WWII and into the 1950s, much of the West drew from another British economist to end their reliance on the gold standard and ease the tension between self-regulating markets and the liberal state. John Maynard Keynes was unwaveringly committed to capitalism, but in a much different way from Ricardo or Malthus.[12] Keynesianism provided ways for the liberal states to allow markets to be free, roaming in great pastures, eating and growing as the market moved. But all this roaming needed to be done within fences, particularly government-guaranteed employment.[13] Markets needed to be

12. Keynes actually found his fame as a participant at the Treaty of Versailles. He was appalled with it. He saw from the start that the reparations were vengeful and promised German default. He wrote a book called *The Economic Consequences of the Peace* that laid this all out and made him *the* economist of the early twentieth century. M. G. Hayes explains, "Keynes made his name by resigning from his position as an official representative of the UK Treasury at the Versailles Peace Conference in 1919 and publishing *The Economic Consequences of the Peace* in protest at the terms of the Treaty. Its rhetorical brilliance and acerbic biography alone make for compelling reading. Its foundation is the claim that the reparations imposed on Germany for the First World War were unpayable." Hayes, *John Maynard Keynes* (London: Polity, 2020), 99.

13. Robert Skidelsky explains in his expansive biography of Keynes, saying, "Keynes emphatically rejected socialism as an economic remedy for the ills of laissez-faire. Its doctrines were ideological, obsolete, irrelevant, inimical to wealth-creation, and likely to involve gross interference with individual liberty. The inefficiency, as well as irrelevance, of socialism as an economic technique had been vividly brought home to him in Soviet Russia. Secondly, Keynes

free, like cattle on a large ranch in Montana. But if the wranglers didn't put up some fences and occasionally impose their will, directing the cattle away from danger and into new pastures, the cattle would die. In the same way, the markets needed to be watched, the fences of regulation keeping the market from wandering into a pasture it shouldn't be in, eating its way into danger, consuming clover, bloating its stomach, and keeling over. Keynesianism allowed the market to be free but no longer wild. Its habitat was now a large ranch with fences and wranglers, allowing the market to roam but always within imposed boundaries, giving people employment and regulating the market so human freedoms were protected, so that all Americans, for instance, had a fair deal—as Roosevelt would say.[14]

Polanyi rushed to complete *The Great Transformation*, hoping it could play a part in keeping the West from making the same mistakes at Potsdam that it made at Versailles.[15] Even if that hope was too ambitious, Polanyi could conclude his magnum opus by at least breathing a sigh of relief and thanking God that the days of the completely wild self-regulating market were over for good. The three-headed monster of the Great War, the Great Depression, and the great fascist dictators showed unequivocally in his mind that wild markets coaxed to behavior by gold was a dangerous business. Polanyi assumed that self-regulating markets encouraged to roam without fences were never coming back!

And by "never," we mean not until the 1980s.

---

objected to the revolutionary strain in socialism. He gave two reasons. He did not regard the existing order of society as so bad that it could not be reformed; and was doubly wrong to have a revolution to establish a system worse than the one being overthrown." Skidelsky, *John Maynard Keynes, 1883–1946: Economist, Philosopher, Statesman* (New York: Penguin, 2003), 371. Nicholas Wapshott adds, "Keynes went out of his way in his Sidney Ball lecture to state that 'for my part, I think that Capitalism, wisely managed, can probably be made more efficient for attaining economic ends than any alternative system yet in sight,' although he conceded that 'in itself [capitalism] is in many ways extremely objectionable.' Or, as he wrote to Sir Charles Addis, a director of the Bank of England, 'I seek to improve the machinery of society, not overturn it.'" Wapshott, *Keynes Hayek: The Clash That Defined Modern Economics* (New York: Norton, 2011), 37.

14. M. G. Hayes provides a nice overview, saying, "The Keynesian era can be defined as a period of three decades . . . during which western governments were committed to full employment. The beginning of the period was marked by the United Kingdom's 1944 White Paper on Employment Policy and by the United States' 1946 Full Employment Act. Its end came shortly after the breakdown of the Bretton Woods exchange rate system and the subsequent oil crisis in 1973–74." *John Maynard Keynes*, 116.

15. The Potsdam Conference happened in August 1945. Roosevelt was dead and Polanyi, in 1944, had no idea that this conference would happen. But he was aware that some kind of Versailles-like treaty would come.

Cold War Contradictions

Potsdam indeed was not Versailles. Lessons were learned. But though the conditions for a precipitous World War III were avoided, a conflict was nevertheless inaugurated. Going into the Potsdam Conference, the Americans and the Soviets warmly celebrated their mutual victory. But they'd leave Potsdam in a chill that would turn frigid. World War III, in another European theater, was avoided, but a Cold War was not. The theater of this Cold War was not the French countryside but the economy. The soldiers of this war were workers, and the most important weapon was growth.

Dwight Eisenhower had already slain monsters. He had defeated the European fascists as supreme commander of the Allied forces in the European theater. As president, following Keynesianism, he assured the growth necessary to battle the Soviets in the cold conflict. From 1950 to 1973, the American economy grew over 5 percent annually. This growth was *mostly* continuous, with only a few years of recession.[16]

This growth came from, importantly, the American consumer. Keynesianism, and the American memory of the Great Depression, caused banking and financial markets to be highly regulated. The field the financial markets roamed in during Keynesianism were lush but small, with high electrical fences. Unlike today, financial markets were *not* able to float the economy. For instance, today, even in the middle of a pandemic during which 10 million American workers have lost their jobs (mostly in the consumer and labor market), the stock market nevertheless increases. The financial markets are now so large and unfenced in our time that they can grow wealth (for the few) even as the unemployment numbers are bleak and other markets collapse. Yet in the mid-twentieth century, this 5 percent growth came almost completely from within consumer and labor markets. America got its 5 percent growth and won (or at least didn't lose) ground in the Cold War by creating a mass

16. Benjamin Friedman adds some more nuance: "Three further recessions followed during the presidency of Dwight Eisenhower, but none of them was long-lasting, and only once, and briefly, did unemployment reach as much as 8 percent of the labor force. After the third of these recessions bottomed, in February 1961, output grew steadily and unemployment remained continuously low for almost nine years—at the time, the longest unbroken American economic expansion on record. From 1946 through 1973, when a quadrupling of the international price of oil by the OPEC cartel finally triggered a sharp recession, unemployment averaged 4.8 percent. After allowing for what had now become a persistent inflation of prices, the economy grew on average by 3.8 percent per annum." Friedman, *The Moral Consequences of Economic Growth* (New York: Vintage, 2005), 183.

society of consumer goods gobbled up by American families. Welcome to the consumer age![17]

This 5 percent growth was dependent on American workers embodying two seemingly contradictory goods. First, drawing from the Protestant legacies of Puritanism (discussed below), workers between 1950 and 1973 needed to embrace a sense of devotion to their work. They needed to put their heads down and do their jobs, not worried about their own selves but about the job at hand. The manager didn't oversee personalities but objectives and quotas. Workers needed to embrace generalized and rationalized systems of the corporation. The workers needed to play their part for the sake of the whole, denying self-gratification to do their duty for the corporation. If the workers did so, whether wearing a blue or white collar, the corporation in this ever-growing economy could promise its workers decades of employment with a pension upon retirement. Mobility was minimal because most workers didn't assume that their job should make them happy or be an expression of their truest self.

The Keynesianism-shaped economy needed workers who were *not* flashy but buttoned-up. The corporations that helped the economy continue at over 5 percent needed workers who stayed organized, functioned rationally, and supported (even embraced) bureaucracy.[18] The best workers, and the best managers, were in the shape of the organization man. The organization man conformed to corporate culture, sacrificing his own individuality for the sake of the corporation's growth (think George McFly from *Back to the Future*).

17. Much like George W. Bush after 9/11, Keynes told English housewives in the 1920s and 1930s to buy. Holding onto capital was the threat. Wapshott says, "The month Hayek arrived in London, Keynes was urging the housewives of London in audio broadcast to spend, spend, spend. The cheapness of goods meant that British shoppers had never had it so good. But while those employed were doing well, millions stood idle. 'Many millions of pounds' worth of goods could be produced each day by the workers and the plants which stand idle,' said Keynes." *Keynes Hayek*, 81.

18. Robert Skidelsky explains the heart of Keynes's perspective, saying, "The simplest, easiest to understand and, therefore, generally most acceptable version of Keynes's argument is his demonstration that economies adjust to a 'shock' to investment demand by a fall in income and output, leading to 'underemployment equilibrium.' 'Quantities adjust, not prices' was the headline version of Keynes's model. In the classical models, adjustment always means a restoration of a unique (optimal) point of equilibrium through movements of relative prices. The theoretical novelty in Keynes's treatment lay in the claim that, when the desire to save exceeds the desire to invest, the only adjustment path open is through a change in aggregate income and output. The excess saving at the initial equilibrium level of income is eliminated by the fall in income, creating a situation of stable output at less than full employment." Skidelsky, *Money and Government: The Past and Future of Economics* (New Haven: Yale University Press, 2018), 118.

The *best* managers of such workers were themselves the bureaucratic high functionalists. They tightly followed the rules, overseeing workers in ways that matched the rationalist foundations of the corporation. The manager's job was to keep the corporate machine of workers functioning by maintaining its bureaucratic shape through organization and conformity. Even if these workers weren't working with machines, they were managed as if they themselves were a cog in the firm's functional pursuit of growth in market share.

Such rhetoric seems so harsh, even unethical to us now, because we live after the dawning age of authenticity, and we have all taken on an ethic of authenticity. The workers of the mid-twentieth century understood that what was most important (particularly inside a Cold War) was doing your duty. Your duty at work was to deny yourself and its wants and *do your job*.

This puritanical self-denying work was only one side of the coin, however. The other side of the coin causes a whiplash contradiction. To get to 5 percent growth, you needed workers who were self-denying organizational men (or women) who accepted bureaucracy and embraced duty, but these same gratification-denying workers needed to leave the corporation at the end of the day and conspicuously consume, throwing caution to the wind to splurge on a new car. Those workers needed to fill their cars with children and take them out for dinner and a movie. The worker may be a cog in the bureaucratic corporation, but he was (at least the men were) king of his own castle, a full-blown consumer on the weekend. The Keynesian growth economy depended on it.

The worker needed to leave delayed gratification at work and seek instant gratification outside it. From nine to five, the post-WWII economy needed puritanical, conforming workers, managed by organizational men for the sake of growth. After five and on the weekends, the economy needed hedonist individuals seeking happiness through consumption. When the workday was over, a new ethic of consumption needed to mobilize the worker. This new ethic was a duty—a gratifying duty, but nevertheless a duty.[19] This duty to

---

19. Daniel Bell states, "The 'new capitalism' (the phrase was first used in the 1920s) continued to demand a Protestant ethic in the area of production—that is, in the realm of work—but to stimulate a demand for pleasure and play in the area of consumption. The disjunction was bound to widen. The spread of urban life, with its variety of distractions and multiple stimuli; the new roles of women, created by the expansion of office jobs and the freer social and sexual contacts; the rise of a national culture through motion pictures and radio—all contributed to a loss of social authority on the part of the older value system." Bell, *The Cultural Contradictions of Capitalism* (New York: Basic Books, 1996), 75.

consume conflicted with the duty (even practice and identity) at work. The conflict between the two became a contradiction. And this contradiction between rationalized worker and expressivist buyer was the road to Keynesian economic growth—over 5 percent every year.

The Time between Times

This reality of rationalized workers and expressivist consumers became what the Harvard sociologist Daniel Bell in 1976 called "the cultural contradictions of capitalism."[20] Into the mid-1960s, no one could look through the Cold War fog and see this contradiction (though many may have felt it).[21] Bell could name this contradiction only because he was writing in the late 1970s. And the late 1970s, in relation to work and the economy, was a time between times. Bell could see the sharp contradictions in Keynesian capitalism because he was looking at work after two important occurrences.

Occurrence One: The Counterculture

The first occurrence was the revolt of the youth. In 1968, young people, raised only in the self-gratification side of the 5 percent growth economy, came of age. No generation had ever been raised in a continuously growing economy won by consumption. These children were the canaries in a mine of this full-blown new economy. A large percentage of the children of the 1950s and 1960s were creatures whose habitat was completely cordoned off from *any* self-denying work for the first time in history. They knew little to nothing of the childhood work on farms and factory floors from earlier American generations. This self-denying work was far removed from the experience and the imagination of the new American suburbs and the children who roamed them.[22]

20. Bell sums up the contradiction when he talks of our North American DNA: "Two images have come down to us as the essence of the American character: the piety and torment of Jonathan Edwards, obsessed with human depravity, and the practicality and expedience of Benjamin Franklin, oriented to a world of possibility and gain." Bell, *Cultural Contradictions of Capitalism*, 58.

21. Some did, but they were pushed to the cultural fringes so that they made no difference until they were recovered and finally given an audience in the late 1960s and early 1970s. I'm thinking here of the Beat Generation, particularly Allen Ginsberg and Jack Kerouac. They denied the contradiction of capitalism on the worker in the 1950s, but they weren't embraced until the late 1960s.

22. Bell discusses the counterculture in *Cultural Contradictions of Capitalism*, xxvii, 141–43.

The context for these children was the glossy, enclosed consumptive side of Keynesian growth economy.

From 1950 to 1968, working parents bore the Keynesian contradictions of capitalism, while their children only knew the expressive and consumptive side. This created, at least from the perspective of the child, a middle-class, white, suburban utopia.[23] But no one recognized that this suburban utopia had a ticking time bomb embedded within it that would explode when it was time for baby boomers to become workers.

The boom of this bomb went off in 1968, as a large number of these children came of age. They were now being asked, almost to their shock, to move from being pure consumers, living only in the self-gratifying and expressivist side of the contradiction (which, being exposed to only this side, felt like no contradiction to them), to being grown up and embracing the other side as well, as their parents did. They needed to be adults and enter the conforming, delayed-gratification, and rationalized side of the contradiction as well. Workers in the post-WWII Keynesian economy of continuous 5 percent growth accepted this necessary contradiction. But being formed entirely in only the expressivist side, the generation coming of age after 1968 was *not* keen to bear the capitalist contradiction.[24] And they let the whole society know it!

They believed the contradiction was unnecessary and an obvious hypocrisy. The fact that their parents didn't recognize this was shocking—even maddening—to them. Their parents should have seen this contradiction as not only hypocritical but a dirty trick. This dirty trick presumed to raise a generation in a historically long childhood (lasting eighteen to twenty-two years), encouraging them to follow their expressive wants, and then abruptly told that younger generation they needed to put that away (at least from nine to five for the next forty years) and be self-denying, rationalized workers who accept the management of rigid bureaucrats. Middle-class children who were

23. The high alcohol use and sexism that would lead to the second wave of feminism shows that this utopia was not really utopian at all. The contradiction of capitalism lay heavily on parents, leading to tensions in gender relations, race relations, and more. But most of the texts (movies, books, TV shows) we get from this period—which idealize it—come not from parents but from how baby boomers remember it. It was a utopia for white, middle-class children.

24. William Davies discusses the importance of 1968 both culturally and economically in his book *The Limits of Neoliberalism: Authority, Sovereignty and the Logic of Competition*, rev. ed. (Los Angeles: SAGE, 2017), xii–xiii.

the benefactors of Keynesianism's consumer-driven 5 percent growth were not willing to accept this, even claiming it to be immoral, calling for revolution against the contradiction.

Unlike their parents, who consented to the contradiction, taking on both sides as their duty, the young people of the baby boom refused. They desired an adulthood beyond the incongruity. But having breathed deeply the air of conspicuous consumption, their strategy for overcoming the incongruity was to try and shape a new adulthood that was fully and completely expressivist (which failed, but not for lack of trying!). This meant that the work their parents did, conforming to a corporation's goals for efficacy by becoming a small, managed piece of the whole, denying their own unique gratifications, was deeply and ethically out of bounds. If that was work, they wanted none of it. The Age of Aquarius was imagined, though never realized, as an age without corporate work.[25] The young people who reaped the rewards of the continuous growth of Keynesian capitalism and modernity's Protestant work ethic decided that the weight of the inherent contradiction was not for them. If they couldn't have an expressivist style of work, they wanted no work at all—to the Haight they went. They decided to grow love, not the economy.

To these young people it seemed hypocritical, downright wrong, to accept this contradiction. Fed like mother's milk on the expressivist and self-gratifying side of the Keynesianism contradiction, the counterculture chose this side alone (which would later create its own contradiction—namely, at some point you need to secure the means to continue in the expressivist consumer glow). But after the 1960s, they built an ethic around this expressivism. The expressivist side became glorified, the rationalist side demonized. They asserted that the organized, rationalized side of the contradiction ("the man") was not simply a necessity of bureaucratic organizations and a growing economy but was itself unethical, even evil. It denied workers their most authentic self. Rationalization, bureaucracy, and delayed gratification—all managed by organization men—for the sake of doing your duty for an impersonal corporation was assumed to be a direct and vicious attack on the self. This kind of work had no place in the younger generation's sense of the good life. Capitalism had a place, but they wanted only its expressive side.

25. Hence the glorification of vagabond artists, farmers, Native Americans, tie-dye, and long hair.

The rational side became an enemy of authenticity.[26] After the counterculture, the contradiction of Keynesian capitalism was clear. Bell could spot it
and name it.

This brings us to the second occurrence that allowed Bell to see the sharp
contradictions in Keynesian capitalism. Coupled with the first, this second
occurrence changed work forever. And in the wake of this change, the rhetoric
of entrepreneurship and innovation entered the scene.

Occurrence Two: Below 5 Percent

In the mid-1970s, Bell could vividly see the contradiction because the streak
ended. In 1973, nearly two and a half decades of 5 percent growth came to an
end with no signs of a quick rebound. For the first time since WWII began, the
American economy showed signs of sluggishness, which opened the door for
panic. We were still in a Cold War, after all. This panic led to opportunism.
Those who hated all the fences of Keynesianism and wanted to return the
economy to its Malthusian state of completely free self-regulating markets
made their move.[27]

These economists argued that the economy was sluggish, losing its streak
of 5 percent growth, because of all those regulations. If we could free banks,
allowing the financial markets to get off the ranch and companies to run
harder for profits, and if we could allow the market to set the cost of labor,
we'd get back to 5 percent and probably even beyond it. Bell wrote his book
at the end of the streak, when talk like this was building. The contradictions
of capitalism were brought into sharp view by the swirling questions of what
happened to all the growth.

When Bell published his book, and the 1970s moved toward their close,
the contradiction of capitalism needed to be reinstated. It was clear by the
late 1970s that the Age of Aquarius would never come.[28] The young radicals

26. I've told the cultural side of this story in Andrew Root, *Faith Formation in a Secular
Age* (Grand Rapids: Baker Academic, 2017), part 1.

27. I'm thinking here of economists Friedrich Hayek and Milton Friedman. The Chicago
school of economics had a huge impact on American economic policy from the late 1970s to today.

28. Robert and Edward Skidelsky say powerfully, "The most obvious reason was the failure
of Western economies to sustain the promise of general abundance. In practice, the protest
movements of the 1960s were rapidly followed by the collapse of the Keynesian state on which
the expectations of imminent abundance had been built. This killed off utopianism. [Herbert]
Marcuse became a museum piece in the West (though not in Latin America) even before his
death. The world of insecure work returned; the trend to more equal income distribution

made their cultural impact but failed to bring forth a new society beyond the contradictions of capitalism. There would be no large-scale work outside the corporation. If we were ever going to return to growth, the worker, even the once-young radical, needed to recommit to this contradiction. But this would be tricky, because while the Age of Aquarius had never and would never come, ending the reign of corporate America, there was also no way of putting the ethic of authenticity, which the counterculture delivered to the whole culture, back in the bottle. That genie was out for good. Somehow the contradiction of capitalism needed to be reinstated, but now coded within the new ethic of authenticity. But before this could be done, the markets needed to secure their own expansive freedom.[29]

EXPANDING THE MARKET

Expanding the freedom of the markets would require a surprising recovery of nineteenth-century ideas. But this time the goal, and the highest good, was growth and more growth. Economic growth had been our day-to-day weapon in the Cold War. In a fascinating turn, this drive for all-out growth, which necessitated the elimination of regulations, remained in place after the Cold War had been won. Even when the war was over, the American economy kept fighting and driving for growth. Growth as our highest good became even more important in the 1990s, and this need for growth settled deeply into our faith communities—only a growing church is a good church.[30]

If economic growth were a high (the highest!) good for society, workers would need to bear the contradictions of capitalism. Workers needed to work even harder than their parents for the sake of the company's profits. But companies could only see those profits if the fences of regulation were pushed down and the markets were free to regulate themselves again (as they were in the nineteenth century).

This time the markets, according to economists such as Friedrich Hayek and his disciple Milton Friedman, wouldn't even need the gold standard to

---

was reversed; creative destruction was back. Under Reagan and Thatcher capitalism recovered much of its old piratical, buccaneering spirit, and the dream of instinctual liberation from a springboard of managed affluence receded." Skidelsky and Skidelsky, *How Much Is Enough? Money and the Good Life* (London: Penguin, 2013), 67.

29. For more on this, see Skidelsky and Skidelsky, *How Much Is Enough?*, 72–73.

30. Growth became so important that neoliberalism would even take over the Democratic Party under Bill Clinton (and the Labor Party under Tony Blair). The party of the New Deal became as anti-Keynesian as the Reagan administration.

babysit them. The gold standard, after all, was shown to be a devious and destructive babysitter. Even Keynes fired the gold standard long ago. No one disagreed with the assessment that it was a poor standard. Hayek and Friedman concurred with Polanyi on this. Yet Hayek and Friedman made an argument inside this assertion that Polanyi would never have imagined (because he couldn't believe it to be true).

Hayek and Friedman argued that, because the gold standard was a very bad babysitter, markets should be free from *all* regulation. All babysitting everywhere was wrong, because markets were always wise and mature. And if markets were always wise and mature, never needing a babysitter, then Keynesianism and its regulations shamefully infantilized these wise markets. Hayek and Friedman believed that markets were so benevolent that it was an insult to even suggest that the markets needed a babysitter. If we could just end the regulation and pull out all the fenceposts, the markets could truly be free, as they deserved, taking complete care of themselves and gifting us, for their freedom, with growth and more growth (even over 5 percent).[31]

In 1979 and 1980,[32] something happened that Polanyi could never have imagined: the West again entertained the idea of completely self-regulating markets. That would be nuts, Polanyi had assumed, like arguing that leeches and bloodletting was good medical practice or that Russian roulette was the best way to deal with a psychological ailment. Though completely self-regulating markets may be a tonic that smells appealingly fruity, to cave to its appeal and drink it would prove it to be poison, not punch. No one, Polanyi assumed, would ever again claim otherwise.

But in 1979 and 1980, Margaret Thatcher and Ronald Reagan were celebrating political victories by touting and toasting this very punch. Two of the largest economies in the West (the UK and US) were taking bold steps to (again!) implement self-regulating market fundamentalism.[33] Those economists who hated Keynesian regulations, and had been sidelined for decades,

31. It takes little imagination to see why some have called this economic perspective a kind of religion.

32. These are the years that Margaret Thatcher and Ronald Reagan won their respective elections. For more on this history, see David Harvey, *A Brief History of Neoliberalism* (New York: Oxford University Press, 2007), 48–52.

33. Many commentators use "fundamental" to refer to the almost religious sense that markets are free, benevolent forces. The only sin that can be done to them is to regulate them. Thinkers like Block and Somers have shown a connection here to religious fundamentalism. The market fundamentalism takes Adam Smith's invisible hand further than he ever would have, turning it into a kind of pseudoreligious commitment.

found frightened policymakers and ambitious politicians who were anxious about slowing growth and ready to accept their updated nineteenth-century economic theory. Polanyi had shown that the heart of this theory had just decades earlier led to deep economic inequalities that eventually bred unimaginable war, famine, and violent, bloody fascism.[34]

This return to updated nineteenth-century economic ideas seemed precarious, but UK and US policymakers decided it was worth the risk. After all, what war can be won without risk? The Cold War was being fought in the theater of the economy, workers were the soldiers, and growth was the weapon. Stagnant economies were not an option. And politicians like Thatcher and Reagan claimed again, as in the nineteenth century, that the best way to be truly liberal, honoring the freedom of the individual, was to allow the companies and businesses that people worked in to be free. To these politicians, freedom meant freedom from regulations to chase the dream of profits.

It brought growth, but not equally. To some, it brought mind-spinning, immediate growth. For others, particularly workers (and, even more so, people of color), not so much. But in the mind of these economists, policymakers, and politicians, this inequality did not violate liberalism but created the conditions for this growth in profits to trickle down to workers. Inequality would have to be stomached—justified—because its rising tide was believed to lift all boats.

This freedom from regulation also freed the very people who could support such political campaigns. For good or ill, the Thatcher/Reagan market fundamentalism (or neoliberalism, as it's often called) was about freeing the Businessman. The 1980s were the dawn of the rise of the Businessman as cultural hero. With regulations stripped, the small business could quickly become

34. Polanyi says this about fascism: "In reality, the part played by fascism was determined by one factor: the condition of the market system." *Great Transformation*, 250. Not to sensationalize, but our self-regulating markets have also led to huge inequality gaps, and in just the last few years, an expansive flirting with nationalism has arrived. Polanyi's ideas from 1944 continue to seem relevant as history repeats itself.

Thomas Piketty, in his award-winning book *Capital in the Twenty-First Century* (Cambridge, MA: Belknap, 2017), says, "I have now precisely defined the notions needed for what follows, and I have introduced the orders of magnitude attained in practice by inequality with respect to labor and capital in various societies. The time has now come to look at the historical evolution of inequality around the world. How and why has the structure of inequality changed since the nineteenth century? The shocks of the period 1914–1945 played an essential role in the compression of inequality, and this compression was in no way a harmonious or spontaneous occurrence. The increase in inequality since 1970 has not been the same everywhere, which again suggests that institutional and political factors played a key role" (339).

the large business. The large business could become the megacorporation. The Businessman himself—now with financial markets off the ranch—was able to secure and multiply his fortune.[35]

WHEN EVERYONE BECOMES A BUSINESSMAN

Neoliberalism brought substantial growth to certain companies and corporations, but what about workers? If these companies and corporations were free to race for the expansive horizon of profits, ignoring all fence lines in their pursuit for more, they would need workers who were willing to accelerate their own lives, working long, taxing hours to achieve profits that would mainly go in the pocket of executives and stockholders.

Now in the 1980s and into the 1990s, in an economic environment that mirrored the mid-nineteenth century, what could possibly cause workers to embrace the contradiction of capitalism? Especially now that they'd had their consciousness raised by the Age of Aquarius and a new ethic of authenticity? What had made the contradiction palpable between 1950 and the late 1970s (besides the glad consumption of all those consumer goods from happy hour on[36]) was that certain protections resulted from the rationalist, delayed-gratification side of the contradiction. Work, even in the rationalist-expressivist contradiction of the post-war era, had been secularized. No one really worked in an organized, self-denying way because it reflected a heart obediently turned to God. Rather, people embraced this rational-bureaucratic form of work because it delivered the protections of full health insurance, retirement pension, and social security. They gave their long hours to a company because the company protected the workers. All the Keynesian regulations were in place to protect workers and their families from the profit motivations of the company.

But in the 1980s and beyond, justified by slow growth, the new rhetoric of zero regulations and freedom won a shift in protections. The protections that workers had received (stable employment, pensions, total health care, disability benefits, union rights) were defined as corporate regulations. Somehow it became logical that corporations, not workers, needed protection in the 1980s

35. Callahan, in *The Givers*, 15, 24, discusses how George Soros became a billionaire almost overnight simply because the restrictions on financial markets were lifted.

36. The fact that it's called "happy hour" shows the contradiction in capitalism that Bell points to. The hour is happy because work is over and you shift from self-denying worker to self-gratifying consumer. What better way to kick off the flip than to flip back a shot or two?

and beyond. For the sake of growth, companies were protected. The corporation needed to be protected from needing to protect their workers so that they could be unencumbered to chase down those fast and free-racing markets.[37]

This shift toward protecting companies makes our question all the more pointed: If protections had shifted from the worker to the corporation, and yet the worker had been imbued with a new ethic of authenticity, seeking expressivism and opposing a conformist, rationalized bureaucracy, how could the contradictions of capitalism be reinstated? How and why would workers drive harder for profits, giving more of themselves, if they got fewer protections and less share of the profits?

The answer was simple: by making each worker their own Businessman or Businesswoman.[38] The 1980s and beyond glorified the Businessman so much that we all became our own business (and the gig economy after the Great Recession of 2008 has only increased this).[39] Neoliberalism had to impose a new form of work that, though it left workers more exposed with fewer protections, gave workers a sense that their labor was an expression of themselves.[40] The worker may have been far from an executive, owner, or even manager (the

37. Skidelsky adds, "Why did this unraveling happen? The accepted answer is that the reaction against Keynesianism was triggered by the failures of Keynesian policy in the 1970s, in particular to control the inflation produced by its commitment to full employment. But in fact the reaction against Keynesianism had been biding its time for many years among those economists who had never accepted Keynes's theory and had acquiesced only reluctantly in Keynesian policy. It can be traced back to the compromise that had launched the Keynesian revolution." Skidelsky, *Money and Government*, 172.

38. William Davies adds, "By switching from a formal-structural emphasis on competition as an essential property of markets, to a psychological emphasis on competitiveness as an essential trait of individuals, these economists occasioned a key shift in how competition (and competitiveness) would later be conceived." Davies, *Limits of Neoliberalism*, 51. The Skidelskys add, "In effect, the governments of Reagan and Thatcher handed economies back to the businessmen. The role of the state in management, ownership, regulation, allocation, and distribution was drastically pared back. Governments gave up attempts to steer market forces to desirable social outcomes, limiting themselves to maintaining framework conditions for successful market performance. The wealth of nations would be made to grow faster by releasing acquisitiveness from its communal restraints, in a reprise of the arguments first advanced by Adam Smith and his followers." Skidelsky and Skidelsky, *How Much Is Enough?*, 184.

39. For an important discussion of the gig economy, see Bruce Pietrykowski, *Work* (London: Polity, 2019), 88–90.

40. Economist Robert H. Nelson says poignantly about neoliberalism and the Chicago school, highlighting how it reinstated the contradiction, "Over the years, the Chicago school of economics has opposed the progressive vision of scientific management, but has typically defended the basic values of material progress and economic efficiency." Nelson, *Economics as Religion: From Samuelson to Chicago and Beyond* (University Park: Pennsylvania State University Press, 2014), 326.

gap in their salaries growing exponentially), but the fluidity of the job market gave each worker the sense that their own self was its own kind of business.[41]

In the "new spirit of capitalism," as French sociologists Luc Boltanski and Eve Chiapello call it, what matters is flexibility and agility.[42] Inside this flexibility and agility, which ultimately exist for the dexterity of corporations to chase down profits, workers are allowed to imagine themselves as expressive little businesses unto themselves, rather than cogs in a rationalist machine. The worker revises and reshapes her LinkedIn profile to constantly update her skills. Her job security is based not on the loyalty of the corporation but on her own ability to make herself more hireable by adding to her profile of skills.

Ultimately, to renew a new generation's acceptance of the contradictions of capitalism, a whole new form of management was needed, leading to a management revolution.[43] This management revolution pushed workers even harder in their efforts for the corporation, but nevertheless each worker put in this effort for their own unique expression of their self. The self, and its project, led a new generation to accept the contradiction of capitalism. The contradiction of devoted work and consumer expressivism remained, but it was brought into a generative tension by a new form of management that used expressivism to renew and refuel the work ethic. Who didn't want to work hard for their own personal business? Who didn't want to invest when the effort was for their own expressive self?

This new form of management was called entrepreneurial leadership. Entrepreneurship brought together, in a functioning form, the contradictions of capitalism.[44] Each worker was their own business because each worker was an

41. Kevin Hargaden adds, "The old liberalism generated a 'supermarket society' but the new liberalism results in an 'enterprise society' where the citizen becomes the 'man of enterprise and production.'" Hargaden, *Theological Ethics in a Neoliberal Age: Confronting the Christian Problem with Wealth* (Eugene, OR: Cascade, 2018), 11.

42. Luc Boltanski and Eve Chiapello, *The New Spirit of Capitalism* (London: Verso, 2018).

43. For a history of this management revolution, see Eugene McCarraher, *The Enchantments of Mammon: How Capitalism Became the Religion of Modernity* (Cambridge, MA: Belknap, 2019), 210–20.

44. Discussing the leading thinker in entrepreneurial business leadership, Joseph Schumpeter, William Davies says, "The entrepreneur enacts 'new combinations' of technologies and practices, so as to inject novelty into circuits of capitalism. A great deal hangs on the psychology of the entrepreneur, which is to refuse ordinary routines and boundaries. The entrepreneurial mentality does not seek success within a given set of institutional rules, but through the invention of new institutional rules, which others will later have to play by. For this reason, entrepreneurs cannot be easily classified or theorized, because by their nature, they move between existing codes, norms and institutions. Nor do they reside in any particular institutional domain of society. In his later life, Schumpeter was even prepared to accept that entrepreneurship may be most likely 'within

entrepreneur of the self. The manager's job was to shape every worker into an entrepreneur for the sake of the firm's permanent innovation.

This form of management washed back into the church. Both Synod Executive Guy and Applebee's Boy were heralding a corporate management strategy that was, without divide, mission. It was the last best hope for Protestantism in the West.

the shell of existing corporations,' where routinization could be disrupted from within. What is clear in Schumpeter's analysis is that the entrepreneurial personality is uncommon. It acts against existing conventions, which structure socio-economic reality for the majority of people, rather than within them. Entrepreneurship operates through counter-acting norms, and for this reason can never be stabilized into any norm of its own." Davies, *Limits of Neoliberalism*, 55.

4

Let's Get Extra

Exploring the Secular Contradiction of Capitalism

Thankfully, it's rare for a lunch conversation to center on toilets. But here we were, Synod Executive Guy and I, discussing not only toilets but also the backwash of sewage. We were light-years away from our Victorian etiquette, but we didn't care, because we were talking TV. We were in the middle of giving our reviews and takeaways from the Netflix docuseries *Inside Bill's Brain*. Synod Executive Guy liked best the episode on vaccinations, but he understood my infatuation for the toilet episode.

"What's amazing about the show," Synod Executive Guy said, now both reflective and passionate, "is the real tangible difference innovation can make in the world. I mean who doesn't want better vaccines or more efficient and creative toilets? It seems undeniable that those innovations in the show are making the world a better place."

I nodded.

"And yet my synod is in a huge conflict over it, ever since the conference you spoke at. It's a big mess."

He told me all about it, careful to avoid names. (Little did he know that I don't remember anyone's name, including his!) Synod Executive Guy was anything but reckless, but I was pretty sure, as he described the characters in this conflict, that Applebee's Boy and Bearded Brown Turtleneck were playing major roles. Because Synod Executive Guy was trying to not talk out of school, being fair to all parties, it was hard for me to completely follow the story. But it appeared that the synod had set up a webinar that was not compulsory but required participation if you wanted to be eligible to apply for the funds.

The webinar, titled "Managing toward Innovation," was a module offered by the local business school. Synod Executive Guy explained that the synod staff had taken it and found it helpful. They had decided that to use the money well they would need to manage the synod's congregations toward innovation. After participating in the class, they realized that these management issues were directly transferable to congregations. If congregations were going to be missional by being innovative, they would need to manage their staff and laity toward innovation. To be missional, they needed to be innovative, but they needed to learn new management skills to do that.

The conflict started in the middle of the webinar for the pastors. The drama began in the chat feed and moved directly, and heatedly, into the discussion period. Bearded Brown Turtleneck blew his top, claiming that the ideas in the webinar were a violation of the call for justice and were a way of allowing usury to colonize the church. No one really knew what "usury" meant in that context, but it sounded important. He referenced something from Thomas Aquinas and then claimed that it was crass and demeaning to equate pastoral leadership and management.[1]

Applebee's Boy couldn't let these accusations stand. Soon multiple people were yelling at each other through their computer screens. The next week, the synod office received a petition calling for the end of any more webinars and the draconian requirements put in place for congregations to receive the funds. Synod Executive Guy had a hard time seeing how these measures were harsh, let alone draconian. But there were twenty-five names of pastors who had signed the petition, and more than a few were shocking to Synod Executive Guy. He decided to call a few to understand why they had signed. They admitted that they weren't totally sure, but that they were definitely confused. They wanted to be missional, even liked the idea of innovation, but though they recognized that Bearded Brown Turtleneck was abrasive, and at times misanthropic, they wondered if this *was* a justice issue. They were worried—even anxious—about being found on the wrong side of any and all justice issues.

So they signed.

1. Michael Krom has a nice discussion of this in *Justice and Charity: An Introduction to Aquinas's Moral, Economic, and Political Thought* (Grand Rapids: Baker Academic, 2020), 75–83.

Welcome to Working in a Secular Age

Whether you identify more with Applebee's Boy or Bearded Brown Turtleneck, there is something important to recognize. The rhetoric and operations of entrepreneurship and innovation can only come to be because of the secular. The secular shapes our modern economy and molds the imagination of workers who act inside this economy. Entrepreneurship and innovation are, from top to bottom, secular realities.

We shouldn't miss this! And yet this fact *should not* keep the church from engaging with entrepreneurship and innovation, leading us to side with only Bearded Brown Turtleneck. We should be aware of the influence of the secular, but also neither glorify nor idealize entrepreneurship and innovation. We should never assume, as Applebee's Boy does, that entrepreneurship and innovation can save the church.

There is a temptation for those who want to justify innovation, fusing it with mission, to assert that the church from its beginnings, and God in God's own being, has championed innovation. Some, for instance, even see the incarnation as proof of God's innovative nature. But we should avoid this temptation because, as we'll see, entrepreneurship and innovation are management technologies forged inside a certain kind of capitalist economy we call neoliberalism. This capitalist economy can only exist in, and is therefore embedded in (even necessitated by), the secularity that Charles Taylor describes as the loss of transcendence.[2]

This chapter develops the important—even essential—role of entrepreneurship and innovation in renewing the cultural contradictions of capitalism. The church obviously has not always found itself living and ministering inside such an economy, so the church has not *always* been about innovation. Talk of entrepreneurship and innovation could not have been on the tongues of our ecclesial ancestors because they were not living and working under the cultural contradictions of capitalism.[3]

2. See the introduction to Charles Taylor, *A Secular Age* (Cambridge, MA: Belknap, 2007).
3. Robert Skidelsky and Edward Skidelsky name this contradiction: "Capitalism is a two-edged sword. On the one hand, it has made possible vast improvements in material conditions. On the other, it has exalted some of the most reviled human characteristics, such as greed, envy and avarice. Our call is to chain up the monster again by recalling what the greatest thinkers of all times and all civilizations have meant by the 'good life' and suggesting changes in current policy to help us achieve it." Skidelsky and Skidelsky, *How Much Is Enough? Money and the Good Life* (London: Penguin, 2013), 3.

Our church forefathers and mothers may have done some innovative things, but they were never seeking innovation itself. Their innovative acts did not bear the same moral weight that innovation does for us. For us, there is a sense that entrepreneurship and innovation can save, as Applebee's Boy says.[4] But what we mean is that entrepreneurship and innovation can save us from decline in the market, *not* from sin, damnation, or the brokenness of the human spirit (living in a secular age allows us to sidestep these realities). As businesses seek more growth in the market, they embrace entrepreneurship and innovation as a form of management (more on this in the next chapter). As institutional religion feels its own decline and loss in the religious market, it too finds entrepreneurship and innovation appealing.

But simple decline isn't enough to make Applebee's Boy come out swinging against Bearded Brown Turtleneck in the webinar. Rather, entrepreneurship and innovation can bear the moral weight of saving because we feel that it satisfies the soul of the self ("Who doesn't want to be creative?" Applebee's Boy stated to me). As we bear the cultural contradictions of capitalism, entrepreneurship and innovation help dull the acute cultural pinch of the malaise of immanence.[5] Now that we must bear our work stripped of divine consequence, we must find some meaning for it. In late modernity, entrepreneurship and innovation feel like they can save because they deliver significance to the very place where secular late modernity (inside the absence of transcendence) shifts meaning—to the inner project of the self.

I'll have much more to say about this below. But for now it's important to see that these cultural contradictions of capitalism reflect an important part of the secular age we inhabit. As the values, commitments, and forms of work shift, those shifts bring with them a secular reality. The cultural contradictions of capitalism, which are formally and directly laid on the backs of workers, disconnect workers, in both operations and (more importantly) imagination, from a sense that their work has divine consequence. As modernity unfolded, work slowly but surely lost connection to the divine or transcendent. This happened as religion was cordoned off as strictly private while work was made public. When these lines of demarcation met Keynesianism in the 1950s, the cultural contradictions of capitalism arrived in full and sharp force. Work

---

4. Entrepreneurship and innovation save by using the win-win perspective, which Anand Giridharadas shows is deeply problematic. See Giridharadas, *Winners Take All: The Elite Charade of Changing the World* (New York: Vintage, 2018), chap. 2.

5. Tipping my hat to Taylor, *Secular Age*, part 3.

had become fully secular, and in doing so, it cut a conflicting duality into the personalities and practices of workers. In the early 1980s, when the sharp contradiction of capitalism could not be managed by the rhetoric of organization and the imagination of duty to the company, entrepreneurship and innovation arrived as the new management technology. It fit hand in glove with both the corporate desire for hypergrowth and the workers' adoption of the new ethic of authenticity.

It would be a major stretch to claim that God's own action to redeem and save the world can be reduced to a form of management in late capitalism. To state that the church and God have always been about entrepreneurship and innovation imposes certain theological problems and overlooks the way cultural histories work. For this discussion to have some coherence, allow me to slow down, step back, and fill in the story. To further make these two points—(1) that entrepreneurship and innovation were not always part of the imagination of the church and (2) that the secular (or the loss of the transcendent)[6] brought a stiff contradiction into work—we can start filling in this backstory by peering into one of the most "innovative" times in the medieval period, what historians call the Cathedral Crusades of the twelfth century.

The New Crusades

When we hear "crusades," we usually think of the knights of the eleventh century. These crusades were just as connected to work as entrepreneurship and innovation are for us today. Yet the medieval imagination, unlike the modern imagination (inside capitalism), didn't accept contradictions (at least not in the area of work[7]).

As Charles Taylor explains, different forms of work were united in their distinction under time, or what he calls *speeds*.[8] Not everyone lived at the same pace. These different speeds were not a contradiction, but like a complicated choreography, they created a unified performance. Some worked at the speed

6. Taylor calls this secular 3—though it is important to remember that secular 3 is an outgrowth of secular 1 (and in a lesser way secular 2). I'm imagining all the stages of secularity in play as we discuss work.

7. For instance, in the area of King Henry VIII's sex life and in hypocrisies over vows of poverty and bishops living in ornate castles. Contradiction was ripe.

8. See Taylor, *Secular Age*, 60–70.

of heaven, such as abbots, nuns, and monks. Others worked at the speed of labor, removing rocks from fields and seeding crops in rows. Still others killed, working at the speed of the warrior, protecting the realm from evil invasion. There were different speeds, but it was one system without contradiction. There was no contradiction at the level of work because there was no sense of the secular.[9] All work was done directly before God. Everyone lived at a different speed, but all these speeds were done in a world (a *cosmos*, as Taylor calls it[10]) that God directly ordered and where spiritual forces were everywhere.[11]

In the eleventh century, warriors and workers, backed by those working at the speed of heaven, went east not to expand markets and find cheap labor but to recover locales of enchanted power—the Holy Land. For them, things themselves were enchanted with divine (or evil) forces. What things could be more holy than the ground and stones upon which Jesus and his mother walked and sat? Such a view makes no sense to us, but our fetishizing of growth and our desire for disposable material products wouldn't make sense to them. Looking at the eleventh-century crusades, we could speak at length on the topics of war, blood, and the Christian justification of violence—but for the story we're exploring here, we're interested in what happened next.[12]

9. Of course, in some ways the Enlightenment elements of modernity sought to do away with contradiction. They saw contradiction not in the psychological constitution of work but in how we understand natural phenomena. The empiricist Enlightenment thinkers imagined that mathematics was a philosophy that avoided all contradiction. But modernity would never settle on such a position. Others, just as modern, argued that contradiction—such as being alive and yet facing death—could not be overcome. This is the Romantic element of modernity. Modernity is a child of contradictory systems.

10. R. H. Tawney says something similar: "[This living before God] is to be found in the insistence of medieval thinkers that society is a spiritual organism, not an economic machine, and that economic activity, which is one subordinate element within a vast and complex unity, requires to be controlled and repressed by reference to the moral ends for which it supplies the material means." Tawney, *Religion and the Rise of Capitalism* (London: Verso, 2015), 73.

11. Andrew Roach adds, "There was a common feeling among clerics that the laity should be kept at arm's length spiritually and physically. Those whose role in life was to fight or to labour should do exactly that and leave their salvation in the hands of those who prayed and were qualified to deal with such matters. When it came down to buildings, the isolation of the clergy performing ceremonies in the chancel or choir of the church at the east end, cut off from the laity in the larger nave to the west, was mirrored by the isolation of monks from society in general, praying for the sins of the world from behind high walls. In terms of participation in the spiritual community of the Church, lay input was minimal. Any significance they had was only as witnesses to what was done on their behalf. But in that lay the key to change as the witnesses started to articulate what it was they wanted to see." Roach, *The Devil's World: Heresy and Society, 1100–1300* (Harlow, UK: Pearson, 2005), 11.

12. For more on the eleventh-century crusades, see Sarah Hamilton, *Church and People in the Medieval West* (Harlow, UK: Pearson, 2013).

In the twelfth century, something changed. The necessity for the encounter with enchantment shifted, moving closer to home. The vigor for crusades flipped from sword wielding to cathedral building.[13] In this period, most of the still-standing gothic cathedrals of Europe were erected. These cathedrals came to be because the crusades shifted from taking lands abroad (which would unfortunately return in the thirteenth century) to building churches at home. One of the main figures behind this cathedral crusade was the French abbot Father Suger (1081–1151). Suger oversaw the building of dozens of France's most beautiful gothic places of worship. Two factors made Suger's ambitious buildings possible.

Factor One

The first factor is that in the twelfth century a certain form of work took on new emphasis. Labor in the field or guilds in the village became more important. Particularly, agriculture improved. These changes created less of a stomach for sending warrior-workers to other lands. There was now a deeper sense that the labor-worker's spiritual needs were more central, because labor-workers' extra crop yields were able to support a stone building containing a relic (this turn to labor-workers' spiritual needs also had something to do with the arrival of the moneyed economy, which we'll return to in chap. 9). These labor-workers in the fields felt no inherent contradiction in their work, as those in modernity would. Their work may have been backbreaking, but it was part of God's cosmos. Though their work may *not* have been done at the speed of heaven, and though it may have been profane and not sacred, it was far from secular. It had its place in a world draped in God's action.

13. Jean Gimpel explains this dynamic, saying, "From the middle of the twelfth century, the idea of going to the Holy Land became less popular. Was it because Jerusalem had been in Christian hands since 1099? Was it because people did not appreciate the continual Muslim threat to the Frankish kingdoms? Was it because of memories of the First Crusade? Or had a taste for luxury and prosperity begun to take a hold? Whatever the case, the Church authorized those responsible for building to grant indulgences to those who helped to erect the house of God. A man need no longer go on a crusade to expiate his sins. The 'cathedral crusade' took shape and the whole hierarchy of the Church, from the Pope to the simple parish priest, took part both spiritually and financially. Thus, after the failure of the appallingly organized expeditions of 1147, 1187, and 1204, crusades to defend Christ's tomb became an idea of the past and the difficulties encountered by St. Louis when he formed his army in the middle of the thirteenth century were characteristic of the spirit of the times. It could be said that the 'cathedral crusade,' in establishing itself, contributed to the weakening of the Frankish kingdom." Gimpel, *The Cathedral Builders* (New York: Harper, 1984), 38.

These buildings, constructed and consecrated by those of the praying class like Suger, brought a slice of heaven to earth.[14] Within their walls of glass and light, these buildings could save your soul from hell. Their stone pillars could protect your hide from storm and fire. These workers were happy to give both sweat and coin to build a space that contained God's heaven on earth. Each guild, like blacksmiths and shoemakers, that gave sweat and coin were remembered in the glass or stone of these holy structures. Work was anything but secular. It was remembered in the holy structure, part of eternity, part of the holy building.[15]

Being a warrior/knight in the first crusades or a laborer in the field in the second crusades infused work with divine consequence. Neither form of work could be confused as divine, heavenly, or sacred work. Neither form of work was done at the speed of heaven, but both warriors and laborers made it possible for sacred work to occur. Theirs was necessary work, done to support and bolster the work of the praying class. It was free from contradiction because it had its place in the divine shape of society.

Factor Two

The second factor that occurred to make this cathedral crusade possible was indeed an innovation. It's hard to know which came first, or at least which was more influential, in making a way for the cathedrals: the different emphasis on labor/work or the discovery of this new building innovation. If we look at this question through the history of one of the oldest and greatest cathedrals of Europe, Durham Cathedral (begun in 1093) in England's Northumbria, we can see it was labor/work that brought forth the innovation.

14. Arnold Pacey states, "A significant comparison is possible at this point. The cathedral as a stone embodiment of the New Jerusalem was a scaled down, material model of heaven, · just as clocks were a scaled down representation of the visible cosmos. Abbot Suger in 1140 said that his church was built 'in likeness of things Divine,' and Pierre de Maricourt could have said the same in 1269 about the magnetic clock he proposed. Thus there was a sense in which the cathedral builders, like the clockmakers, had a celestial prototype." Pacey, *The Maze of Ingenuity: Ideas and Idealism in the Development of Technology* (Cambridge, MA: MIT Press, 1996), 45.

15. Steven Epstein gives some context to guilds and the sense of work being connected to the divine: "Religious and charitable duties were partly an internal matter, but their primary focus was, in most ways, the next world. These spiritual concerns resulted from a guild's frequent status as a confraternity—a fact that attracted the Church's interest. A guild often possessed a strong religious character that provided a grander purpose as well as common spiritual ideals that the masters shared along with their apprentices and journeymen." Epstein, *Wage Labor and Guilds in Medieval Europe* (Chapel Hill: University of North Carolina Press, 1991), 156.

As builders of the Durham Cathedral sought to heighten the walls, able to reach heaven, without enclosing the building in small, dark rooms with thick walls to support the roof (which had been done many times before), they discovered the pointed arch. From the pointed arch, and the way it was used in Durham, came another building breakthrough: the flying buttress.[16] These two innovations allowed buildings to be constructed like never before. They allowed a slice of heaven, in light and glass, to be manifest on earth. After a few of these buildings had been constructed, more were needed. Working for such spaces that hummed with eternity was more than a good reason to labor.

Suger mobilized the funds and secured royal decrees for such buildings of pointed arches and flying buttresses to rise throughout the French countryside. He convinced both workers and royals alike that it was necessary not to mobilize knights to go crusading in foreign lands but instead to bring to their own lands the beacon of divine beauty. But Abbot Suger was not without his critics and rivals. The most famous was his fellow French abbot, Bernard of Clairvaux (1090–1153). Bernard was Martin Luther or John Calvin before there was Luther or Calvin. Or perhaps it's better to say that Bernard was a seventeenth-century Puritan, five hundred years before the Puritans.

Bernard saw a great need to reform monastic life and thereby all of Christendom. He hated Suger's drive for opulent structures. Instead, Bernard ran his monastery in Clairvaux with severe austerity and deep devotion. Neither he nor his monks depended on the purse of the rich or even the small gifts of laborers. The monks themselves would labor.[17] They remained part of the praying class, offering intercession for all workers, whether stationed with hoes in the field or swords to protect the realm. But these monks of Clairvaux now worked while they prayed and prayed while they worked.[18] Soon Bernard had forged a great social entrepreneurial endeavor; he made

16. "At Notre Dame, one can see two of the most spectacular features of construction that were characteristic of the cathedral crusade—the systematic exploitation of flying buttresses and the tendency toward enormous size, especially in the height of the vault. Whereas, prior to the 1160s, the vault of a large church might be 70 or 80 feet (about 23 meters) above the floor as at Sens, at Notre Dame it was 110 feet (34 meters). The church was made exceptionally wide as well, with an extra aisle on each side." Pacey, *Maze of Ingenuity*, 19.

17. Cultural evolutionary thinker Joseph Henrich believes that this turn to labor and hard work in the Cistercian order shifted the whole of Western society. It made the ground fertile for capitalism. See Henrich, *The Weirdest People in the World: How the West Became Psychologically Peculiar and Particularly Prosperous* (New York: Farrar, Straus & Giroux, 2020), 370–71.

18. Work had been part of monastic life long before Bernard. See, for instance, Basil's monastic reforms. But never before had commerce and the creation of products been a central element of monastic life until Bernard.

his monastery self-sustaining.[19] Bernard's monastery became a business of artisans, the Cistercian order a network of skilled laborers.[20] Even though Bernard of Clairvaux and Suger had opposite stances, both could be accused of being innovative.

The Land of No Contradictions

Bernard and Suger did entrepreneurial and innovative things. Even so, neither Bernard nor Suger directly sought entrepreneurship and innovation. They never thought to call what they were doing "entrepreneurship" or "innovation."[21] They couldn't have. True, the flying buttress was a technological

19. Arnold Pacey explains this further: "The little abbey at Citeaux remained an obscure foundation until the year 1112, when a young nobleman and some of his friends decided they had a vocation to become monks there. This man, known to us as St. Bernard of Clairvaux, provided the dynamism that, by the time of his death in 1153, had led to the foundation of 340 Cistercian abbeys all over Europe. In a Cistercian monastery, there were particular times laid down during each day for different activities. The lay brothers were supposed to devote seven or eight hours to manual labor, and the fathers four or five hours; this did not differ much from the Rule of St. Benedict, which allocated five and a half hours to manual work. Intended as part of a spiritual discipline, the work done was supposed only to make each abbey self-sufficient. But it was often done so effectively that products like wool and iron were turned out in far greater quantities than were needed by the monks themselves. There was a market demand for these things, although the monks were warned, 'Let not the sin of avarice creep in; but let the goods always be sold a little cheaper than they are sold by people of the world, that in all things, God may be glorified.' This injunction was perhaps too finely balanced, for the abbeys were soon in receipt of a large money income. In the course of time they became very wealthy, and the monks found themselves acting as estate managers and businessmen rather than laborers." Pacey, *Maze of Ingenuity*, 10.

20. For more on Bernard, see Brian Patrick McGuire, *Bernard of Clairvaux: An Inner Life* (Ithaca, NY: Cornell University Press, 2020). Joseph Henrich discusses further what these monasteries actually did: "The Cistercian Order . . . built a sprawling network of monastery-factories that deployed the latest techniques for grinding wheat, casting iron, tanning hides, fulling cloth, and cultivating grapes. Most Cistercian monasteries had a water mill, and some had four or five such mills for different jobs. In France's Champagne region, for example, the Cistercians were the leading iron producers from roughly 1250 to 1700. The motherhouse in Burgundy planted vineyards, which produced one of the world's most famous vintages, and houses in Germany devised ways to cultivate vines on terraced hillsides. At mandatory annual meetings, hundreds of Cistercian abbots shared their best technical, industrial, and agricultural practices with the entire order. This essentially threaded Europe's collective brain with Cistercian nerves, pulsing the latest technical advances out to even the most remote monasteries. With their strict devotion to an austere life, monks freely dispensed their know-how, strategies, and skills to local communities." Henrich, *Weirdest People in the World*, 446.

21. Lindy Grant points out that the drive for innovative newness was not something Suger considered. Grant says, "The irony is that the last thing Suger was trying to get his workforce to do was to create something new. He was trying to recreate the abbey church's former glory; trying to make it look as much as possible like the Carolingian church which he inherited, and

breakthrough, and the monastery at Clairvaux was a clever and industrious endeavor. But Bernard's and Suger's aims were much different from the goals of entrepreneurship and innovation inside late modernity.[22] This is mainly because entrepreneurship and innovation are the late (youngest) children born out of the womb of the contradictions of capitalism. Even if we find ways of affirming entrepreneurship and innovation, we must recognize that they are fundamentally children of capitalism. Entrepreneurship and innovation are in no way the bedrock of an ecclesial or theological imagination and action. They cannot be in the world without their conflicted contrarian capitalist parents (think of it as the entrepreneurship and innovation family tree).

Bernard and Suger were not living inside a capitalist system, and therefore they felt little need to pacify an acute sense of contradiction between devoted work and consumer expressivism. There simply was no contradiction in work. They would never have imagined that what they were doing was for anything close to the ends and aims that we think entrepreneurship and innovation are for today. Their actions were motivated not by growth in relation to markets or the necessity of the project of the self but by the draw, and even the demand, of transcendence. They worked to make their stone building or praying monks a reflection of God's divine order. There were tensions, but no inherent contradictions. The earth was God's, and it was the abbot's job, whether by stone or by monk, to make this earth reflect the divine order. Bernard's and Suger's supposed entrepreneurship and innovation existed not to cope with contradictions in their work; instead, they were the manifestation of how all forms of work have a place in the economy of God.

My intent is not to idealize Bernard and Suger or the system of work in which they existed. (I personally don't want to return to an economy based on subsistence farming and its cycles of famine.) After all, the medieval system of work became corrupt, with crusades to foreign lands and the lands at home used to exploit peasant laborers. But all this is to say that arches were pointed

---

which he believed to be the original church built by King Dagobert. His inspiration came from splendid new buildings associated with the Gregorian reform that he had seen in and around Rome, which themselves attempted to revive a lost Early Christian past." Grant, *Abbot Suger of St-Denis: Church and State in Early Twelfth-Century France* (London: Longman, 1998), 30.

22. Pacey explains, "Work done in the monasteries was part of a spiritual discipline and was not aimed at producing goods for market. The improvements made by the monks in water supply, building techniques, and agriculture might therefore be seen as to some degree the result of an 'idealistic' approach to technology. Though . . . the monks did in time become businessmen and sell much of their produce, initially the direct influence of the profit motive on their practical and technical activities was probably very limited." Pacey, *Maze of Ingenuity*, 15.

and candles were formed not to solve the problem of slowing capital growth, giving builders and monks an identity as original, unique, or even creative, but to respond to the transcendent quality of existence.

A breakthrough in building construction occurred for the sake of transcendent space. A monastery found a unique way to support itself for the sake of obedience to the divine call. The moral good its monks sought in their action had little to do with catching up to change. The breakthrough therefore had little to do with innovation and entrepreneurship.[23] Bernard and Suger stumbled upon (what we call) innovation and entrepreneurship, but the aim of their action stood far outside either. We can call Suger a great innovator, or Bernard a magnificent entrepreneur, but only if we admit that we're imposing on them what they never could have known—the constraints, freedoms, and strictures of a secular age.

Entrepreneurship and innovation are what they are because of their place inside a secular age. The secular age births the contradictions of capitalism. Or, better, the secular age keeps us coping with, and therefore accepting, the piercing sharp edge of this contradiction of capitalism. The secular age, then, imposes a certain stringent contradiction into the reality of our cultural work lives. Entrepreneurship and innovation are never free of this modern contradiction. They therefore cannot save, as Applebee's Boy wishes, because as the children of capitalism, entrepreneurship and innovation exist to continue the contradiction of capitalism. This *does not* mean the church cannot learn from and even engage in entrepreneurship and innovation. But we need to think more deeply about it. Our discussion of Bernard and Suger shows that we should not assume entrepreneurship and innovation are realities (or even platonic life forms) that are eternal and therefore de facto morally good. Entrepreneurship and innovation are historical-cultural realities inseparable from our secular age.

But a further question is, Why is there an inherent contradiction in capitalism in the first place? And what makes this contradiction inseparable from the dawning of our secular age? Answering these questions will provide a bridge from Bernard and Suger back into the story we explored at the end of the previous chapter. Walking over this bridge will allow us to discover how the contradiction of capitalism got reimposed in the 1980s—even after markets slowed and young people revolted.

23. Entrepreneurship and innovation are inseparable from the race to catch up to the pace of change.

It's So Extra, but for Hard Work

In 1904 a man who had grown up in the Charlottenburg area of Berlin was struck by a question. Standing at the end of the nineteenth century (which, remember, started and ended a decade and a half late), he wondered what produced capitalism. The nineteenth century, and Berlin as one of its city centers, saw the triumph of capitalism. Capitalism had become as common and as ordinary as paved roads and top hats.[24] Capitalism had become so embedded in European society that it seemed to most people to have always been there. But Max Weber knew better, and he wanted to peel back this assumption and seek capitalism's origins.

Though we rarely notice it, Weber pointed out that capitalism is a strange kind of action. Kathryn Tanner explains Weber's position: "For all the careful means/ends, and in that sense rational, calculation typical of capitalism, there is something unnatural, even irrational, about all this when considered from the standpoint of the satisfaction of basic material needs—if, that is, one's end is simply to live well."[25] Capitalism irrationally imposes on us a deep sense that we need more than what is necessary to live on because we need more than what will allow us to live well today. Living well today, capitalism says, is having more than you need for today. Capitalism demands that we work hard to create something extra (which we call "capital").

Good work, inside capitalism, is finding the means for living well today *and* upping the effort to drive harder to produce something for today and, just as importantly, something extra for another day. This is capitalism at its core. Capitalism is ultimately these two realities: (1) the need, even drive, for the extra and (2) the necessity to work hard to get this extra. These two realities directly shape what we consider to be good work. Good work produces not just the means for today but the extra of capital. In turn, the good worker is the hard worker. The good worker is willing to give the extra effort to procure extra capital.[26]

24. It's not necessarily that capitalism was not thought about. The Marxist movement in the 1870s was also reflecting on capitalism. But the Marxist movement assumed that capitalism was a firm reality. Communism or socialism in its Marxist form was caught in a Hegelian struggle that presumed capitalism.

25. Kathryn Tanner, *Christianity and the New Spirit of Capitalism* (New Haven: Yale University Press, 2019), 2.

26. Stephen Kalberg explains Weber's position: "Similarly, the reinvestment of profit and surplus income signified loyalty to God's grand design and an acknowledgment that all riches emanated from the hand of this omnipotent deity. Because believers viewed themselves as merely

Neither Suger nor Bernard can truly be considered entrepreneurs or innovators because neither lived inside this form of action. Their motivation to
build cathedrals or reorder their monastery was not for the sake of the extra.
Entrepreneurship and innovation are appealing to us—but would have made
no sense to Suger and Bernard—because both are dispositions or styles for
achieving the extra (the growth of capital) through hard work.

The sharks on *Shark Tank* always remind the people making their pitch that
you can't be an entrepreneur unless you hustle 24/7, working harder than your
competitor to procure the extra that your bottom line and investors demand.
"He wasn't all in" is Mark Cuban's refrain on why he passes on a pitch. Entrepreneurship and innovation, as we'll see, are post-1980s capitalist forms of
action that renew the idea of getting the extra through hard work. The Age
of Aquarius was so unique, infuriating, and ultimately short lived because
its hippie middle-class members wanted consumer expressivism without the
hard work of procuring the extra (which is why, to this day, there are those
who are disgusted by hippies). The counterculture kids wanted capitalism's
goods without capitalism. When this desire ran its course, capitalism welcomed them back through the rhetoric of entrepreneurship and innovation.
In 1978 the counterculture hippies Ben and Jerry started selling exceedingly
delicious and expensive ice cream.

Yet to truly understand how capitalism imposes a cultural contradiction,
we need to further explore this idea, focusing on the need for hard work in
capitalism. Weber was not puzzled by the desire for the extra as he worked to
trace the origins of capitalism. Human beings have always desired and even
been tempted to want something extra. Every parent throughout time has
noticed that small children desire—will even lie and cheat—to get the extra
goody or turn. Hoarding the extra for yourself has always been labeled as
bad. Even capitalism believes this (capitalism is even dependent on the extra
capital not being hoarded but invested, an impulse that interests Weber). Or
at least early and middle capitalism believed hoarding the extra was wrong,
even sinful. It was best to reinvest that extra, allowing it to become more

---

the earthly trustees of goods awarded by their divinity, all wealth had to be utilized on behalf of
His purposes only—that is, to build the affluent kingdom that would praise His glory. Hence,
the devout practiced frugality, restricted consumption (especially of luxury goods), and saved
and invested in large quantities. A preference to live modestly characterized the Puritan outlook, for to indulge desires would weaken the required focus on God's will, the faithful knew.
Indeed, and although wealth was now created on a large scale, its enjoyment became 'morally
reprehensible.'" Kalberg, *The Social Thought of Max Weber* (Los Angeles: SAGE, 2017), 20.

extra by allowing the profits of capital to reach others who were working hard procuring their own extra. Late neoliberal capitalism doesn't seem to believe this anymore, contending that growth can only occur if some have huge amounts of extra capital compared to others. I personally am committed to capitalism, so much so that I find late capitalism and its glorification of the few hoarding the extra capital abhorrent. Those who are full-on advocates for entrepreneurship and innovation, like Applebee's Boy, have to contend with the fact that these forms of work have been used to justify the hoarding excesses of late capitalism. This, I think, is what Bearded Brown Turtleneck meant when he talked about a justice issue.[27]

It wasn't this drive for the extra that Weber found so unique in capitalism; it was how capitalism shifted what counted as good work. The ethic that it was good to work hard Weber saw as a uniquely capitalist creation. The idea that the best workers were the hardest workers was not something the medieval period would have affirmed. It was quite the opposite. The best workers—those living at the speed of heaven as the praying class, as well as the royals and landed genteel—were lauded and favored because they avoided all hard work. They sat and prayed. At its most extreme in Louis XIV's court at Versailles, the landed genteel played cards, drank punch, and ate cakes from dawn to dusk.[28] Hard work was not assumed to be a good. Before the arrival of full-blown capitalism, the good worker was not necessarily the hard worker. The ethic of work in the medieval period was something other than expending large amounts of energy. Of course, Bernard's monks certainly worked hard.[29] But it made them strange, which is why I've called Bernard a Puritan five hundred years before the Puritans. For Bernard and his monks, the point of hard work was not to gain something extra but to bear the direct suffering of Christ. Hard work was intended to cause a kind of sacramental

---

27. Of course, it is a sneaky kind of justification. Entrepreneurship and innovation seem to invite all to take their own shot at being a hoarder of capital. The markets are open to all; if you are a good enough entrepreneur and innovator, you too can have excess capital.

28. Of course, Louis XIV's court occurs after the Reformation, which brings a change in the form of work. But France under Louis XIV was a rigid Catholic nation that was more like the medieval period in religious disposition—though radicalized in many ways.

29. C. H. Lawrence states, "The thing most conspicuously absent from the Rule is any provision for leisure. 'Idleness,' Benedict observes severely, 'is the enemy of the soul.' His insistence upon the value of manual work is in the Eastern monastic tradition. It had an ascetical as well as an economic function; it kept men humble, and it provided for the material wants of the community." Lawrence, *Medieval Monasticism: Forms of Religious Life in Western Europe in the Middle Ages*, 4th ed. (London: Routledge, 2015), 30.

encounter, not to gain extra capital. No one in Bernard's day really wished to be known as a hard worker.[30]

This is difficult for us to relate to. We tend to hold up hard work—being a hard worker—as a very high good. The ethic of work is to work hard. We want many things for our children, but we hope that even if they discover that they're lacking in talent, they'll have learned to work hard. As the venerated (at least in Minnesota) 1980 gold-medal-winning hockey coach of the "Miracle on Ice," Herb Brooks would often repeat the adage, "Hard work beats talent when talent doesn't work hard." If you grew up around hockey rinks in Minnesota in the 1980s and '90s, as I did, this proverb of Herbie wisdom was nearly tattooed on your young forehead. As middle-class parents, we hope to impose a work ethic that affirms the importance of working hard. Outside the unrealistic dream of your child being a first-round draft pick, you drive across the state for tournaments every weekend with the hope that it will at least teach your child to work hard. We know somewhere deep down that learning to be a hard worker is how you survive in all forms of a capitalist society.

The Odd Birth of Capitalism

Weber wants to know what brings about this shift that moves work from being just one element in a society before God to being a means to attain extra capital. Weber believes that this change requires some kind of mechanism. It can't just happen. There must be some cultural source that triggers and normalizes this odd action that works hard so that you can have more than you need. Weber's answer has been one of the most influential and contested theories of the last hundred years. It may not be completely right, but it is insightful, helping us see why the cultural contradictions of capitalism are present. And it opens the door for us to understand how capitalism and its cultural contradictions relate to the secular.

Weber's answer is that *what produces capitalism is contradiction itself.*[31] Capitalism and contradiction are inseparable. Particularly at capitalism's

30. For more on this, see Lawrence, *Medieval Monasticism*, 160–63.

31. Robert H. Nelson calls "irrational" what I'm calling "contradictory." He says, "Although scholars have criticized a number of the details of Max Weber's interpretation of the role of Calvinist religion in the development of capitalism, he was probably correct to argue that there was something 'irrational' about the motivations that were required. A good capitalist should pursue the accumulation of capital beyond what would be rationally sensible; he thus forgoes hedonistic pleasures and may be serving society's interest more than his own." Nelson,

beginning, Weber believes, it's the cultural contradictions of Calvinist Protestantism that produce capitalism. Working hard to reach for the extra is ironically (to say the least) born out of the abundance of God's free grace. The odd contradiction is that the people of free grace and election produce an economic system necessitating hard work. People of devout austerity and self-discipline, who worship in empty spaces, made the pursuit of the extra the outward sign of faithful work.

As we discussed in chapter 2, the Reformation equalized all work. Everyone was a priest and more. All work in ordinary life was completely affirmed. Being a priest in the market or the field meant doing your duty passionately and fully for God. Everyone worked at the same speed. It was no longer just those few in the praying class who were moving at the speed of heaven. All of us were priests. All of us were part of the praying class in our ordinary life. You worked hard in your ordinary life, in all its forms of work, as direct obedience to God.

Yet you knew that your hard work was indeed faithful in that it gained enough for today and also some extra. This assured your anxious soul (which was committed to live each minute as a priest) that you were doing your duty for God. God desired faithful work from you. And faithful work was self-disciplined, and therefore hard, work. Hard work was verified by the small (or large) amount of extra capital your diligent work produced.

Because this work was motivated by your duty to God in your ordinary life, you'd never think to hoard the extra, spending it on yourself or status symbols, thereby releasing yourself from labor for opulent leisure.[32] Rather, you reinvested that extra, allowing *the extra itself* to work. You needed to remain

---

Economics as Religion: From Samuelson to Chicago and Beyond (University Park: Pennsylvania State University Press, 2014), 270.

32. Gordon Marshall states, "Since one has only a limited time on earth in which to give glory to God, and to make sure of one's election by attaining that quiet self-confidence of salvation which is the fruit of true faith and of proving one's regeneration in the conduct of one's daily life, then every moment spent in idleness, leisure, gaming, idle talk, excessive sleep, unnecessary recreation, and enjoying luxury is literally a waste of time, is worthy of moral condemnation, and is a sign of imperfect grace. How, then, ought the faithful to employ their time? That first of all they must fulfill their spiritual duties—prayer, attendance at church and sacraments, Sabbath observance, and the like—goes without saying. But equally they must work hard in their lawful callings. Hard, methodical, continuous, manual and mental labour in a legitimate calling is required of all: it is God's commandment that they who shall not work shall not eat. Idleness, like time-wasting, is the mark of a reprobate. Finally, we must guard against the dangers and temptations of wealth, which are principally idleness itself and hedonism. We are put on earth to glorify God, not to enjoy a carefree and comfortable life. Social drinking, delicate foods, fine clothes, excessive decorating of the home, sexual pleasures, and material comforts in general encourage the unprofitable use of time and turn people from the diligent pursuit of their lawful

disciplined, choosing the austere over the opulent. You therefore reinvested your extra capital to feed the markets. Not for the sake of the markets but for the sake of your soul. Nevertheless, this duty to work hard for the extra and the impulse to reinvest the extra would make the markets flush. This in turn allowed others, in their own priestly affirmation of their own ordinary life, to work hard and achieve some extra themselves.

Weber's point is that the hard work for the extra, mobilized for the sake of duty to God, created capitalism. As Kathryn Tanner says, "If one is graced by God, among the elect, one's ordinary pursuits will be coolly self-disciplined, restrained, non-hedonistic, and in that way amenable to capitalist requirements as a kind of unintended consequence."[33] Weber's point is that capitalism is the unintended consequence of all work being equalized as duty before God. Work takes on a new Protestant ethic that states that good work is hard work, because ordinary life had been affirmed as the place to directly encounter and obey God. Work, not the Mass in the cathedral, is where we directly do our duty to God.

Capitalism's origin, inside the devout interests of Reformed Calvinism, makes contradiction real and endemic—though not yet completely secular.

Contradiction in a Presecular Age

The idea that you need to work super hard (imposing a strict Protestant work ethic) because works themselves didn't matter (justification by faith alone) is a seemingly deep incongruity. The sense that God is full of grace and yet predestines some for eternal salvation and others for eternal damnation is a heavy paradox that must be borne for the early Calvinist Protestants. And the notion that you can get only the haziest of hints about whether you're bound for salvation or damnation by how hard you're willing to work for extra profits places an innate, and never-departing, contradiction inside the DNA of capitalism. Capitalism will always demand hard work, claiming that it is always what's best for the worker. Capitalism is inherently contradictory because it legitimately cares about the freedom of its workers but also believes this freedom is only actualized by constant and consistent hard work. Capitalism wants to honor work but also get as much of it as it can for as

callings." Marshall, *In Search of the Spirit of Capitalism: An Essay on Max Weber's Protestant Ethic Thesis* (New York: Columbia University Press, 1982), 76.

33. Tanner, *Christianity and the New Spirit of Capitalism*, 3.

cheap as it can so the extra (or profits) can expand. Capitalism is conflicted because it cares for its workers but knows no other measure for work than the gain of extra capital.[34]

What balances this contradiction signals whether we're in a secular age (what Taylor calls an immanent frame). Weber saw that, in the early days of capitalism, the contradiction was balanced or appeased by duty to God. What made the contradiction palatable, even generative, was how it was held together by duty to a living and speaking God. The contradiction— like the dialectical paradoxes of Protestant theology—could be generative because the economy of God's act stood above the economy of markets. Your work was both freeing and arduous because it was done as an oath before God.

In the medieval period, only some workers were compelled to give their oaths of duty. Those in the praying class gave oaths to God. The knight pledged his sword and honor to the sovereign. But the largest group, the laborers working in the field or village, needed to accept their station, but they gave no real pledge of duty.[35] Laborers never gave oaths because their work did not participate directly in the transcendent economy of God to call for such a pledge.

But that changed with Reformed Protestantism. All work, especially labor, began to participate directly in the economy of God. The praying and killing classes were over. All laborers were priests. All work was now totally and completely done before God. All were simultaneously priest, laborer, and warrior. Protestantism ended the divisions of work, fusing them into one. Being a warrior no longer included blood, sword, and violence but instead order, manners, and the self-disciplined hard work that gains the extra (welcome to the rise of the

34. R. H. Tawney gives some nuance: "The Calvinist applications of the doctrine of the 'Calling' have, doubtless, their significance; but the degree of influence which they exercised, and their affinity or contrast with other versions of the same idea, are matters of personal judgment, not of precise proof. Both Weber and his critics have made too much of them, as I did myself. His account of the social theory of Calvinism, however, if it rightly underlined some points needing emphasis, left a good deal unsaid. The lacunae in his argument cannot here be discussed, but two of them deserve notice. Though some recent attempts to find parallels to that theory in contemporary Catholic writers have not been very happy, Weber tended to treat it as more unique than it was. More important, he exaggerated its stability and consistency. Taking a good deal of his evidence from a somewhat late phase in the history of the movement, he did not emphasize sufficiently the profound changes through which Calvinism passed in the century following the death of Calvin." Tawney, *Religion and the Rise of Capitalism*, xi.

35. In some places there were pledges to princes and landowners, but these were never assumed to hold the same weight as the oaths of priests and knights.

polite society).[36] The new knights were the merchants in Protestant lands such as Holland. Ultimately, after the Reformation, all workers needed to give an oath of duty to work hard for God. This oath to God balanced the early contradictions of capitalism. The oath balanced equity in the markets as it counterweighed the cultural contradiction of unrelenting hard work with the free grace of God. The extra was a sign that the hard work was on track.[37] The reinvestment of the extra was each person's obedience to the God whom they dutifully worked for.

The Continuation of the Contradiction

From its very beginnings, capitalism should be understood as a form of action that seeks to heighten our devotion and duty to God. At the time of its origins, we were far from the loss of transcendence and a secular age. Capitalism makes accountability central and all work accountable to God. The centrality of accountability never leaves capitalism, but the source of accountability changes. At the beginnings of capitalism, all parties in work—whether employer or employee, buyer or seller—are accountable to do their duty by working hard and fairly before God. Capitalism, if Weber is right, is a cultural creation of hyper-devoted and committed believers. As Charles Taylor says, you can be a society where belief is completely optional only if you come out of a society where belief was once everything.[38] So it is with capitalism. You can have an economic system where work has no relation to God only because this economic system is birthed out of a commitment that every minute of every day of hard work is accountable to God.

Therefore, capitalism and the dawn of a secular age—while not necessarily the same—share a deeply intertwined history. Capitalism and its contradictions set up the conditions for a secular age.[39] The capitalism born out of Protestantism intends to do something different: make obedience to God

36. This brought about what Taylor calls "equal mutual regard of peace" (see Taylor, *Secular Age*, 190–208). Peace is seen as much more advantageous for business, so Europe transitioned from a land of warriors and knights to one of merchants and businesses.

37. This is far from the prosperity gospel, because you would never assume that opulence and riches were a sign of God's favor. Rather, to have such things showed disobedience, that you were not willing to reinvest your capital. But the prosperity gospel came to be because it had its DNA inside this cultural reality.

38. See Taylor, *Secular Age*, part 1.

39. It's no wonder that many of the architects of the immanent frame and dawn of the secular age—people like Descartes, Locke, and Spinoza—spent a good chunk of their time in the Netherlands, where the kind of capitalism Weber is describing had its most concrete

universally shared by all. It desires that everyone be a priest giving an oath of duty to God in all and every kind of work. The contradictions of capitalism are managed by loyal duty and accountability to God. But, of course, this framework for capitalism depends on the oath of duty staying directed to God. If the oath and accountability that capitalism demands (which it always will demand) moves to another entity other than God, the secular age and its immanent frame can come rushing in, playing a major part in moving our most practical forms of life away from the imagination of transcendence.[40]

How this oath embedded in capitalism is moved off of God, allowing the secular age to emerge and shifting the direction of accountability, is not with a frontal attack on God or transcendence. Rather, it occurs with a divide that places faith and work on different sides. The Calvinist creators of capitalism could never have imagined that it was possible to divide belief and work. Capitalism was the outworking of holding them together. Nevertheless, in the late eighteenth century and throughout the nineteenth century, modernity imposed a demarcation. In an inadvertent homage to its Calvinist forefathers, the architects of a secular age and its immanent frame kept both belief and work as important. But they didn't see why belief and work needed to be held together. They saw no reason why belief and work needed to operate under the same kind of oath and accountability, why both needed to be done as a duty to God. So they divided them.

On one side of the demarcation were things deemed *private*: marriage, family, love, and most importantly, religious belief. On the other side were *public* things: institutional structures, political orders, and of course work. The legacy of Reformed Protestantism demanded that oaths of accountability, which produce duty, be given in all forms of life. But now that there were private and public spheres, these oaths could be divided. You gave oaths in love, marriage, family life, and religious belief. These oaths in the private sphere, if you wished, could still be directed to God. But the public sphere, while also needing an oath of duty, no longer needed or wanted that oath of accountability to be given before God. Making an oath to God was your own personal choice in the private sphere, not something to be publicly imposed. The drive to work hard for the extra was no longer supported by an oath to God at all.

---

locale. Deep inside the early contradictions of capitalism, new thoughts about immanence and a world no longer ordered by transcendence were permitted and affirmed.

40. Tawney adds, quoting Keynes, "'Modern capitalism,' writes Mr. Keynes, 'is absolutely irreligious, without internal union, without much public spirit, often, though not always, a mere congeries of possessors and pursuers.'" Tawney, *Religion and the Rise of Capitalism*, 280.

The secular age dawns by imposing a public-private divide between the oath of loyalty to God (faith) and the oath to work hard (embedded in something other than faith). The secular age arrives when the cultural contradictions of capitalism are used to impose a divide between our oath to God and to work. We are moved into a secular age when our duty is divided, when belief and work are no longer one and the same, because one oath is given in our private lives and the other in our public lives. In this secular age, the contradictions of capitalism can no longer be held together by an oath to do our duty before God. We accept that as fact because capitalism and its contradictions make it obvious. Belief and work can never again be united under one oath, making Protestant ecclesial conversations of vocation difficult in late modernity. As Protestant theologians try to revive the vocation talk of the Reformers for late-modern people, the fractious break between belief and work is so jagged that it seems no amount of theological and practical jerry-rigging can possibly put them back together.

To summarize my point, building off Weber, capitalism is inseparable from duty and accountability. Capitalism necessitates duty because it is built on the ground of cultural contradictions. Like a tool in the belt of a plumber, duty is the wrench that directly joins together the innate contradictions in capitalism. Duty takes pipes like *justification by faith alone* and the *Protestant work ethic* and fits them so firmly together they can hold water. Yet in the dawning of a secular age, the oath to work hard was no longer connected to duty to God—but to something else. It's to this something else we now turn.

The New Duty and Its Limits

As capitalism moved into its industrial and then corporate stages, duty was remade and the contradictions shifted. Because work was cordoned off in the public sphere, and the public sphere kept belief and faith in the private realm, duty and accountability shifted from God to the company.[41] From nine to five, your work is no longer accountable to God but to the manager who stands in for the corporation. You no longer worry if God is watching, but

41. Eventually this gets shifted to the union for the sake of (at least some) workers. Loyalty and duty to the union, because you can't trust the company, becomes a major part of the late nineteenth century and first half of the twentieth century. Neoliberalism breaks union loyalty. Margaret Thatcher, the warrior knight, fighting for corporate company executives, does this breaking, upending union duty. However, loyalty still stands today, but loyalty has shifted to the self.

you do care a great deal if your manager is watching. You work hard because you're accountable to the manager and, through the manager, the company.

Though not the same, the company also has a kind of accountability to you as the worker. If you do your duty, giving your oath to work hard for the company, it promises to give you the protections of regular pay, benefits, and pension. If you do your duty of working hard for the corporation, then the corporation will do its duty of giving you the promised protections that produce stability, even gain, in your private sphere. This is why you work hard. It's your duty to the company and your company's duty to you in this period that fuels the hard work of capitalism—not God.

Capitalism in this stage (as in every stage) needs duty to join together its imposed cultural contradictions. In capitalism's earliest days, the cultural contradiction of free grace and anxious hard work was held together by intense duty to God. But a new cultural contradiction arrived, which Daniel Bell named and we discussed in the previous chapter,[42] and this entered the scene as the mass society arrived and Keynesianism reigned from 1950 to 1976. This new cultural contradiction of capitalism needed Puritan-style hard workers who were, on the one side, orderly and self-disciplined in their duty for the company and, on the other side, hedonist consumers after hours (this is the story Matthew Weiner told in the hit series *Mad Men*).

Yet there is another dimension to this contradiction that Bell doesn't articulate. This dimension of the contradiction of Keynesian capitalism imposed an oddity in American religion that has never left. We can see it when we place Taylor next to Bell. Inside the cultural contradictions that Bell names, you were called to be a Puritan-style hard worker in the public sphere of labor but oddly without God. God was shut out of the corporation (Puritanism without God is harsh: no wonder it, and the 1950s as a whole, would be rejected). The hard work due to the corporation was not in relation to duty to God but duty to the corporation itself. Yet, though at work you were supposed to be a Puritan-style laborer without God, you were also supposed to be a consuming hedonist at home, more oddly, *with* God.

This strange contradiction has persisted in American Protestantism, causing the shape of religious devotion to impact work in the public sphere but

42. I'm skipping ahead from early Reformed Calvinism to the mid-twentieth century. There is a deeper story to tell here about contradictions and the secular in the eighteenth, nineteenth, and early twentieth centuries. I simply don't have the space to do so. My objective is to get us back to entrepreneurship and innovation.

without any oaths or commitment to God. At home you *could* (and civic religion made it good to) give such an oath to God. But it was now much harder for this commitment to be anything beyond a personal consumerist choice. In the same way that you leaned into the hedonist duties of consumption, so you made your religious choices. It's no wonder that at the end of the twentieth and into the twenty-first century, Protestant belief gets nearly completely merged with consumer want (see the megachurch movement, for example).

What allows for this contradiction to hold water, until it doesn't, is duty directed to company and country. You could accept the drive of being an organized, self-disciplined, hard-working Puritan employee without God or transcendence because you were accountable to the company (and the company to you, even if you were nameless to it). And your hedonist drives too were for duty. It was your duty to country to buy and spend—that's what good old Keynes wanted. We were at war, after all, against a Red enemy, a war in which growth and employment were the main weapons. It proved a difficult task to be a hedonist who consumed for the sake of duty, and even accountability, to a bureaucratic country; it was so hard it couldn't hold.

As we've discussed above, the youth of the late 1960s rejected these modern cultural contradictions of capitalism. They marched, sang, and took on a style (in dress and language) that refused to give duty to country or company. They refused to live under the judgment of the manager. Management was seen as a form of corporately imposed fascism. These young people of the '60s gave no duty to the corporation by being accountable to the manager. They wanted to end all contradictions and free themselves from duty completely. But burying duty in a shallow grave was possible only if they could end capitalism. Capitalism always needs some form of duty. Ending capitalism was much harder than any member of the Age of Aquarius thought it would be. After coming of age inside Keynesian capitalism, consumer hedonism felt too much like freedom for these young people to take the bold steps to abandon capitalism (plus, where would you get your music?). Capitalism was in their bloodstream.

The Arrival of Entrepreneurship and Innovation

The 1970s were a quagmire. The Age of Aquarius was sputtering out, as was Keynesian capitalism. The contradictions of capitalism, borne in the duty to company and country, were neither overcome nor producing growth. This made everyone discontent, from executives and managers to workers.

They could have returned to God. But the secular age and its immanent frame was too fully imposed to make that a realistic response. The public-private divide (as well as many more changes) made a perspective shift toward God appear impossible. If capitalism was going to be restored, reinstating its drive for the extra (growth) through hard work, then a new source of duty was necessary.

This new source of duty became the self. It seemed perfect. It felt like a freedom beyond the contradiction of capitalism for the worker. But it wasn't. It was deeply expressive and bound within *you*. But it was still a duty. You were now accountable to the project of your own self.[43] You owed it to your self to work hard and advance. This new duty imposed a new contradiction. For example, it imposed the feeling that we never have enough time to really be the selves we wish we could be. The project always remains open, imposing on us a drive to work harder to be the self we should be. We no longer are guilty before a righteous God, as the early Calvinist Protestants would have claimed; we are guilty before ourselves. We are guilty for not being the self we could or should be. We imagine that if we only worked harder, having more or different training or techniques, we could be the authentic, unique self we wish we could be. Our freedom to be a self, and yet the way that freedom judges us for not taking full advantage of our freedom, is the newly imposed cultural contradiction of late capitalism.[44]

Inside the new contradiction, your loyalty was obviously not to God, company, or country but to your own most authentic way of being you. You were now your own business, your own project. You needed to work hard, but again, not for God and your covenant election, nor for the eye of manager and corporation, but for the sake of your own self. You became your own

---

43. Peter Fleming says something similar: "The neoliberal dream of turning us all into our own individual micro-enterprises—or what I will call in this book the 'I, Job' function—appears to have succeeded. But of course, here is the downside. Taking on capitalism's structural weaknesses as our own entails a serious price. The crisis of economic reason is lived as an internal social/existential crisis. . . . I term this the 'I, Job' function because work is transformed into something we are rather than something we simply do among other things. Work becomes an inescapable way of life, 24/7. For example, when we enter the workplace today we are not only selling our skills as potential labour power but also ourselves as certain kinds of people." Fleming, *The Mythology of Work: How Capitalism Persists Despite Itself* (London: Pluto, 2015), 6, 37.

44. For more on this, see Andrew Root, *Congregations in a Secular Age* (Grand Rapids: Baker Academic, 2021), chaps. 1–4.

manager. And your manager became your coach, helping you reach a constant state of innovation as an entrepreneurial self.

Work became a place to work on the self. And working on the self became your motivation to work hard. Because you weren't accountable to the company but to yourself, you owed it to yourself to work hard and with creativity. The manager's job was not to oversee you (you were managing that) but to guide and encourage you as you worked. You worked not in a department but on a team to accomplish a project—not just do a job—for the company but also for yourself. The self (as we'll explore below) was always a site under construction (the new heavy contradiction of neoliberal capitalism). And so too was the company. Just as the self moved from one project to the next, so too did the company. As the company was in a constant state of innovation, so too was your own self.

The company sensed that it could renew hard work by allowing the duty and accountability of the worker to be on himself or herself. This greatly benefited the company, especially as it sought to run fast, free of regulations on the plains of the unfenced and freer markets of a post-1980s neoliberal economy. By making the self the object of duty, the corporation could renew the push for hard workers and could be released from the demands of giving protections to its workers. Because as a worker you were loyal to the duty of your own self (not the company), the company was accountable only for allowing you to work on yourself as you worked for the company—connecting your project of the self with the company's projects. That setup seemed nice. But though they offered this new shape of work, they took something else away. Because the obligation of duty was now on the project of the self, the corporation no longer felt accountable for other forms of protection. By the early 1990s, with laws changing, pensions and benefits were cut so that the company and its workers could be accountable to their own selves.[45]

The Dawn of Entrepreneurship and Innovation

Inside this late-modern transition in capitalism, entrepreneurship and innovation start populating business literature. Only in this period does talk of

45. The arrival of the 401(k) over the pension is one example. The 401(k) allows the worker to work on their own personal and individual portfolio. The worker's retirement is disconnected from the company's direct obligation to the worker. It's a good financial retirement tool when the duty, for both worker and employer, is carried by the self.

entrepreneurship and innovation become exciting. It becomes *the* new way of bringing growth to companies and, at the same time, the self.

What neither Synod Executive Guy nor Applebee's Boy realized is that entrepreneurship and innovation do *not* come from nowhere. They come from somewhere specific. Entrepreneurship and innovation are fundamentally the children of late capitalism. They come from the capitalist apparatus used as the new form of duty that holds together the contradictions of capitalism in late modernity.

Therefore, by historical fact, entrepreneurship and innovation cannot (and should not) be considered to have always been part of the church. Nor are they a form of action that has direct correlation with God's own act and being. This does not mean the church cannot engage with entrepreneurship and innovation. But we should realize that if we do, entrepreneurship and innovation will seek to function out of their own inherent capitalist contradictions. *Though entrepreneurship and innovation may be able to motivate a certain kind of creative action, they will in turn overinflate the self.* If we are not very careful, this inflation of the self will get smuggled in, which is a pastoral and theological problem! The overinflation of the self must be dealt with, never overlooked.

Entrepreneurship and innovation are late-modern management strategies of workers wherein the self is the new source of duty. Because entrepreneurship and innovation are inseparable from late capitalism, they are nearly always tangled up with the driving ambitions and anxieties of the project of the self. It was for this reason that some of the pastors signed Bearded Brown Turtleneck's petition. They wanted to be a self that embraced innovation, but they didn't want to violate even an unknown justice issue (Bearded Brown Turtleneck was no dummy!). They signed because the pinch of contradiction still bites (and hard). The contradiction is heavy and toothy when the self is the source of duty and when entrepreneurship and innovation are the way of being in the world.

These pastors had to bear the anxiety of this contradiction. The contradiction was the need to innovate their selves and their congregations, with no real direction for the purpose or end of this innovation. Inside neoliberal capitalism, there is no end to innovation, in the sense of both direction and momentum. Innovation has no end (no larger moral vision or purpose) in neoliberalism other than more growth. Innovation is seen as fully and finally the best way to keep compounding the extra. In turn, innovation has no end; it never stops. The company's permanent innovation is possible if the workers concede that the project of their own self is also under permanent construction as well.

But how do you connect—or synergize, as the business literature would say—the corporation's drive for permanent innovation with the workers' desire to be an entrepreneurial self?

By a management revolution.

Bearded Brown Turtleneck could not abide this. He was wrong to assert that the church could not faithfully embrace entrepreneurship and innovation. But he was right that it all started as a management strategy.

Synod Executive Guy was now not only swimming in the backwash but also diverting it into congregational life. The new management strategy was reversing the flow. Protestantism's deep commitment to belief, which washed into work and created capitalism, was now moving the other direction. The secular age and its immanent frame kept capitalism, but it disconnected work from being a duty to God. Therefore, new forms of managing capitalism and its contradiction needed to arise. In early and mid-capitalism, the rising tide of these new forms of managing the work of capitalism came nowhere near the doors of the congregation. But when late modernity brought forth the capitalism of the post-1980s, its new form of managing work washed directly back into the church, reversing the flow completely. No longer did Protestantism and belief in a living and watching God shape work. Now what was considered to be good ministry was shaped by the new management technology of managing workers in a neoliberal economy.

As we finished lunch and rose from the table to head back into the conference, Synod Executive Guy asked, "Did you watch *Challenger: The Final Flight*?"

His question brought the memories rushing back.

5

———•——————————•———

Leave It to Management

Managing for Permanent Innovation

In fall 2020 Netflix released the four-part docuseries *Challenger: The Final Flight*. It explores the tragic explosion of the space shuttle *Challenger* in January 1986. Watching the docuseries imposed a heavy, bitter nostalgia on me.

I was in fifth grade, with a teacher, Mrs. Lenter, whom I hated, when the shuttle exploded. The *Challenger*'s mission was particularly poignant to all American elementary-age children. The first civilian nonastronaut was on the flight, a teacher named Christa McAuliffe. There were plans for her to teach us lessons from space. It was going to be cool. But it never happened.

When the day of the launch came, my suburban school wheeled out big TV carts, placing them in the hallways. Midmorning, as was my custom, I asked for a hall pass to the bathroom. It had become a common way for me to waste time and avoid Mrs. Lenter. By 10:30 a.m. I needed a break from her, and her from me, I imagine. I walked as slowly to and from the restroom as my eleven-year-old legs could go.

On this day, on my return journey, I stopped to watch the TV with others gathered there. Why not? And I saw it! The shuttle rose and then exploded into a ball of fire and smoke. An adult ran from the TV with her hand over her mouth. The man on the TV repeated over and over that something terrible had occurred. An explosion. I completed my slow return to the classroom, and when I entered, I announced, "Mrs. Lenter, the space shuttle just exploded."

This pronouncement was the first time I'd participated productively in class in weeks.

"Andy!" she yelled at me, "That's a terrible thing to say!"

She figured my comment was a sadistic joke, a primal wish that teachers like her would be launched into outer space to explode. I pleaded my case. I wasn't that kind of person! But she only accused me further. I pleaded more. She finally marched out of the room, leaving the class alone. My classmates peered at me in perplexed silence while she was gone.

When Mrs. Lenter returned to the room, she was in tears. The soon-to-be space-teacher was dead. Mrs. Lenter and Mrs. McAuliffe were near the same age, both with small children. It could have been her. It shouldn't have been Christa. Mrs. Lenter sobbed. But I had no empathy for her. I just peered coldly at her swollen face and red eyes. She never apologized. Our grudge deepened.

With my fifth-grade experience in the background, watching *Challenger: The Final Flight* was uncomfortably nostalgic. What became clear, as the four parts unfolded, is that indeed Mrs. McAuliffe should never have died. The explosion was the result of hubris in the management practice. NASA's management practices, so successful in the 1960s and '70s, catastrophically detonated in the '80s with the *Challenger*. NASA may have had cutting-edge technology in the area of boosters and rockets, but they lacked the one technology that was promising to return the American economy to growth: the new entrepreneurial management strategy.

The Dawn of the Managers and *Leave It to Beaver*

Just months before the *Challenger* burst into flames in the Florida sky, the renowned business professor Peter Drucker released his classic book, *Innovation and Entrepreneurship*. Drucker was the foremost thinker on how companies manage workers.[1] He was *the* management guru. Drucker's book signaled a

1. Eugene McCarraher provides some context on Drucker, saying, "The most prescient managerial philosopher was Peter Drucker, who produced a voluminous body of work that three generations of managers have revered. Drucker's frequent description as a management 'guru' only hints at his moral and spiritual concerns, and it helps explain his renown outside

major change. The America economy was now into Reagan's second term. Keynesianism had been replaced by neoliberalism over five years earlier. And Drucker saw that this new economic system was changing the shape of work.

In the introduction to the book, Drucker steps back to show us how things have changed in the new economy, post-1980s. Drucker reminds us that management had not really been a focus for most companies in the pre-Keynesian economy. Of course, workers were managed, but there was no real sense of management, particularly management as a science. Workers were being managed, but the science of management was not impacting businesses and other social structures (government agencies or denominations or congregations).

Drucker contends that the rise of management as a science began slowly right after the Great War (WWI). This first massive-scale, industrial war made the science of management (of men, matériel, and information) essential. Into the 1930s, few enterprises were interested in the science of management. Businesses like DuPont, General Motors, and Sears Roebuck started to dabble, but most companies ignored it. There was little sense that it mattered or could be the catalyst to success, and there was little sense that management could be a distinct area of expertise—but this all changed with World War II.

Even more than WWI, WWII was won only by the use of both science and management. Coming out of WWII it was understood that the science of management had won the war. In 1955, five years after Eisenhower's Keynesian consumer economy had been put in place, Drucker explained that the American business world found itself in a "management boom." Almost overnight every business was dabbling in, if not fully embracing, the science of management. Managers themselves were colonizing the work force, popping up everywhere like dandelions after the first warm rain in spring. New management jobs became ubiquitous. The goal for many was to rise and become a manager.

---

corporate business circles. (By the 1940s, even W. H. Auden—a socialist a decade before—was recommending Drucker's work to friends.) A consummate corporate humanist, Drucker glided easily through the corridors connecting finance, journalism, academia, and industry. Born and raised among the liberal burghers of pre-World War I Vienna, Drucker had been a rising star in Catholic political thought; a financial reporter in Europe in the early 1930s; a political commentator for *Harper's*, the *New Republic*, and the *Saturday Evening Post*; an editor at the Luce manors of *Time* and *Fortune*; a professor of economics and humanities at Bennington College; and a much sought-after consultant for General Motors and other corporations." McCarraher, *The Enchantments of Mammon: How Capitalism Became the Religion of Modernity* (Cambridge, MA: Belknap, 2019), 399.

As a practical science, management was now seen as a social technology. The Keynesian economy was a managed economy. Every agency, organization, and company needed management.

The church and its denominations were some of the only cultural collectives that didn't need this new social technology of management in a Keynesian economy. Between the 1950s and 1980s there was little sense that the pastor was managing a congregation. The practical pastoral material of this period contains some, but very little, literature on managing a congregation. This kind of material would explode in the mid-1980s, when the identity of the pastor, following the economy, shifted toward the new kind of management. But in the period between 1955 and 1985, the new science of management was cordoned off from congregational life, because the church (like the family), for good or ill, was placed in the private sphere. The new science of management, post-1950s, was for public work, not for home or church.

All the classic sitcoms of the period are based at home, and we almost never see work. For instance, we're never really told what Ward Cleaver does for a job in *Leave It to Beaver*.[2] There are only a few times we even see Ward at work (much different from, say, *Modern Family*, where Phil's work as a real estate agent is central to much of the comedy). Rather, in almost every episode, Ward enters the show through the front door as he returns home from work. Seeing him walk through that door, we're supposed to understand that Ward has left the sphere of work for the sphere of home. He is putting away the logics of one world for the other. The show doesn't care about the work world because work is supposed to be divided from the world the show is set in, the world of the home and family.

This separation of work from home reveals something important about this period in American work life. The comic engine of the show is that Beaver can't be managed, because he's not a worker but a boy living in the private, not the public, sphere. This made Beaver iconic for those living in this period. In a time of the heavy management, Beaver represents the opposite. Beaver loses things, gets distracted, always arrives late, dirties his good clothes, and says things he shouldn't. All this behavior was managed out of

---

2. We do meet his boss, Fred Rutherford. I grew up as a big *Leave It to Beaver* fan. Watching it in syndication in the late 1980s and 1990s was oddly appealing. Teaming the lost world of *Leave It to Beaver* with Nirvana's "Smells like Teen Spirit" encompasses for me that time and my own existential state then.

workers in a Keynesian-born science of management. At the beginning of most episodes, Ward forgets this. Instead of remembering that Beaver is just a boy, Ward tries to manage him. It always fails. By the end of each show, it never disappoints that Ward comes to realize that the home is no place for management. Ward learns that you can't manage your kids, because the family is not work. Middle-aged men in the mid-1960s, like my own grandfather, loved Beaver Cleaver, delighting in his antics. They loved Beaver, I think, because living deeply inside the science of management in their work lives, Beaver reminded them of something they had lost. He reminded them of a time when they weren't managed. Beaver assured them that the home could be this kind of space.

From 1955 into the 1980s, the science of management was not designed to shape the raising of children or the leading of a church. Not even the grandmasters of the science of management at NASA would assume so. No NASA manager thought to raise their children or shape their church by the logic of the science of management. The barrier that separated the public from the private delineated where this new science could be appropriately used. It wasn't assumed in the 1950s, '60s, and '70s that our private lives of religion and family, or even our most private experience of our own self, needed managing.

Yet this all changed by the mid-1980s. Soon enough, the science of management was crashing through the levee, and private lives were now being flooded with management techniques. Bookshelves, conferences, and talk shows (every week Donahue and Oprah hosted another expert manager on the self-help management of the self) were filled with people who could use management techniques to help you get the most out of your spouse, sex life, children, and more. At the same time, church growth conferences started proliferating. The church growth movement invited pastors to adopt the new management style of the neoliberal economy. If these new management practices promised growth to businesses, why not use them in the church? For good or ill, through management, the shape of secular work was washing back into the church. Now the pastor needed to think about himself or herself as a manager.

The 1980s ended the days of Ward Cleaver. Management was no longer left at the door of the private sphere. Management was now a science for every part of the private life as well. Most significantly, it stretched to the most private realities of the private sphere—the self. The evolving management science of the mid-1980s grabbed hands with psychology. This new management style could help you manage your very self so that you could become, through self-management, the self you always wanted to be.[3]

But to gain the volume and speed to break the levee and race over the walls of the private sphere, management needed to be reworked. It needed to come under a great technological transformation.

The Cold Manager

The Keynesian economy built after WWII was made to last, with sturdy pillars and beams of thick stone. Its heavy regulations demanded this. Businesses needed to be stable and structured. The crafters of the Keynesian economy thought it was necessary for companies and businesses to be strong and durable, able to withstand the high winds of global conflict. Not only had the pre-Keynesian economy been battered by the winds of wars and inflation, but the opposing economic ideology of the Communists was blowing hard across Europe and Asia.

Organization directly made the companies in the Keynesian economy sturdy and durable, able to withstand the winds. When the Keynesian mass society of a consumer economy arrived, companies got bigger and more complicated. To keep them growing and not ground to a halt, that complication needed to be organized. Management became essential to organization. Management became a science. Hence the arrival of the management boom in 1955. The manager, for the first time in history, was indispensable.

But this is where an important distinction comes in. We need to see clearly what this management *was directed toward*, because it shifted hard in the 1980s, allowing even families, churches, and the self to become open to new psychomanagement techniques. From 1955 to 1980, the manager was managing technical operations and bureaucratic systems. NASA is the greatest example of the height of this organized management. NASA's genius was as much its ability to manage an initiative as to create a lunar module. Obviously, to put people on the moon was a complicated endeavor, to say the least. To make it happen, the manager was essential. The manager was neither an engineer nor a pilot. The manager's job wasn't to create the equipment or to test it, but to make sure all the complicated systems of each component of the mission came together, on time and on budget. The manager made all the

3. For a more contemporary example, see David Allen, *Getting Things Done*, rev. ed. (New York: Penguin, 2015).

complicated bureaucratic systems work. What was managed between 1955 and 1980 was bureaucratic operations and systems.[4]

The workers' job was to do their part inside the system, dutifully working hard on their small part of the larger operation. The manager wasn't directly managing the worker, but instead the system. Or maybe it's better to say that the manager was managing the worker by focusing completely on the objectives of the system. There was a kind of quasi-military sensibility to all forms of work in the first management boom of Keynesianism (which makes sense, since it came out of the successes of WWII). Most managers didn't really care about you or your feelings, but about how your work participated in the objectives the manager was overseeing. The shared duty of the manager and the worker in Keynesian capitalism was directed toward the company. As the pinnacle of the organization man, the manager's job was to maintain the system that allowed the objectives of the company to be reached. The workers' job was to follow the manager and do their small (or large) part. It was the duty of the manager to oversee the systems; the duty of the workers was to play their part and receive direct management.

Keynesian economics worked to great success as long as workers had *Leave It to Beaver* private lives. The ethic of authenticity had not yet dawned, and the profits of companies and the overall growth for the economy continually increased. But none of these held in the 1980s. Five years into the Keynesian economy, when it was running full throttle in 1955, the first management boom arrived. In the same way, five years after the arrival of a neoliberal economy in 1980, an all-new management strategy arrived in 1985.

The Exploding Bridge to a New Style

When the *Challenger* exploded, the country grieved like it hadn't since the assassination of John F. Kennedy. Mrs. Lenter and millions of others cried. Yet within months, the grief turned into red-hot anger. It was discovered that Christa McAuliffe and the six other astronauts died not because of an unforeseen technological malfunction but because of bad management. Engineers, both at NASA and Morton Thiokol (the private contractor that built the boosters), advised

4. If the global pandemic of 2020 had happened during this time, these management experts would have had it figured out in six months. But now what counts as management is not operating complicated bureaucratic operations and systems. Since management now largely entails curating the self, we no longer know how to do what we could have done forty years ago.

against the launch. It was too cold. The engineers knew that the O-rings in the boosters were compromised. The O-rings had held through other launches, but the unusual freeze in Florida made it advisable to wait for warmer temperatures.

But the managers at NASA and Morton Thiokol couldn't wait. This launch was already two days behind, and the whole operation was lagging and running overages. If the managers were to meet the objectives of the program and hit the number of launches scheduled for 1986, this launch, with Christa McAuliffe aboard, needed to go. The managers asked for risk assessments. Though advised to wait, the caution in the managers' minds couldn't be justified. They were responsible for making the systems run to meet the objectives of the organization. The managers were directly managing the successful operations of the organization, not the life of Christa McAuliffe and the others aboard the shuttle. The managers and Christa McAuliffe, as a worker, were to do their duty for the objective of the organization. To everyone's surprise, the managers gave the go-ahead.

In early summer 1986, the American public learned at the Rogers Commission that these managers knew the risk was elevated but gave the go-ahead anyway. They bore the country's scorn. Lawrence Mulloy and his boss William Lucas were released from their duties and painted as terrible managers. Lucas couldn't understand it. Even thirty-five years later, Lucas believed he operated (managed) correctly. He said in a recent interview, "I did what I thought was right in light of the information I had, and if I were going over it with the same information I had at the time, I'd make the same decision, 'cause I thought it was right. I didn't do anything that I thought was wrong then, and I didn't do anything that I think was wrong in retrospect."[5]

Lucas explained that losses are necessary for advancement. Though he regretted the losses, his job was to meet the objective of advancement. No great advancement comes without loss. Any good Keynesian manager knew this. But Lucas was one of the last of the old-school managers, and the Rogers Commission proved that NASA needed an update in management style. In 1986, Lucas needed to be retired as a dinosaur. Into the mid-1980s, the American worker was entering into a new management revolution that stood in direct opposition to old Keynesian managers like William Lucas.

5. See the 42:20 mark of *Challenger: The Final Flight*, episode 4, "Nothing Ends Here," directed by Daniel Junge and Steven Leckart, September 16, 2020, on Netflix.

Innovate or Die

This new management technology, as Peter Drucker called it, was to shift the objective of management from bureaucratic operations to people.[6] The new managers of the neoliberal economy were, of course, still managing objectives, seeking profits and growth for the company (even more profits and more growth than Keynesianism could produce). But it was discovered that this happened best not by managing workers as if they were small pieces of a larger bureaucratic system but by seeing each worker as a distinct and unique self.

This sounds like music to our ears. Nearly utopian! But we should remember where it comes from and why this new management style arrived, and ultimately what it meant for workers. It meant a *new* jagged and heavy contradiction of capitalism, because utopia was not the objective of this dawning management style.[7] Exponential growth in profits was.

Management needed to change in the mid-1980s and beyond because a new neoliberal economy arrived, pulling up almost all the fenceposts of regulation and protection, making it possible for companies to run faster than ever, chasing innovation after innovation. If a company could string together a couple of these innovations, an avalanche and not just a trickle of profits would ensue. For the new neoliberal economy that dawned in the 1980s and moved with force into the 1990s, the route to huge leaps in growth was to shape the company or organization into a state of *permanent innovation*.

True, Keynesian companies sought innovation, but not permanently. The Keynesian company was built in such a way that once the innovation arrived, it moved into modes of ordered operation. No one between 1950 and 1980 wished for permanent innovation—that would be crazy. After all, innovation was a disruption and, therefore, a difficult and costly management issue (involving the new machining of equipment, new systems of oversight, and the new training of workers). Like rich Black Forest cake, every Keynesian company wanted a slice of innovation, but not more. Too much cake would leave the company incapacitated with a severe bellyache.[8]

6. Peter Drucker says, "And the vehicle of this profound change in attitudes, values, and above all in behavior is a 'technology.' It is called management. What has made possible the emergence of the entrepreneurial economy in America is new applications of management." Drucker, *Innovation and Entrepreneurship* (New York: HarperBusiness, 1985), 14.

7. Karl Polanyi discusses this market utopianism in *The Great Transformation: The Political and Economic Origins of Our Time*, 2nd ed. (Boston: Beacon, 2001), 267.

8. Lee Vinsel and Andrew Russell, in their important book *The Innovation Delusion: How Our Obsession with the New Has Disrupted the Work That Matters Most* (New York: Currency,

Yet the companies of the neoliberal economy saw things very differently. They were built with iron stomachs. These companies could stomach much more than a slice of the cake of innovation. They went much further and decided to make the rich cake of innovation nearly the only component of their diet. The goal was to shape the company for a state of permanent innovation. Permanent innovation had the excitement of promised profits, and it became a necessity inside neoliberalism because business was now an all-out guerrilla war.

Innovation needed to become permanent and continual, because laced inside the "freedoms" of neoliberalism was a menacing threat. The dial on business-based social Darwinism was turned way up inside neoliberalism. The competition was white-hot. The environment for profits in business became much more bountiful in the 1980s. Business was now a lush landscape. But the possibility of being eaten by a predator, even a much smaller one, was heightened. If the smaller company innovated in the right way, a larger company that slumbered by maintaining and not innovating could be maimed with one strike. Soon the larger company would be bleeding profits. Apple, the standard for permanent innovation, did just this. What had seemed impossible in the early 1970s Apple was able to do in the mid-1980s: severely wound a giant of corporate Keynesianism, IBM. The innovation of Steve Jobs and Steve Wozniak, in a Northern California garage, was a stone that wobbled the giant and its army of Keynesian-style managers.

The neoliberal environment for business was lavish but dangerous. If you weren't constantly evolving by always innovating, you'd be lunch. The elimination of regulations and projections freed the economy in a way that incentivized innovation (which was good). But in turn, the only way to maintain the company's newly achieved growth, and not see it bleed out to zero, was to enter a constant state of innovation and then seek more innovation. The company could never have enough innovation. Like Darwin's finches, the company needed to innovate its beak or bear its bleak end. But unlike Darwin's finches, which took centuries to adapt, each innovation from the business required another immediate innovation. There was no time to rest. The competition

---

2020), state, "At a deeper level, innovation-speak is built on the hidden, often false premise that innovation is inherently good" (11). The authors show that innovation being inherently good is not the case. They give context for why this was assumed: "Our point is this: By the late 1970s, economists, policy makers, and others had grown seriously worried about productivity, and these anxieties have been crucial ever since to how we talk about innovation." *Innovation Delusion*, 28.

was too heated. Deep inside neoliberalism, the company needed to constantly innovate and kill the competition or be killed.

The Management Revolution

Needing to innovate or die (a state of permanent innovation) meant the company required a new kind of worker. Old-school Keynesian workers, formed by old-school-style managers, were of little help. That was no longer the kind of army necessary to fight this new kind of business war. Such old-school workers were even portrayed as major detriments, promising the bloody death of the company. The new business literature painted such workers, and particularly their dinosaur managers, as the enemy within. It soon became clear that the only way to get new-school workers, which neoliberal companies of permanent innovation needed, was to create them. This approach demanded a whole new form of management. A new management revolution emerged that sought both to attack the ideas of the science of management that came from the boom of Keynesianism and to re-create the worker for a new capitalism.

Peter Drucker titled his book *Innovation and Entrepreneurship* because the two main words were linked as a kind of one-step/two-step inside new capitalism. The necessity of a state of permanent *innovation* (step 1) created the demand that all workers follow suit and, from top to bottom, embrace *entrepreneurship* (step 2). Drucker uses "entrepreneurship" in two ways. First, he points out that the new innovation-based economy means that a sole entrepreneur, with the right innovative idea and drive, can garner significant profits, creating a large, successful business almost overnight. But more importantly for his readers, Drucker uses "entrepreneurship" in a broader, second way to mean that, following this leading entrepreneur, all workers who labor for the founding entrepreneur also need to see themselves as entrepreneurs. For this to happen, a whole new style of manager was needed that could get each worker committed to the state of permanent innovation. In Drucker's mind, the manager was no longer managing a system, keeping a bureaucratic machine running. Rather, the new managers were managing people toward this entrepreneurial state that would produce permanent innovation for the company. This, Drucker thought, was a management revolution.

The state of permanent innovation meant there was now little need for an army of Puritan company loyalists. That had been one side of the old, and now dying, cultural contradictions of a passing form of capitalism. Instead, the new form of management needed to raise an army of entrepreneurs (there could never be enough!). But this new style of entrepreneurial work didn't end the contradictions that workers had to bear in capitalism. Rather, it created an all-new cultural contradiction for workers in this new capitalism.

The Background to the New Capitalist Contradiction

The dawning of this management revolution was unable to alleviate the secular cultural contradiction of capitalism. Rather, it helped make a sharp new contradiction that workers now needed to bear. *And they needed to sustain this contradiction directly at work.* This new contradiction took a new shape, distinct from the old cultural contradiction. To understand its distinct edges, we need to view it against the contrasting backdrop of the old cultural contradiction of capitalism.

Remember, the old Keynesian contradiction asserted that workers needed to be Ward Cleavers, smoothly leaving behind the public world of work for the private life. These workers needed to be Puritans in the office but loving and, importantly, product-consuming fathers or mothers at home. This old Keynesian contradiction was real, but it was ultimately not the company's problem. Between 1950 and 1980, the tension of this contradiction rarely if ever landed on the manager's desk. It may have been a contradiction felt deeply by workers, but it was not a contradiction that could muck up the gears of the bureaucratic systems the manager was overseeing for the corporation. This was the case because, put simply, the other side of the contradiction was located outside the realm of work. The contradiction was not caused by the company, and therefore it was not the manager's concern. Helping workers cope with the contradiction was not an issue the company, or the manager, needed to deal with. How you *felt* was a private matter. In the Keynesian economy, private matters, like some YouTube videos today, were not suitable for work.

To say it another way, the concrete locale of the Keynesian cultural contradiction of capitalism was *not* located at work. If it had a concrete location, it was the bar. Happy hour and the stiff drink after work before returning to being the perfect consumer father/mother was often the pained liminal act that eased the pinch of the Keynesian contradiction of capitalism. The drink was the elixir that helped you cross from one world to the next (some, like Don Draper, did this more clumsily than others).[9] Inside this Keynesian contradiction, all the company knew or honestly cared about was the Puritan side of the contradiction. There was no real need to manage *people or their feelings*, because for workers there was no operative contradiction inside work hours. The internal psychological constitution of the worker mattered little to a Keynesian manager. The science of business management could be purely and completely rationalized science, producing what the sociologist Herbert Marcuse calls *technical rationality*.[10]

The Keynesian contradiction was located right at the liminal place between work and private life. The bar was the O-ring that cushioned the tension between work and home, Puritanism and hedonism. The bar was the best that the mid-twentieth-century secular age could do (it took on a pseudoreligious function, providing a kind of community, the drink serving as a kind of sacrament for entering another world). The original thick and dependable O-ring of the Calvinist sense of duty and calling to God was lost completely inside twentieth-century capitalism.[11] Without this O-ring of belief, Keynesianism could only create an O-ring that was as compromised as the *Challenger*'s. This made the transitional point between the two worlds rub hard, creating uncomfortable sparks of contradiction.

With this background, we're better prepared to see the distinction between the Keynesian contradiction and the new contradiction of neoliberal capitalism and its permanent innovation.

Locating the New Contradiction

Inside the need for permanent innovation and the drive for every worker to be an entrepreneur, the location of the contradiction of capitalism significantly shifted. When the corporation began to function out of a sense of permanent

9. This is not to say that workers in the new capitalism don't have happy hour and a drink after work. But I think this has changed. Entering bars after work hours has taken on a different form. The Don Drapers are gone. In these bars now are two groups: older executives and managers who are actually still working, entertaining clients, etc. and, more prominently, young workers who don't yet have families (marriage and family occurs much later in life in the new capitalism than in Keynesianism). They drink not to gain the nerve to jump from one world to the next but to have fun and hook up.

10. See Herbert Marcuse, "Some Social Implications of Modern Technology," *Studies in Philosophy and Social Sciences* 9 (1941): 138–62, available at https://courses.cs.washington.edu /courses/cse490e/19wi/readings/marcuse_social_implications_1941.pdf.

11. Secular 1 had taken it away.

innovation, and therefore asked all workers to be entrepreneurs, the cultural contradiction of capitalism swiftly relocated. The contradiction moved from being in the fictitious space between work and private life to being fully and completely locked inside work itself. In the new capitalism of permanent innovation, work became the land of contradiction.

We can see the bold outlines of this contradiction and how deeply it's planted inside the late-modern worker by listening to the important German social theorist Andreas Reckwitz. Reckwitz, in a chapter called "The Rise of the Aesthetic Economy" in his insightful book *The Invention of Creativity*, discusses the management gurus who followed Peter Drucker. In discussing them, he lucidly names this new piercing contradiction. Reckwitz says, "The theories of [Tom] Peters, Rosabeth Moss Kanter and Charles Handy took off from the idea of permanent innovation borrowed from innovation economics. [These approaches of leadership and management were] predicated on a presumed tension between the organization's need to innovate, on the one hand, and employee inertia resulting from routine and security, on the other."[12]

The new contradiction is that, inside the drive for permanent innovation, routine and security are problematic. The winning company will continually, without stopping, disrupt and risk for the sake of constant innovation. It needs new innovations on top of more new innovations to survive and thrive. (Inside a neoliberal economy, surviving and thriving are the same thing. You can't survive, keeping your stock price up, if you're not thriving. Slow growth is death.) Yet Reckwitz's point is that human beings, who of course happen to be these workers (until sophisticated AI and robots can replace them), seem to always slide back into routines to create security. This psychological, even biological, fact imposes lethargy on the race for more innovation. Human beings need to equilibrate and seem to thrive on rich routines that give them ontological security.[13] *But in the neoliberalism of the new capitalism, this is bad for business!* Too much routine and security within a company causes a drought of innovation, and a Darwinian bloodbath of decline and corporate insecurity will follow.[14]

---

12. Andreas Reckwitz, *The Invention of Creativity* (Malden, MA: Polity, 2017), 118.

13. See Anthony Giddens, *The Consequences of Modernity* (Stanford, CA: Stanford University Press, 1990), 92–98.

14. Reckwitz adds, "A further typical character trait of the entrepreneur is the ability to cope with uncertainty—a trait which Frank Knight would later see as the entrepreneur's crucial feature. Making novelty successful is thus for Joseph Schumpeter not an achievement primarily of perception or cognition but, rather, of energy, will and the desire to succeed. . . . The

Somehow the company needs to get workers to do what is unnatural to the human spirit, and by doing so it creates significant psychological tensions—to live in a constant state of disruption and insecurity. This makes late capitalism somewhat inhuman. The need for constant innovation imposes endless disruption and insecurity on workers, going directly against the grain of the human spirit. Of course, work has been a fundamental category for *Homo sapiens* for hundreds of thousands of years. Like all other animals, human beings need to eat; but unlike other animals, human beings thrive when meaningful routine produces symbols, which give us an appropriate sense of security.

Late capitalism, as Karl Polanyi foresaw, becomes something unnatural, even inhuman. The company needs workers. But the only kind of workers it can choose from are beings in ontological need of routine and security. For the company to compete, these human beings who work for the company must abandon their very ontological needs. After all, the company can only grow if these workers can move past those ontological needs and embrace a state of constant disruption and risk. To survive, the company needs workers who have the psychological capacity to participate fully and energetically in neverending innovation by choosing for forty-five (even sixty-five) hours a week to operate outside their ontological need for routine and security and reach for more and more innovation. But to truly be effective at work, accepting the strains of this way of working, it's best if the worker imposes this need for permanent innovation on every part of their life. They must seek permanent innovation and its unnatural disruption and insecurity in love and leisure. Even in their own identity.

This is the heavy cultural contradiction of the new capitalism. It is the face-off between the company's needs and the workers who must abandon all routine for the sake of constant novelty, always seeking growth over security. Yet the worker's finite humanity can't really stand this open-ended uncertainty that the company in the new capitalism seeks. Human beings need rituals of dependability, order, and constancy that lead to some security.[15] Without these, the human spirit can be overrun by anxiety. One symptom of this contradiction

---

entrepreneur experiences a 'joy of making, of the creation of novelty as such,' but also a sporting ambition to win at any cost. Yet for Schumpeter these emotional qualities are strangely contrasted to the entrepreneur's outward blandness, his unattractiveness in the public eye of his time." Reckwitz, *Invention of Creativity*, 97.

15. The Korean-German philosopher Byung-Chul Han has offered a rich text on this: *The Disappearance of Ritual* (Cambridge: Polity, 2020). Chaps. 1 and 2 are particularly splendid and fit perfectly with the argument I'm making.

is the spiking mental health crisis we're facing across innovation-based economies. The other symptom is depression, which also comes to be inside the
same phenomena.[16] Depression, Alain Ehrenberg argues, is the fatigue or
burnout of needing to always (without dependable routine, ritual, or security)
innovate the self (more on this soon).[17]

The company has the difficult challenge of keeping the one-step of permanent innovation going by getting the worker to accept (and psychologically
bear) the contradiction. But the trick is that it's best if the workers don't just
accept but embrace, even choose, the contradiction, constant disruption, and
insecurity. The way to make this contradiction seem appealing, Drucker believes, is through the second step of turning every worker into an entrepreneur.

The new management revolution was fueled by the realization that human
beings are willing to bear long stretches of disruption and insecurity for a
greater good. Soldiers live in long stretches of disruption and insecurity for
the greater good of country. Parents welcome an intense period of disruption
and insecurity of birthing and bringing home a child for the good of loving
the child. But what greater good could workers possibly recognize inside the
drive for permanent innovation? They're inside a company that is giving its
workers fewer protections, always cutting costs, benefits, and salaries as much
as possible to win the Darwinian war.

Accepting the reductions of the immanent frame, late capitalism and its
management revolution didn't make this greater good something outside or
beyond the self. Rather, they made the self the greater good, period. The
lauded company builders of late modernity swallowed oceans of disruption
and insecurity (sometimes to mythological levels) all for the sake of building

16. Ulrich Bröckling adds insightfully, "Depression, irony, and passive resistance are certainly
not the only causes of friction in the regime of entrepreneurial subjectification. They have been
presented here as anecdotal evidence and are of differing importance. None of them are suitable
as models for the kind of tactical, critical practice needed to obtain a different freedom than the
freedom of the market. They themselves testify both to the impossibility of truly becoming an
entrepreneurial self once and for all and to the impossibility of escaping the demand to nevertheless work on becoming one. . . . The force of the entrepreneurial call can be weakened by its
own inherent excessiveness. The entrepreneurial self is a 'weary' self. The individual is always
lagging behind because the demands are principally incapable of final satisfaction. She is always in
danger of being eliminated because the 'categorical comparative' posed by the market maintains
a permanent contest of exclusion. Since recognition is contingent on success, every failure stirs up
the fear of social death. There are no stable compass points and no places of respite." Bröckling,
The Entrepreneurial Self: Fabricating a New Type of Subject (Los Angeles: SAGE, 2016), 200.

17. See Alain Ehrenberg, *The Weariness of the Self: Diagnosing the History of Depression
in the Contemporary Age* (Montreal: McGill-Queen's University Press, 2016). See also my
discussion in *The Congregation in a Secular Age* (Grand Rapids: Baker Academic, 2021), chap. 1.

their own business. If it's your own, the logic goes, you'll accept truckloads of disruption and insecurity. The way to get workers to accept what the founder and CEO does, even without any of the payoff, is to get workers to also be invested in the business—not necessarily in the business of the company but in the business of their own selves. Workers accept permanent innovation and all its disruption and insecurity because it allows them to be entrepreneurial selves, to run their self like their own small business.[18]

Making workers into entrepreneurial selves for the sake of a company's permanent innovation became the heartbeat of the new management revolution. The manager's objective is no longer to oversee impersonal systems but to manage people. Though this sounds nice, we shouldn't miss that people are the attention of management only because of the inherent contradiction the company has thrust upon those people. What is often missed in the church's adoption of innovation language and strategy is that the reason people are the focus of this kind of management (even calling the manager to be empathic) is to make workers into entrepreneurial selves, which makes them accept the unnatural end of permanent innovation. When the church adopts this innovation language, what washes back into the church is a heightened obsession with the self.

Managing the Unnatural

We are now faced with an important question: If permanent innovation—and the entrepreneurial selves it births and which companies need—is fundamentally unnatural, why is it accepted and even lauded today? Why does Applebee's Boy think it's the best way to be a pastor? Why does Synod Executive Guy even equate it with mission? Understanding why this unnatural contradiction is accepted will help us see how permanent innovation and the entrepreneurial self are held together. It will show us why this management perspective has been so appealing to denominations and pastors.

The unnatural realities of permanent innovation and entrepreneurial selves are accepted because the new management style ingeniously found a natural tendency. It wouldn't have worked without finding and linking permanent innovation and the entrepreneurial self to this natural tendency. The gurus of the

18. For an important and intricate discussion of the rise of branding yourself, see Ryan McAnnally-Linz, "An Unrecognizable Glory: Christian Humility in the Age of Authenticity" (PhD diss., Yale University, 2016).

new management revolution knew that if the one-step, two-step of permanent innovation and an entrepreneurial self were going to hold, there needed to be a firm natural ligament to keep them together. To switch the analogy, in the same way one might give a dog medicine, this natural tendency functioned as the smear of tasty peanut butter on the jagged pill of the new work-located cultural contradiction of capitalism that made it go down.

This natural tendency was *personal development*. Reckwitz explains that the new neoliberal managers took up the "idea from personality and organization theory [and from psychology more broadly] that every worker has a natural tendency towards personal development. By thus redefining the economic subject and the organization, post-bureaucratic management envisages an easy convergence of dynamic individuals with dynamic institutions." Reckwitz continues, explaining that through the natural drive of personal development "the worker is redefined as naturally innovative on two levels: as a creative individual striving for personal development and constantly new ideas; and as an entrepreneurial self, searching for challenging ways to assert himself and his ideas in a dynamic environment."[19]

Workers could accept the disruption and insecurity of permanent innovation. They could invest deeply in a war for new innovation as entrepreneurial selves. They could deliver new ideas and solutions at a fast pace for the company that cared more for profit than the worker's protections. Workers could do all this because they believed that working for the firm—even amid exhaustion and anxiety—allowed for personal development.[20] If workers were allowed to deepen and develop their selves, they were willing to accept (until they couldn't) the contradiction of late capitalism that came as constant disruption and insecurity. It didn't matter if they lacked routine and security,

19. Reckwitz, *Invention of Creativity*, 118. David Frayne adds, "It is clear that work represents much more than an economic necessity and a social duty. In affluent societies, work is powerfully promoted as the pivot around which identities are properly formed. It is valorized as a medium of personal growth and fulfillment, and constructed as a means of acquiring social recognition and respect. All of this we recognize, even if work's ultimate function is in most cases to generate private profit." Frayne, *The Refusal of Work: The Theory and Practice of Resistance to Work* (London: Zen Books, 2015), 15.

20. Peter Drucker points to this reality, saying, "Successful entrepreneurs, whatever their individual motivation—be it money, power, curiosity, or the desire for fame and recognition—try to create value and to make a contribution. Still, successful entrepreneurs aim high. They are not content simply to improve on what already exists, or to modify it. They try to create new and different values and new and different satisfactions, to convert a 'material' into a 'resource,' or to combine existing resources in a new and more productive configuration." Drucker, *Innovation and Entrepreneurship*, 34.

because while that was difficult, they had in return the latitude to develop their personal selves.[21]

I think both Applebee's Boy and Synod Executive Guy sensed this peanut butter smear of personal development that covered the contradiction. But they were tasting only the peanut butter and not the jagged little pill of contradiction. Tasting only the peanut butter gave both of them a hope that innovation could be merged (directly) with ministry. Like a Labrador retriever, they swallowed it too quickly, unable to taste the heavy contradiction it covered. They failed to realize how, if not careful, this innovation and entrepreneurial focus can overinflate and burden the self.

To better see how this overinflation happens, we need to ask a question: What did personal development actually mean inside the companies of neoliberalism? In the twenty-first century in Silicon Valley, it meant that coders were given lunchtime yoga sessions, breaks for mindfulness, and more so they could bear the inhuman pace of permanent innovation, feeling compelled as an entrepreneurial self to win market share and even to find new markets for the company. But these Silicon Valley ways of inviting personal development at work rested on something more fundamental that stretched back to the late 1980s and '90s: creativity. Inside decline and the cultural sense that religion is boring, the focus on creativity makes both Applebee's Boy and Synod Executive Guy ready to embrace permanent innovation for the synod.

For companies of permanent innovation, an imposed ethos of creativity within the company could solve the problems of permanent innovation and its unnatural tendency on workers. Through an ethos of creativity, the company positioned itself for the pursuit of permanent innovation. After all, new innovation demands new creative ideas. And creativity could also signal to workers that their labor could scratch their natural itch for personal development, keeping them pushing continually for more innovation. In stark difference from the Keynesian company and its bureaucratic management, neoliberal companies ordered themselves around (even for) creativity.[22] Imposing and protecting this creative ethos became the central job of the manager.

21. David Frayne, drawing from André Gorz, says, "In today's society, growing numbers of people live in a condition of what Gorz called 'generalised insecurity,' always aware on some level that they are potentially unemployed or under-employed, potentially insecure or temporary workers." Frayne, *Refusal of Work*, 74.

22. Frayne reminds us, "The trouble with defining work in these terms, however—as a form of creative activity—is that it becomes difficult to know what we should call work that is not creative but menial and routine. Workers who complain about their jobs in call centres, on supermarket

To maintain this creative ethos, the manager had to build an environment and a culture where "the employee functions as an interpreting and emotional entity."[23] In the time before permanent innovation, the culture of the company was not really a concern, not really something to think about. But inside permanent innovation, the culture of a company becomes nearly everything, because the culture moves workers to cross the Rubicon and accept the unnatural tendency of constant disruption and insecurity.

The manager was no longer stewarding a firm bureaucratic system. Now, instead, the manager was responsible for the culture of the company (a Keynesian manager would have no idea what *culture* even meant).[24] The manager did their job by managing an elusive, emotionally constituted environment.[25] If the workers felt like the environment was conducive to their own personal development, through their creative self-expression, they'd accept the inhuman drives for permanent innovation. Innovation could be accepted as good (even glorified!), because it was itself a creative operation. This is what Synod Executive Guy wanted to accomplish with the funds: to create a synod culture conducive to permanent innovation. For the neoliberal company, an environment with the *feel* of creativity (even more than actual creativity) could move workers to accept the contradictions of late capitalism and seek profits over their natural tendency for routine and security.

---

checkouts, or at computers, inputting data day after day, are more likely to view their work as a means of self-preservation rather than self-expression." Frayne, *Refusal of Work*, 18.

23. Reckwitz, *Invention of Creativity*, 118.

24. As an example, Clayton Christensen and Michael Raynor say, "The answer lies in the process by which the ideas get shaped. Midlevel managers play a crucial role in every company's innovation process, as they shepherd partially formed ideas into fully fledged business plans in an effort to win funding from senior management. It is the middle managers who must decide which of the ideas that come bubbling in or up to them they will support and carry to upper management for approval, and which ideas they will simply allow to languish. This is a key reason why companies employ middle managers in the first place. Their job is to sift the good ideas from the bad and to make good ideas so much better that they readily secure funding from senior management." Christensen and Raynor, *The Innovator's Solution: Creating and Sustaining Successful Growth* (Boston: Harvard Business School Press, 2003), 10.

25. Here is an example from a popular business book: "What we observed across all the diverse individuals and organizations we studied was a surprisingly consistent view of the leader's role in innovation, which can be expressed this way: Instead of trying to come up with a vision and make innovation happen themselves, a leader of innovation creates a place—a context, an environment—where people are willing and able to do the hard work that innovative problem solving requires." Linda A. Hill, Greg Brandeau, Emily Truelove, and Kent Lineback, *Collective Genius: The Art and Practice of Leading Innovation* (Cambridge, MA: Harvard Business Review, 2014), 3.

In the late modernity of the new capitalism, creativity has become defined as an expressive act of the self, which is fundamentally unique and courageous. A good self is creative, unique, and brave in its expression. Therefore, a good job is a job that allows for the development of your creative—unique—self. Of course, we must recognize that this personal development is an emotional feeling. It doesn't necessarily mean that your specific task in the company has to be creative. After all, the one who is responsible for you being a certain kind of self is you. But it would help if the environment (the culture) where you work (even if you just made copies) were creative. Being in a creative culture would assure you that your self is developing well. In such a culture you can feel like your work is giving you the freedom for creative self-development through expression, even if it isn't.

Because the manager is responsible for a culture of self-development and not a bureaucratic structure, the manager can no longer be a rationalist scientist as in Keynesianism. The manager must become a romantic coach of expressivism.[26] This type of manager fits perfectly with the ethic of authenticity. The manager as coach of expressivism shapes the culture of the company so that workers interpret it as creative. It shouldn't be missed that the manager is overseeing and seeking to shape workers' emotions. Emotions had no part in the workday of Keynesian laborers (they only came out in the bar after work). But emotions are central and constant—even the very thing to be managed—in the neoliberal company. (Enter the hilarity of the UK and US versions of *The Office*, *Office Space*, and *Superstore*.)

The manager now needs to manage the emotional tensions of the contradiction delivered to workers by work itself. The manager must deal with these tensions not because the company is necessarily altruistic but because permanent innovation is the objective. The manager manages people's interpretations and feelings of the culture, not the apparatus of the structural systems.[27] The manager becomes coach and pop psychologist so the company

26. Reckwitz explains, "The work practices in aesthetic capitalism are borne along by a culture of motivation based on a neo-romantic model of work and profession which identifies satisfying work with creative work, supplanting the repetition of technical or administrative processes with the variable and challenging production of new and especially of aesthetic objects and events. This creative work can and should produce a personal transformation. Innovative enterprises with their symbolic, aesthetic modes of operating require people with creative motivation. These workers should have an emotionally charged, enthusiastic self-image and approach to work." Reckwitz, *Invention of Creativity*, 91.

27. Bröckling adds, "For employees to be entrepreneurial, creative and innovative, the company needs a climate favourable to challenging old ways. A BMW management guide includes

can keep all workers in a state of permanent innovation, making everyone a creative entrepreneur. The new capitalism of permanent innovation becomes inseparable from psychology and its language of the personal development of the self. In other words, the company can obsess over profits because the workers are obsessed with the development of their selves.

This detailed explanation of the history of entrepreneurship and innovation gives us some insight into Russ and his young adult group that was nominated for a grant from his alma mater seminary. Innovation was a powerful initial hook that engaged his young adults. But Russ discovered that innovation soon became an imposition that produced a confusing lethargy. Russ had discovered that innovation, and the drive for the creativity of entrepreneurship, was both exciting and defeating.

---

the maxim, 'it is everyone's duty to become an initiative taker.' When total flexibility is required, then the expert-governed regimentation of the old Taylorism inevitably looks counterproductive. A company run on TQM [total quality management] fines will still need a large number of standardized procedures which will determine the way workers act. But the aim is no longer to adapt behavior to a fixed production quota that is regularly raised, but rather to ceaselessly cultivate the ability to improvise in order to reach a preset goal. In other words, TQM replaces continually raised quota fulfillment with the norm of continual improvement." Bröckling, *Entrepreneurial Self*, 153.

6

The Viennese Worm That
Exposes the True Self

When Work Becomes about Flexible Projects

As Russ's group worked on its innovation, Fiona, a twenty-three-year-old, kept asking the group, almost as a verbal tic, "Is this dumb? I think this might be dumb." Russ had to keep assuring them all that it was a good idea worth *not* abandoning. Instead of doing something epic, the group should just do something, he pointed out. The group was filled with confidence at the beginning of the grant. But now half of them were anxious, and the other half had a fraction of the energy they started with.

Russ, too, was exhausted. The leaders of the grant kept telling him (and the group) that cultivating innovation and creativity was hard but exciting work. Moving into year three of the grant, Russ was feeling the hard more than the exciting. If he had had the energy to reflect, it didn't feel like innovation and creativity was the burden. Rather, reaching for innovation and creativity foisted something on his young adults. The reach for innovation and creativity seemed to impose something on them that made Russ have to work hard to manage all their feelings, upping his own emotional output to cheerlead them beyond self-doubt.

Russ's congregation was asked to join the grant initiative at his alma mater seminary because of its work with young adults. The grant was built on many important, good assumptions. The goal was to simply but profoundly draw young adults into relationship, connecting them to their congregation by working on a project together with other adults. It seemed advantageous to do this in and through innovation. After all, there is an implicit (even explicit) assumption that young adults are drawn to innovation and entrepreneurship like moths to a porch light. Innovation and entrepreneurship are considered somehow instinctive to these younger people in a way that it's not for older ones. Innovation and entrepreneurship make up the air that young people breathe, we assume. To keep our Darwin analogy going from the previous chapter, young adult lungs have evolved, it's believed, to effortlessly take in the air of innovation and entrepreneurship.

This assumption about young adults meets another assumption. The grant contended that the church needed to catch up to permanent innovation. It appears to be an objective fact that the church (at least the mainline church) is in decline. Inside the imagination of a secular age of neoliberalism, the medicine for decline is always growth won by innovation. For those who have been shaped by this secular imagination, it's only obvious that decline can be countered only by entering a state of permanent innovation. The answer to lost market share in neoliberalism is not more organization, better bureaucracy, and therefore higher efficiency (as Keynesianism would presume), but innovation and then more innovation.

What better option, this grant team at this seminary assumed, than to turn entrepreneurial young adults loose inside the church to move it toward this needed state of innovation? Young adults, so inherently entrepreneurial, could create for the church, almost as a reflex, a new spirit of innovation. But, as we lick the peanut butter from our lips, it only makes us more susceptible to swallowing without noticing the jagged pill of the new cultural contradiction of the new capitalism. It took a year or two, but Russ noticed it. By year three of the grant, Russ felt that jagged little pill scrape down his throat.

The Innovative Generation

It's true that young adults, to their great credit, have adapted to the new capitalism of neoliberalism. They are natives to this economic dispensation. Of course, so are many of the rest of us who are *not* so young. Yet what distinguishes young adults from not-so-young adults is that while the latter may have also come of age in the new capitalism, they didn't do so with the same (or any) digital tools. They weren't natives to the internet, particularly Web 2.0.

The absence of these digital tools gave the earliest generation of the new capitalism (those born between 1965 and 1980) an edgier discontent. Hence, we see the arrival of the Seattle scene. Young adults in the 1990s realized that the future belonged to the creative entrepreneur. But for most of us, even middle-class young adults in the 1990s, there was no real access to the tools of innovation and entrepreneurship. To say it bluntly, there were no seventeen-year-olds in 1992 holding meetings with venture capital firms (which became a common story beginning around 2010). Stripped-down, commercially apathetic, and creative outlets like grunge and hip-hop came rushing to the surface. Particularly, the Seattle scene was for a short time an almost anti-entrepreneurial movement.[1] Its most popular voices didn't even want to be rock stars. They had no desire to conquer the world with their innovative sound. They just wanted to express their discontent and point out the contradictions of the new capitalism, deconstructing the music industry.

What makes us assume that the young adult is inherently an entrepreneur, and what even makes young adults themselves look affectionately on entrepreneurship (something Kurt Cobain would have never done, hating all those Microsoft stiffs!), is the way the internet delivers access to, and even the tools for, entrepreneurship. We assume young adults are more entrepreneurial, able to win permanent innovation, because they are natives to a digital world. The digital space is where innovation and entrepreneurship now seem to be proliferating. Young adults have been raised on this kind of Silicon Valley innovation and entrepreneurship. So we assume that empowering young adults in the church will consequentially produce what we want: innovation for the church.

The Tensions of the Self

This assumption about young adults makes good sense. But as Russ discovered, it's not as straightforward as it appears. His young adults loved

---

1. Not surprisingly, in 1999 one of the most important events of the decade, which got some of the most confusing and distorting media coverage, happened in Seattle—the World Trade Organization protests. This was a revolt against the new capitalism and its innovation and entrepreneurial drives. Of course, what makes for an even more interesting story is that Microsoft, one of the core leaders of the new capitalism and maker of tools for the new spirit of innovation, was also located in Seattle.

the idea of innovation and entrepreneurship. There was something intoxi-
cating about consuming other stories of creativity and the direct products
of innovation. The first few years of the grant were filled with energy. But
something changed when it was time for Russ's young adults to become innovative themselves.

The assumption that innovation was effortless and would just happen
concealed an invisible burden that Russ couldn't name. Switching from consuming innovation to doing the work of innovation was entirely different.
The difficulty was not that it was hard work. It's a stereotype that young
adults shirk hard work: it's not true and it misses something deeper they're
acutely feeling. Most of Russ's young adults were anything but lazy. It was
something else more significant: to enter into doing the work of innovation
was *to expose the self*. It was to step out on stage to perform the self before
others. Thanks to management practices that birthed the permanent innovative economy, to enter the process of innovation is to ask the self to enter
into a process of its own entrepreneurship. The grant was unintentionally
asking these young adults to bear the burden they were already carrying at
work (and in the digital spaces they entered 24/7). They were being asked to
enter another self-development process that was fundamentally competitive.

The new management revolution wanted to make self-development and
the emotional expressivism of the self the payoff for accepting the unnatural
work-state of constant disruption and insecurity. But inside this new form
of managing workers, there was no desire to eliminate competition (actually quite the opposite). Competition was necessary.[2] Each worker needed to
show how their own self was developing by producing creative ideas for the
company that could fuel new innovations. The best worker had the most (or
best) creative ideas. This self became known as a star or legend at the office.
By having a whole firm of entrepreneurial selves, the company can achieve
permanent innovation.[3]

---

2. Michel Foucault explains, "Now for the neo-liberals, the most important thing about the
market is not exchange, that kind of original and fictional situation imagined by eighteenth
century liberal economists. The essential thing of the market is elsewhere; it is competitions."
Foucault, *The Birth of Biopolitics: Lectures at the Collège de France, 1978–1979* (New York:
Picador, 2008), 118. He continues, "This means that what is sought is not a society subject to
the commodity effect, but a society subject to the dynamic of competition. Not a supermarket
society, but an enterprise society. The *homo oeconomicus* sought after is not the man of exchange
or man the consumer; he is the man of enterprise and production" (147).

3. Ulrich Bröckling, in his field-defining book, *The Entrepreneurial Self: Fabricating a New
Type of Subject* (Los Angeles: SAGE, 2016), adds, "The bestsellers of Peters and Waterman and

When it came to doing innovation, Russ's group doubted their ideas. They kept looking over their shoulder at other groups who seemed more innovative, because innovation itself is bound inside the logic of the entrepreneurial self. The goal of the grant was *never* to impose this comparison or competition, but it happened because the practices of innovation are tightly wound by a certain form of work in the neoliberal economy. To ask these young adults to innovate, even for the church, was to ask them to carry a further burden of competing against other entrepreneurial selves to substantiate their own entrepreneurial self using their own ability to access a truly unique idea. To not meet the threshold of a truly unique idea would reveal that their own self-development process, even their own selves, were generic. An ordinary idea would unveil an ordinary self, because innovation, through the new management revolution, was mobilized as a direct process of working on the self.

Russ became frustrated in the innovation process because he was forced to switch from being a pastor to a manager. It became his job to create a culture where the group had the emotional resiliency to design an innovation that revealed that they were all unique selves with creative depth. Russ was now managing the group as therapist and coach. He had to keep his group from accepting that it was better to never settle on an idea than to go for it and discover it wasn't very creative, particularly in comparison to other groups.

This process was much more complicated than the grant team had assumed. The grant team unknowingly built a canal where the spirit of the new capitalism and its form of work could wash directly back into the church. This wash, no doubt, brought some good things. Creativity is rarely bad. But with these good things came an inflated view of the self.

The Rise of Emotional Capitalism

In 2004 Eva Illouz, the feminist American-Israeli sociologist, gave the renowned Adorno Lectures in Frankfurt, Germany. They were published as

---

Pinchot mark the transition from the role model of the 'organization man' to the entrepreneurial self. The organization man is not a model for ordinary people to follow but rather for employees in leading positions. The recommendations are directed at large companies who want to break up ossified structures by simulating entrepreneur functions (see Peters and Waterman) or by integrating entrepreneur types in the company (see Pinchot)" (31).

Cold Intimacies: The Making of Emotional Capitalism. The first lecture is a tour de force in which Illouz shows that modernity, and particularly capitalism, is dependent on a certain kind of management of emotions. When Russ and his group decided to participate in an innovation process, they were entering squarely into the realm of capitalism. The group would never sell anything, but all the practices and imagination for innovation and entrepreneurship were directly birthed from the womb of neoliberal capitalism. It would have been naive for Russ to assume he could use the practices and imaginations of innovation without also deeply breathing in the fumes of the contradiction of the new capitalism. What Russ didn't realize is that leading his group into innovation was not possible without him becoming a manager of emotions.

In her lecture, Illouz shows that all twentieth-century capitalist forms realized that emotions needed management. Both the management boom of post-1955 Keynesianism and the management revolution of the post-1985 neoliberal innovation economy were, in much different ways, managing the emotions of workers. In the twentieth century, management became fused with psychology. Since at least the 1950s, to be a manager was to operate out of a psychological framework. Illouz shows that psychology became the science of the twentieth century because of how it was used in the workforce.

As we said in the previous chapter, the Keynesian management boom adopted rationalized science into work. The manager was a dispassionate scientist organizing the bureaucratic systems. While the Keynesian manager was focused more on managing systems than people, people were nevertheless in his charge. To make the systems efficient, people's emotions needed to match those of the manager. The worker needed to be cool and steady. But workers were bearing the cultural contradictions between work and home. Getting the jagged pill of the Keynesian contradiction of capitalism to go down was not the manager's job (that was the job of happy hour and the stiff drink). Nevertheless, the manager did need to regulate workers' emotions, cooling frustrations and steadying irrationality.

Continuing in the vein of a scientist, the Keynesian manager drew from psychology, which was, after all, the science of emotions. To protect the efficiency of the company's bureaucratic systems, the manager needed to draw from the science of psychology to manage workers' emotions. Elton Mayo, one of the early management scientists writing and doing experiments at General Electric in the early twentieth century, told managers to be good psychologists. This meant something much different from the model of the coach as manager in the innovation economy of today.

Coaches passionately manage the emotions of their team by being the most passionate and emotional of them (which is what exhausted Russ). The coach in the economy of permanent innovation is hot with emotions, seeking to infuse energy into the teams they're managing. The Keynesian manager cools emotions. The neoliberal manager stokes emotions. Their leadership must turn up the emotions of their team. At the same time, they must direct those emotions toward their shared goal of victory. The neoliberal manager is not a scientist but a coach. The coach as manager is not a cold scientist but an emoting artisan of self-development processes who by an energetic manner wins the workers' emotions and energy.

The manager in neoliberalism is as much a cheerleader as coach (much like Pete Carroll, the Super-Bowl-winning coach of the Seattle Seahawks). This romantic/bohemian turn, which shifted the manager from dispassionate rationalist to passionate coach, had to wait until after the dawn of the age of authenticity.[4] Until then, the Keynesian manager oversaw workers' emotions like a psychologist sitting behind the client in a dark room. They dispassionately listened and took notes, allowing the emotions, like the steam running the machines on the floor, to be released so the systems could return to efficiency. Yet overall, while the Keynesian manager was told to draw from the science of psychology, the average worker had little sense that they were interfacing with psychology at work. If they had any sense of an imposing psychological frame, it was at home.

The Self at Home

When the Keynesian management boom arrived in 1955, it was entering a weird time. The 1950s were just odd. They were scientifically and politically progressive but culturally regressive.[5] The middle decade of the twentieth century was an oasis, when nineteenth-century Victorian cultural forms were

4. For more on coaching, see the rich discussion in Luc Boltanski and Eve Chiapello, *The New Spirit of Capitalism* (London: Verso, 2018), 76–79.

5. By *scientifically progressive*, I mean that they sought progress as a high good. As *politically progressive*, I don't mean this as we might say today, meaning open to multiple identity options, but progressive in the sense of organization toward the objective of the New Deal (progressive in FDR's way). And by *regressive*, I don't mean bad or deformed but backward looking.

readapted. Suburban America in the 1950s sought to out-Victorian the Victorians. Most primarily it reinstated the separate spheres, once again hanging a thick curtain between the private world of home and the public world of work (a move that kick-started the economy but further imposed the Keynesian cultural contradiction of capitalism, which lasted until 1980).[6] Ward and June Cleaver were twentieth-century Victorians.

The division in spheres, Illouz explains, is best understood as the management of emotions. In the nineteenth century, the Victorians set a certain emotional climate by dividing life into the spheres of public and private.[7] To impose this emotional climate, the spheres were divided along gender lines. The public sphere was a place without emotion, or where emotions were cold. Therefore, the public was assumed to be a place best fit for men. The private sphere was to be emotionally warm. The Victorians may have wanted or accepted cold work, but they desired an emotionally warm home environment. (Not surprisingly, Christmas as we know it today, as the great emotionally warm festival of the private sphere, was created in the Victorian age, thanks in major part to the Victorian writer Charles Dickens, whose antagonist was a frigid public man named Ebenezer Scrooge, who we knew was bad because his home was cold.) It made sense to the Victorians that this private space of a warm emotional climate would be best managed by women.[8] Of course, this put a lot of pressure on women. They were painted as the emotional sex, but it also became their job to set and maintain the emotional temperature of the private home. It was their duty to make the home a warm bath that their husbands could slide into after a hard day in the emotionally frigid public sphere.[9] The wife and mother

6. Keynes himself was British and grew up at the end of the Victorian age.

7. Which, of course, further imposed the secular age that Charles Taylor describes.

8. Linda Simon, in her biography of William James (the nineteenth-century American philosopher), explains this view of family, marriage, and women: "William learned from his father—and found echoed in the culture at large—that women were at the same time intellectually inferior to men, but spiritually purer. 'In your intercourse with pure women study to do nothing and say nothing and feel nothing but what would elevate them in their own self respect and the respect of their kind,' he once counseled Bob. Marriage to a good woman allowed a man to reject his baser instincts and attach himself to 'a more private, a more sacred and intimate self than that wherewith nature endows him.'" Simon, *Genuine Reality: A Life of William James* (Chicago: University of Chicago Press, 1999), 97.

9. John R. Gillis provides texture in discussing the changes in educational institutions of Victorian England. In his fabulous book *Youth and History: Tradition and Change in European Age Relations, 1770–Present* (New York: Academic Press, 1974), he explains a shift in education from resembling the monastery to resembling the military. This had the effect of not only excluding women but making the cold public realm a place constructed without emotion, or better, tenderness. This in turn made the private sphere a longed-for haven of emotional softness. He

was the emotional manager long before emotional management became a norm of work life in the late twentieth and early twenty-first centuries.

This clear and firm distinction between spheres didn't last. After a decade and a half of updated twentieth-century Victorianism, it was over. This revived Victorianism of the 1950s couldn't last, because a kind of Viennese worm had entered the imagination of 1950s people that wasn't there in the Victorian age. This worm ate so many holes in the curtain that separated the two spheres, and the beams that held the curtain, that by 1965 it all fell. The curtain and the beams were so damaged they could never again be rehung in their large cultural form. The worm attacked the beams and curtain between the two spheres, but ultimately the two spheres were neither the worm's direct objective nor the worm's host. Instead, the worm took habitat in the very conception of the self.

The Victorians maintained their two spheres and the dual emotional climates because, as Illouz explains, they had a certain understanding of the true self. Charles Taylor has taught us that, since the days of Augustine, Western people have contended that there is a kind of "true self."[10] There is a core essence to us, a true us, the real me. Illouz says, "For Victorians, finding and expressing the true self did not pose a special problem—the true self was always there and it was only to be entrusted to a person worthy of one's self-revelations."[11]

The challenge for the Victorians wasn't to find the true self but to find someone who was worthy of entering into an emotional space to receive the revelation of this true self. No honorable woman (or man) would reveal their true self to just anyone. The true self was meant for only the emotionally warm private sphere. This search to find a worthy person to whom to reveal

---

says, "Sport was taking over many of the functions of the rite of passage once reserved to Latin language study, for it, too, ensured the separation of boys from the world of women during the critical transition from childhood to adulthood. There was an important social change involved in the substitution, however. The model of the earlier Latin school was the monastery; the ideal of the public school was increasingly military. Women were to be avoided by adolescents because femininity was now associated with weakness, emotion, and unreliability. So strong was the avoidance of female traits by 1860 that men no longer dared embrace in public and tears were shed only in private" (111). Only in the private sphere was it appropriate to share the feelings of the true self. Gillis points out that the separation of spheres (and of bitter gender roles) was imposed by secular educational institutions, not the church. Regardless, shifts like this birthed the public-private divide.

10. See Taylor, *Sources of the Self: The Making of the Modern Identity* (Cambridge, MA: Harvard University Press, 1989), part 2.

11. Eva Illouz, *Cold Intimacies: The Making of Emotional Capitalism* (Malden, MA: Polity, 2007), 28.

the true self is one of the main driving plots of Victorian author Louisa May Alcott's *Little Women* (published in 1868). The women, particularly Jo, know who they are. Jo needs no help, nor has any doubts about her true self. Rather, the struggle is to find the right person (outside of her sisters) to reveal this true self to. Whomever she reveals this true self to will be who she loves. The revelation of the true self is what creates an emotionally warm private sphere.

The Victorian self was like hickory. The self was made out of solid, hard wood. It was not always easy to reshape. You weren't able to easily carve a new self. But the self was stable and resistant to the Viennese worm. This wasn't the case in the 1950s. The wood that made up the self of the American Victorians of the 1950s was much softer. Its grain was susceptible to the worm, which would be this retro-Victorianism's demise.

The Viennese Worm

The doctor of the late Victorian age did more than his part in ending Victorianism. Sigmund Freud from Vienna ended the Victorian age by opposing the solid self with his new science. Illouz pinpoints 1909 as the year when the West embraced a much different emotional relationship to the self.[12] In 1909 Freud crossed the Atlantic to lecture at Clark University in the US. By the early twentieth century, Freud and psychoanalysis made psychology a broad-reaching science. By midcentury, America was a land open to the new science at work and home.

In a profound way, Freud reversed the Victorian conception of the self. A worm was planted in the self that would eventually, in the late twentieth and early twenty-first centuries, shape a culture in which it would be viable and coherent to look to the fully secularized work world as the primary place to find the self. This worm in the self began by crossing a boundary that the Victorian self held sacred. From within this new conception of the self, the worm started eating away at the beams that held the curtain that separated the public and the private spheres. Once the beams were compromised, the curtain between the spheres could eventually fall.

12. Illouz is actually uncomfortable with pinpointing a moment; she makes a parenthetical statement that explains that she doesn't think one moment can make a cultural change. Like Taylor, she doesn't believe in subtraction stories or cultural home runs. But for the sake of the lecture, she believes it helpful to have a point in time to examine. I'll follow both her unease and her use of 1909. See Illouz, *Cold Intimacies*, 5.

To accomplish this, Freud reversed two Victorian realities. First, he argued that the true self was anything but solid and completely known by the subject. Whereas the Victorians didn't think it necessary to go looking for the self (the true self was known and treasured), Freud believed the true self was actually deeply hidden. The Victorians always knew the self. The challenge was who to share this true knowledge of the self with. Freud, on the other hand, claimed that the true self was hidden from the self and therefore needed to be excavated. The true self could be discovered by freeing the self from layers of deceptive emotions and narratives. Freud claimed that the individual was mostly a stranger to himself or herself. The true self was so buried that excavating it could usually not be accomplished by the effort of the self alone. Rather, to find the true self you needed a doctor like Freud who specialized in the science of excavating true selves buried within human minds and burdened by distorting emotions. You needed someone to analyze your feelings and uncover your hidden narratives.

Jo in *Little Women* knows exactly who she is. Her task is to discover the person to whom she'll reveal this true self. Freud asserted the opposite. The true self was fundamentally unknown. The task was to reveal the true self not to an intimate other but to one's own self. This was the only way to find intimacy with one's self. To reveal the true self to the self, the self needed to go digging for this true self. The true self could now, as in a scientific project, be discovered. The self was no longer just given.

Freud's theories had major ramifications. Your emotions were no longer trustworthy. The Victorians embraced emotion. They believed emotions were straightforward and true representations of reality, and therefore emotions needed to be protected and treasured by restricting them to certain appropriate zones. Emotions were so straightforwardly true that they were not to be shown in much of the public sphere. They were to be revealed in an appropriate manner (with the appropriate manners!).

Freud hatched the Viennese worm when he claimed that, because we don't *really* know our true self, our emotions themselves can't really be trusted. We had no real grasp of our true self. When we concealed our emotions, it wasn't us being appropriate; it was us repressing those emotions. We were repressing the emotions under which the true self was buried. Freud believed that at least some of our emotions lied by attaching to the false self. We needed a doctor or scientist to tell us which emotions were part of our true self and which were attached to our false self. The Victorians knew who they were and therefore rarely doubted their emotions. Their emotions could be ordered and differentiated between the public and private sphere. The twentieth-century person, on the other hand, had little idea what to make of their emotions. Were these emotions coming from the true or false self? You could only know if you were confident that the new science had excavated the true self, confident that your digging hit the ground of the true self.

Not having a grip on our true self and therefore doubting the validity of our own emotions played its part in pulling down the curtain between the public and private spheres. If emotions had no clear correlation to the true self, then they no longer needed to be protected in only the private sphere. Emotions of longing, love, desire, and more were now loosed from the home. Such emotions, by the mid-twentieth century, could even drive a budding consumer economy. By the late 1960s, buying was feeling. What you were feeling through your buying was your true self. This kind of marketing only perpetuated the Freudian sense that our true self was deeply buried some-where within, needing to be found. It could be found only by emotionally departing from the strictures of the private sphere of the home and family. This consumer society asserted that the true self was found through internal self-development. This self-development and discovery of the true self only happened for those in the twentieth century when you left the home. Because in this post-Freudian and anti-Victorian world, the home was assumed to repress the emotions that revealed the true self.

Freud's second reversal of a Victorian reality targeted the home, the private sphere. As a good Victorian, Freud followed the "bourgeois cultural revolution which moved away from contemplative or heroic definitions of identity and situated [the true self] in the realm of everyday life, chiefly in the workplace and in the family."[13] Taking a page from Puritan Calvinists, Victorians contended that it was not in prayer or in heroic acts that you found the self but in the direct emotional responsibility you performed at work and at home. Freud affirmed, as a good Victorian, that particularly the home mattered. But as a bad Victorian (who did his part in ending Victorianism), Freud contended that the home was not a protective haven but instead ground zero to losing your true self.

If, as Victorians believed, the self could be solidly known and emotions could be understood as the true feelings of this true self, then the private sphere—the home—was sacred. You were most free to be your true self at

13. Illouz, *Cold Intimacies*, 8.

home. Jo felt this with her sisters and mother. Jane Austen's characters often have such a relationship with their fathers. Home is a haven for the true self, the place where the intimate feelings of the true self are revealed and shared. The Victorians highly venerated love (particularly romance) as the revelation of the true self by making a home of warm feelings with another.

Yet for good or ill, Freud used psychoanalysis to attack this private space. The home became no longer a haven but the origin and place where you lost touch with the true self (your id). For Freud, the home was no longer a haven but the location where your true self was lost under the layers of misdirected and confused emotions. The self was buried under false conceptions and negative emotions (almost all stemming from sex) that, according to Freud, started in childhood experiences at home. We needed to dig out the true self that our childhood experiences buried under piles of confusing emotions. In childhood the home imposed emotions on us that disconnected us from our true self. The home was no longer haven but hell.

American suburbia in the 1950s tried to recover this retro-Victorian separation of spheres, returning to the home as a haven. The Keynesian organized economy made it possible for many American families to thrive with one income. As in the Victorian age, the curtain between the public (work) world and the private (home) world could be rehung. Ward Cleaver returned from the unknown world of work to be home in June's haven. Ward was reminded again in every episode that Beaver was a boy whose habitat was the haven-home. Beaver's boyhood was his truest self. Beaver was not an employee to be managed for efficiency but a true self we all could learn from.

But this retro-Victorian period of the 1950s could only be a blip on the radar of American life. It ended quickly because Freud's Viennese worm had compromised both the beams on which the curtain was hung and the wood that made up the true self—the Cleavers were only a repressive illusion. This worm quickly infected the home, making it no longer the place to find the true self. The countercultural kids of the late 1960s were sure that the emotions of the home were more repressive than freeing. They left home for university and then left the university for the Haight in search of the true self deeply buried under the organized, separate spheres of controlled emotions. To find the self, they needed to find the path of self-development, taking on public practices of emotional expression (becoming expressivists, adding a romantic edge to individualism). That path, at first, would reside nowhere near work, until the dawn of neoliberalism and its management revolution of the late 1980s and '90s.

The management revolution of the 1980s and '90s turned to a Freudian-inspired psychology, just as the management boom had in 1955. But instead of psychology being seen as a rationalized science that could solve emotional problems that hindered organization and efficiency, psychology was used to create a self-development process that would make work the place to find your true self. The psychological forms were now more romantic, more self-help, more enamored with creativity rather than efficiency. The new manager used psychology to coach workers toward permanent innovation, reminding them that they were in a permanent search to find the true self. *The permanent innovation of the company cleared a path for the post-Freudian worker to be permanently searching for her or his true self at work.*

Work within a disruptive and insecure environment may be stressful, but it allows for discovery. It supposedly allows for the discovery of your true self through the discovery of new creative innovations for the company. It became the manager's job to correlate these two pursuits—the company's permanent drive for product innovation with the worker's permanent drive to discover a deeply hidden self.

Finding the Hidden Self through Innovation

The grant project in Russ's congregation brought together young adults and the church, believing that, like a chemical reaction, innovation and entrepreneurship would follow. Indeed, innovation might! But the project missed what so rudely met Russ in year three. Washing back into the church with innovation and entrepreneurship is an anxious obsession with the self. In direct contrast to the Victorian home, in late modernity, innovation and entrepreneurship cause work to become the place to find and, more importantly, work on the self. The home buries the self under repressed emotions. Work (at least in its ideal form) releases the self, it is believed, to find its true self through creativity. It's assumed that while home thwarts creativity, work causes it to bloom inside each worker.

What reveals the true self, what ensures that you've found the true self that was buried at home, is the creativity of your own entrepreneurial spirit at work. The self can be found through innovative ways of making money or, even more importantly, winning recognition.[14] In the attention economy of the

14. See Axel Honneth, *The Struggle for Recognition: The Moral Grammar of Social Conflicts* (Cambridge, MA: MIT Press, 1995).

new capitalism, recognition *is* money. Through recognition you have a solid, true self. When your self is so creatively innovative that it is recognized as singularly unique by an audience of people (by coworkers, Twitter/Instagram followers, executives, or headhunters), then you've unearthed your true self.

But if you don't receive the recognition you wish, if your idea or style or creation receives negative recognition or, worse, is ignored (too flat to even create haters), then your true self remains buried under a fresh load of dirt and stone. Failure thrusts doubt on you that just maybe you don't really know who you are after all. The prospect of failure made Russ's group unsure of moving forward, worried that their idea wasn't good enough. They needed Russ to manage their emotions and give them the nerve to try. They needed help in mustering the courage to vulnerably open themselves up to the possibility of not having met some threshold of creativity. Not meeting that threshold would cause their true self to go unrecognized, even to themselves.

This dynamic of recognition and failure has made Brené Brown the über-sage of our time.[15] She is deeply sought after by corporations and companies to speak to managers. Brown gives managers across neoliberalism new ways of framing permanent innovation and its offer of personal development. If workers are going to find their true selves, they must embrace their vulnerability and risk negative recognition. The manager can use this need for vulnerability (and its promise of self-development, which Brown's research points to) to get their workers to again and again risk a creative innovation, even though its potential failure will cause them to doubt themselves. Vulnerability becomes the way to grow into your true self as a self-development process.[16] Because vulnerability can be a self-development process to find the true self, the worker can accept the constant disruption and insecurity of permanent innovation. Vulnerability becomes the necessary risk in finding the true innovation that both the worker's self and the company needs.

15. For a long, insightful discussion on Brown and thought leaders in general, see Anand Giridharadas, *Winners Take All: The Elite Charade of Changing the World* (New York: Vintage, 2018), chap. 4.

16. Boltanski and Chiapello add, "Another seductive aspect of neo-management is the proposal that everyone should develop themselves personally. The new organizations are supposed to appeal to all the capacities of human beings, who will thus be in a position fully to blossom. 'Coaches' will support people in this endeavor, and everything will be done to ensure that they attain a better knowledge of themselves, and discover what they are capable of. The new model proposes, so we are told, 'genuine autonomy,' based on self-knowledge and personal fulfillment, not the false autonomy, framed by the career paths, job descriptions, and systems of sanctions-rewards, proposed by the 1960s." Boltanski and Chiapello, *New Spirit of Capitalism*, 90.

Freud takes us down a road where the self becomes fundamentally our own project. But the Viennese doctor's greatest legacy is in convincing us that we can never be like those Victorians who were confident in themselves. Freud's framework makes us always unsure of ourselves, never trusting even our own emotions. Therefore, we are bound inside the conundrum of late modernity, which tells us to be concerned only with being our unique self. This uniqueness can be validated as truly our self only by the recognition of others who affirm our self by liking our creations, styles, and ways of being. Their liking is now the pickax and shovel that uncover our singularly creative and true self.

Work inside the permanent innovation economy of the new capitalism can't give you the stability and security of protections. But it *can* give you a manager who will be a coach, helping you develop innovations on a team for the company that will in turn help you uncover your true entrepreneurial self—though only if you're willing to accept vulnerability.

The Shape of Management

Directly entering into the innovation process in the grant turned Russ into a manager (being a manager also caused Bearded Brown Turtleneck to resent his synod's turn to innovation, yet his anger also included, unfortunately, a disdain for creativity and coaching, which Russ didn't share). Pastors at bigger churches have more experience and honestly more interest in management. They need to manage staffs, hundreds of volunteers, large budgets, and a calendar filled with programs.

That wasn't Russ. He specifically chose a medium-sized church because his gifts were more in the area of pastoral care and teaching than management. He didn't know—because he didn't know where innovation and entrepreneurship came from—that entering an innovation and entrepreneurship grant would invariably thrust him into management. Synods, seminaries, and congregations should be aware that innovation and entrepreneurship always lead to a form of management. That doesn't mean synods, seminaries, or congregations should avoid innovation and entrepreneurship, but they need to realize how it causes the role of the pastor to shift. To call pastors of small churches to enter into innovation is to move pastoral identity, at least to a degree, in the direction of management. Innovation and entrepreneurship sound exciting and appealing, because they *are* indeed creative activities, but they are inseparable from management in neoliberalism. Innovation and entrepreneurship are always tangled up with a particular pursuit of the self.

The manager's unique job inside the new capitalism is to marry the company's drive for permanent innovation with the worker's pursuit to find the true self. The best managers are able to show how expressive creativity at work—which is just what the company needs to innovate inside free, deregulated markets—can uncover and develop the true self. This was squarely where Russ now sat. Without knowing it, he was being called to marry the church and the denomination's need for innovation with young adults' fragile quest to find their true selves.

Neoliberalism and the ethic of authenticity link at the intersection of the expressive and creative drive for more innovation (whether in products or self-expression). This true self, inside the innovation economy, is nothing like the homebound Victorian self but is instead an entrepreneurial self who never stops developing. The manager brings the company to a state of permanent innovation by encouraging workers to be obsessed with the pursuits of the self. Workers should not desire routine or security from work, but instead the ability to work on the self. Workers should therefore accept, even welcome, constant disruption and insecurity. Such an environment invites and produces expressive creativity, which unearths your true self, winning you the recognition you need to find this self.

Yet it's never quite so easy. It being difficult is good for the company because, if the manager continues to do their job, the workers remain in a state of constant entrepreneurship. They are kept from complacency. Inside this environment of disruption and insecurity, the true self always seems illusive and unsettled. The Viennese worm remains embedded in the self. But rather than this being a spiritual or existential problem, the manager's job is to frame this discontent as an invitation to race harder for more creative entrepreneurial ways to more fully excavate the true self. We're susceptible to this because the Freudian worm keeps us worried that the self we have isn't really the true self at all.

The new capitalist economy and its new contradiction confirm this constant search for the true self. We're asked to continue going harder and faster, giving more to innovate for the company, believing that *this* time, inside *this* project, we might find the creative innovation of our own self to finally be satisfied that we've uncovered the true self. But the new capitalism of the late-modern secular age has no interest in us being satisfied with the self (the worm wouldn't let us anyway). It doesn't pay for us to ever lose our concern for ourselves in something bigger than us (even something transcendent). It doesn't boost growth or profits for us to ever find our self inside a greater self.

How It's Done

If the job of the manager is to marry the company's drive for permanent innovation with the worker's pursuit to find the true self, how is this done? It's rarely done in a direct, planned way. There are no companies holding meetings on how to marry the company's drive for innovation with the worker's pursuit of their true self.[17] Marrying them just more or less happens, rather than being directly planned. It occurs because of a shift in the practices and imagination of both companies and workers.[18] The first step in marrying permanent innovation with the worker's pursuit of the self begins with the shared belief that *flexibility* is always a high good.

Flexibility

Managers have the difficult job of leading two distinct entities—the company's goals and the desires of the workers—into a state of unremitting flexibility. They must do this while never causing the company to lose profits. This flexibility needs to invite workers to use that flexibility to find their unique, true selves, even to recognize that a true self is a flexible self, creating their self anew from within new experiences. Workers will benefit from these new experiences by remaining flexible and open to change.[19] If innovation is to happen (and continue permanently), both the company and the workers have to embrace flexibility as a high good. For Russ to lead his congregation into innovation, he has to manage it into a state of constant flexibility. His congre-

17. Companies don't attempt this in an overt way because even executives are not exempt from the pursuit of a true self. They are caught in it themselves. The innovative drive across the company is fueled not just by the hunger for profits but by the deeper longing to find the true self inside the creative expression of running a successful business.

18. I'm following Boltanski and Chiapello, *New Spirit of Capitalism*, in which they lay out the changes in management that dawned since the 1990s.

19. The Victorian self is not flexible. It is firm, known, and trusted. To obtain to a flexible self, we need Freud and his worm to lead us to question if we have a handle on our self at all. Because of Freud, we need to be flexible because our emotions do not straightforwardly tell us who we are. We have to analyze these emotions, being flexible that their interpretation may tell us something different about our self, changing us.

gation has to welcome a constant drive to change. Both the institutional parts of the church and the young adults working for innovation in the grant must fully embrace flexibility. If one side does and the other doesn't, the manager will eventually fail, with plenty of headaches along the way.

The manager, like Russ in his situation, can feel squeezed between the different ways that both entities fear flexibility. Both institutions and persons can only take so much flexibility.[20] The flexibility that the neoliberal economy demands is often beyond what persons or institutions can handle.[21] The manager needs to get both people and institutions to acclimate to the furnace of high flexibility. On one side, the manager has to "teach a giant to dance," as Rosabeth Moss Kanter says in her bestselling management book.[22] The manager needs to keep the big company from getting too stiff in its forms and structures, keeping it agile, never becoming IBM of the early 1980s. A company needs this agility so it can run fast inside free markets. Its budget and organizational chart need to be built with flexibility in mind. The manager has to help the giant keep changing its shoes so it can be fast and nimble.[23]

On the other hand, in a much different way, the manager needs to reframe the dangers of flexibility in emotionally positive terms for workers. As it relates to workers, this need for constant flexibility is fundamentally the management of emotions (the fact that it's concerned with emotions gives it voice in regard to the self). Flexibility in relation to corporate structure is organizational. But flexibility in relation to workers is fundamentally emotional. It's an emotional state that allows workers to accept the disruption of newness, to even find excitement in insecurity.

Kanter quotes workers who voiced emotions of excitement, as if they were X Games participants, in companies in constant states of flexibility and permanent innovation. These workers say the following about working inside companies of permanent innovation: "It's like riding a bucking bronco." "It's

20. We are now seeing that most of our institutions can no longer handle the flexibility, which is why so many are failing.

21. At the institutional level, we could call this move away from flexibility, drawing from Max Weber, routinization. Institutions tend to move from a charismatic start to routinizing. Weber thought this was normal, even good. But routinizing has become the enemy in neoliberalism.

22. Rosabeth Moss Kanter, *When Giants Learn to Dance* (New York: Simon & Schuster, 1989).

23. For more on flexibility, see Boltanski and Chiapello, *New Spirit of Capitalism*, 71–74.

like riding a roller coaster." "It's exhilarating." "It's fun." "There's never a dull moment." "Time flies here."[24]

These are emotionally infused statements. The constant flexibility for the worker *can be* experienced as good, because it so directly includes emotion. It's the opposite of boring. Inside the drive to uncover your true self, to find your uniqueness, boring is the enemy of authenticity. A boring job cannot be a place to work on the self, because it is void of creativity and therefore emotion. But the job that demands flexibility because of the company's fast pace can produce the emotions necessary to be a place to work on the self. The manager has to avoid allowing the giant to become too stiff or too frantic that it smashes workers under its new shoes. In the end, there is no way to completely avoid this. It's the risk of working on the self inside the new capitalism. Getting stomped on is worth the risk because flexibility infuses work with emotion, even excitement, making work fertile ground to find your true self—supposedly.

Team Projects

From this contention that flexibility produces a mutual good for the company and the worker, a new organizational form of working is born. This new form is imbued with flexibility. Luc Boltanski and Eve Chiapello state, "The workers themselves, we are told, must be organized in small, multitasked teams (for they are more skilled, more flexible, more inventive and more autonomous than the specialist departments of the 1960s)."[25]

Management in Keynesianism was a rational science. Therefore, workers were arranged in departments organized around ranked specialists. Such organization could achieve efficiency but not permanent innovation. Ranks and overspecialization create intransigence. In the new economy of permanent innovation, working as a specialized rational scientist (even if you weren't one) was out. Instead, neoliberal companies needed workers who were organized in flexible teams. These teams needed to be constituted not of ranked rational scientists but romantic artists. As artists, they could put their selves into a project.

24. Rosabeth Moss Kanter, *The Change Masters: Innovations for Productivity in the American Corporation* (New York: Simon & Schuster, 1983), 129, quoted in Andreas Reckwitz, *The Invention of Creativity* (Malden, MA: Polity, 2017), 119.
25. Boltanski and Chiapello, *New Spirit of Capitalism*, 74.

The project replaced the specialized task. The self of the worker was a project, and likewise the self at work was to invest in a project. The company benefited from this turn away from ordered and static tasks in a department to team projects. Just as the self is a fluid and open project, swiftly changing, so too are the projects of the company. The worker has security as long as the company is committed to the project. The company can promise commitment only as long as the project is going. When the project is done, so too is the company's commitment to workers whose team is working on the project. Arranging workers on teams working on projects allows the company to remain flexible and fluid. And having project teams allows workers to attend to the project of their selves as they focus on the project at work. Protections and duty no longer create commitment between companies and workers in neoliberalism; instead, that comes about through the dual commitment to the project. Companies are committed to workers for the sake (and duration) of the project. Workers, too (at least skilled ones), are committed to the company as long as they find the project advantageous and, at best, *meaningful*. Their commitment lasts as long as the project means something to the workers' own project of finding their own true self.[26]

The project is like the doted-upon child in a marriage that has just come undone. Neoliberalism, for the sake of growth in deregulated markets, imposes a divorce on companies and their workers. Yet both partners must stay together, even if the commitment to each other is gone. What keeps them together is that both need to raise the project. But because the project is the only thing keeping them together, they also fight over the project. Executives and workers blame each other for the project's failures, questioning the other side's commitment to the project and each side's importance in raising the project well. Both partners now have their "freedoms" in neoliberalism, but not outside the dual commitment to the project. The project alone holds them together (tenuously). How the project is managed will determine whether these "freedoms" and dual commitments to the project are agreeable or contentious (again showing how important management is in the new capitalism).

This centering of the project is acceptable—even logical—to most workers because working on the project equates to working on the development of the self in the secular age of authenticity. A pivot in the project may cause a pivot in your own project of the self. Such a change might incite you to leave and

26. Andreas Reckwitz, *The Society of Singularities* (London: Polity, 2020), 137.

search for a new, more authentic project by which you can work on the project of the self. Commitment to a project rather than to a company can feel like freedom. Of course, if your third child was just born and your husband was diagnosed with colon cancer, the dependability and security of a department and rank may be more appealing than the free-flowing flexibility of a project. But there is no such security in this economy of permanent innovation. You are offered only the linking of projects (the project you and your team are working on with the project of your own self).

As for stability, you are offered, if you're lucky, only a succession of projects. Though that's risky, causing you to cope with disruption and insecurity, late modernity and its age of authenticity has taught us that flexibility of projects is just what the self seeks. The self in late modernity becomes a succession of projects to uncover the true self. Each project, and the recognition received for it, unearths, even makes, bit by bit, our true self.

This leads us back to the importance of the team.

The Team

The work project wouldn't really have the dynamism (or spirit) necessary to be a means of working on the project of self if it were not done on a team. The team, not a department, produces flexibility and emotional inclusion. The supposed equality (deemphasizing of rank), shared goals (completing the project well), and leanness of the team (being small for the sake of budget and overall flexibility) makes each individual on the team matter. Your necessity on this small team and the role you play in the project fuels the unearthing of your true self. Working on the team can especially do this if the role you're playing on the team is expressively creative, or at least if you're recognized as being invaluable to the innovative outputs of the team. Remember that the self needs recognition to find itself. The self needs feedback on its expressive ways of being a self. Other people must be present. The team becomes a (even *the*) form of community, or human encounter, or shared collective needed to know the self in late modernity (think of TV shows like *The Office*, *Community*, or *Superstore*).

In neoliberalism, particularly since the early 1990s, participation in non-commercial/nonwork collectives has plummeted.[27] In my mind, involvement in

27. See, e.g., Robert Putnam, *Bowling Alone: The Collapse and Revival of American Community* (New York: Simon & Schuster, 2000).

such noncommercial collectives continues to plummet in major part because the human necessity for a social collective has been dynamically co-opted by work in the project-based team. People have less interest or need for bowling teams, local political groups, and, importantly, churches, because they are intensely (in the sense of emotions and hours) invested in their work team. The risk, insecurity, and cutthroat competition of winning with your project is a rush that makes other noncommercial collectives seem boring and pointless. Or maybe it's just that you've given so much to your team to win that you don't have the energy or time for any other demands that move at a much different (noncompetitive) speed.

In a secular age, noncommercial collectives, particularly religious and spiritual ones, have been devalued as places to find meaning and therefore discover the self. There has been a rise in spiritual activities, but not ones that demand a commitment to a collective. People find their spiritual needs met through an individual choice. Spiritual practices like yoga and meditation are usually done outside of collective commitments.[28] The team and its project have replaced people's need for a collective commitment, for something like community.

When the grant initiative gathered teams of young adults from congregations to create projects of innovation, it unknowingly allowed neoliberalism's forms of work to wash back into the church. Again, this may not be entirely bad, but we should be aware of it lest the unhelpful elements of this backwash coat the church's confession with a residue of idolatry. We should be particularly aware of how the team and its project cause work to become *the* place for the self's development, the location where the true self is unearthed. This may have faith-formation repercussions.

By seeing the importance of the team, we can spot more clearly how the project at work becomes the self-development process that the manager promises the recruited worker. The project leads workers to accept disruption and insecurity over routine and security because the project is done on a team within a network that offers recognition. The team or the network's responses to your work give you the direct emotional sources you can use to excavate your true self.[29] As you work with a team, you develop and succeed

---

28. See Jeremy Carrette and Richard King, *Selling Spirituality: The Silent Takeover of Religion* (London: Routledge, 2008).

29. Reckwitz adds to this network sense by discussing the profile self. He says, "In general, the format of the profile is fundamental to the subjectification of the late-modern self. In the economy of singularities as well (and especially so), subjects are profile subjects. The 'profile' is a metaphor from physiognomy: whoever has a profile is as clearly and sharply contoured as the

in delivering an innovation for the company. In the heat of competitive team-work, you discover what you're made of, who you really are (at least until the next project). As sociologists Boltanski and Chiapello explain, "The project does not exist outside of the encounter. . . . Hence the activity *par excellence* is integrating oneself into *networks* and exploring them, so as to put an end to isolation, and have opportunities for meeting people or associating with things proximity to which is liable to generate a project."[30]

If you spend any time in airport lounges or hotel bars, you'll witness teams planning, partying, or commiserating. The communion that rests on the project's victory or failure is palpable. Fragile confidence or stabbing disappointment surround them. Some drink to victory, their words of praise for each team member flowing with the wine. For others, the whispers are poison. When one team member leaves for the restroom, two or three others talk with brewing anger about how he failed the team ("that pitch sucked!"). The coldness among the team is frigid. Win or lose, you receive direct recognition for your part. Each self is directly and intensely evaluated through negative or positive recognition of the other team members. The team does what the Keynesian manager used to do: manage workers to high output. Shifting this job to the team allows the manager to remain a positive cheerleading coach (as discussed above).

The team, like the self, is not solid. Because the project duration is limited, so too is the team.[31] Work is fundamentally disruptive and insecure because innovation is done best by teams formed for the duration of a completed

silhouette of his or her face viewed from the side." Reckwitz, *Society of Singularities*, 147. He continues, "In order to build an attractive profile, it is thus essential to have a variety of skills and a whole palette of interesting or intensive professional and non-professional experiences. In late-modern working culture, such things are always showcased on the CVs of high-potential employees; to expert job applicants, they lend something unusual and serve as a 'distinguishing feature.' In this sense, profiles can be enhanced by one's experience on various projects in various professional contexts as well as by internships abroad, social or political engagement, or special hobbies. All of these activities and the experiences associated with them contribute to rounding out the personality of the working subject. Although they were of little if any significance to the 'organization man' of industrial society, they are indispensable to working subjects in the society of singularities" (148).

30. Boltanski and Chiapello, *New Spirit of Capitalism*, 110.

31. Even those who are not officially assigned projects—such as administrators for institutions like seminaries, churches, and denominations—nonetheless support projects, such as evangelism or a youth gathering. If the institution stops doing that project, your position is vulnerable to elimination unless you're moved to another project or department. If an institution as a whole pivots its focus—moves toward a new project—your position or the positions in your department could be cut. Flexibility makes it so that your position could theoretically disappear at any time.

project. By riding this wave of insecurity, you can find your next project and therefore your next team. Through the networking connections you make with your team, or through your team with other teams (inside or outside your company), you find your next opportunity for pay and self-development in the new capitalism. Unlike in Keynesianism, the company owes you nothing. You choose to be part of the project. They choose to fund a team to work on the project. Eventually, your team finishes the project (or the company decides to defund the project). There is no more security offered to you. When the project ends, you find a new team and new project or else starve. But you do get to take something with you from your now-debunked team and its project: your networked contacts. Your next job and next project (which allows for your next self-development process) will more than likely come from the networking that your current team did in its previous project.

This insecurity makes it all the more important that you see your work on every project with every team as a way to deepen your own personal development. You must curate a self that will be valuable in the free-agent market that is flush with workers switching projects. Your network becomes like gold; it both connects you to other teams and projects and signals that you're a valuable asset for another team. You are the kind of creative self that can bring recognition to the team. Your vast network proves this. Adding your network to a new team adds recognition to each team member's own self, giving them more contacts through which to be perceived by others and their own self as an entrepreneurial self. This gives you some stability but never outside your own self-development. If you have anything like stability, it's bound in the depth and extent of your contacts, not in the commitment of the company. In the new capitalism, your contacts are your scorecard of how developed and recognized your self is.

Russ's team of young adults felt all of this. They worried that their idea was too mediocre to qualify for an abundance of networked contacts. The other teams seemed so much more creative, working on more interesting projects. What kind of selves were they if their project was just okay? What if their idea was good, but not good enough to be considered a creative self that others would want on their next team, or at least a contact in their growing network? The grant did not intend to make the young adults feel competitive, but innovation is fundamentally worked out in these project-based teams of networks that always seek to build winners (even if that's not the goal!). Because these teams are fundamentally flexible, disruptive, and insecure, they are always competitive. Whether or not Russ or the grant team wished it, to push the congregation into innovation is to allow all of this competition and insecurity to wash back into the church and its frameworks of ministry.

———————

As Russ's team needed to finalize and pitch its idea to the leadership of the grant, Fiona texted. Out of the blue, she was out. She gave vague excuses laced with emojis about her busyness. Russ was frustrated. Fiona was now the sixth person to quit Russ's group since the grant began.

7

Justification by Creative Works Alone

When Creativity Becomes King, the Self Becomes a Star

Each team from each congregation in the grant was made up of eight people: five young adults, two lay leaders, and a pastor. Since starting the grant, almost everyone had turned over on Russ's team. That hadn't been the plan. Every few months, someone had a reason for why they couldn't participate any longer. Russ was directly experiencing the fact that commitment and the neoliberal economy of permanent innovation don't necessarily go together. Innovation produces engagement, but not necessarily long-term commitment. Many innovative firms in Silicon Valley even dream of a quick and lucrative exit. The goods of congregational life cannot and should not match this pattern. But such goods inevitably wash back into congregational life from the culture of work. Russ was now swimming in this backwash.

Fiona had been one of the first young adults Russ recruited to the grant team. She seemed the perfect fit. She was twenty-three when the grant started. She'd grown up in the congregation, but had participated sporadically. She made it through confirmation and had months, even a year, of being a regular participant in the youth group. Her hit-or-miss participation never worried Russ too much. Fiona had been a faithful participant in the local Young Life

137

club. But in her senior year of high school, she was MIA from both. The last Russ had heard, she'd been admitted to an Ivy League school in upstate New York.

You couldn't blame Russ for not recognizing her three years later, when, out of the blue, a much different young woman showed up at the congregation's young adult gathering. Fiona had left for college as a preppy, honorable-mention soccer player and pre-med major. She returned as an artist who had found her true (or at least truer) self. Her hair was cut and colored in a way that high-school Fiona could never have imagined. She explained to Russ that she had felt suffocated after a year and a half in a highly competitive and conventional academic environment. Somewhere deep within, she found a truer self, a more artistic and creative Fiona. To her parents' disappointment, but with their support, she left the university and moved to Philadelphia to take art and design classes. In her final year of that program, she started participating in the young adult group back at her home congregation. Soon after her involvement, the group started regularly going to shows and exhibits with Fiona. A Fiona-show and drinks in Philly became a regular outing for the group.

Russ would never have assumed so when Fiona was in high school, but she was one of the most creative people he'd ever met. She exhibited her paint-ings and photography, but for fun (and extra cash, which at times was her only income) she cut hair, sold original T-shirts, created logos for companies, took portraits, and designed websites. Each of these "for fun and extra cash" activities was its own little business. Fiona explained that these little busi-nesses were the only way to fund her "real" art. Plus, creating and running a little business was an expressive, creative activity in itself. She loved it. Fiona called herself a serial entrepreneur. The day Russ got the invite for the grant and called Fiona, she was making an Instagram story to sell hundreds of peaches she'd just bought from the farmer's market. She figured that with some good marketing, she could double her money and, more importantly, get the suburbanites in South Jersey some delicious fruit.

When Russ thought about a team of young adults from his congrega-tion for the grant, Fiona was a must. Having Fiona on the team assured him (and the others who joined) that the congregation was the perfect fit for this grant. With Fiona on board, they couldn't help but do something epic. Like the Lakers must feel with LeBron James on their team, a surge of confidence spilling into their bloodstream, so Russ's team felt with Fiona.

Just as LeBron falls out of bed hitting jumpers, so Fiona falls out of bed an entrepreneur.

Weird Dispositif Talk

Fiona was lauded as the entrepreneurial LeBron of South Jersey, giving her team confidence, because we all find ourselves in a creative dispositif. *Dispositif* is an odd word that comes from the LeBron (or at least Kobe) of social thinkers, Michel Foucault. It brings to mind something disparate and yet somehow connected or related in its unrelatedness. Foucault uses this word to describe how a historical moment, even our own, operates. We can't understand a time as one solid reality. What constitutes a time is not one or two institutions, functional systems, or sets of values and norms. Rather, what makes up a given time is encompassed in "a whole social network of scattered practices, discourses, systems of artifacts and types of subjectivity, recognizably coordinated with one another by orders of knowledge without being thereby entirely homogeneous."[1] Fashion, figures of speech, political hot-button issues, technologies and tools, political organizations, economic functioning, even trends in food are all part of a historical moment.

To live inside a particular time is to be swept up in the river by all of these disparate things. All these dynamics—related and unrelated—are swirling together in the current of the river that carries and soaks us. We are caught up in this river, often without realizing it. We are unconsciously part of an epoch, part of a time. Being a person of your time means the dispositif is saturating you and carrying you along. Your imagination, practices, values, and forms of knowledge are shaped by it.

While a dispositif encompasses all these distinct (even opposing and unrelated) practices, discourses, artifacts, and patterns (of identities, sensibilities, and desires), it is nevertheless coordinated, a current with momentum in a single direction, a way of being. There is always a culturally dominant dispositif in power, one that simply but profoundly shapes our unreflective imagination of the good way to live in our historical period.[2]

1. Andreas Reckwitz, *The Invention of Creativity* (Malden, MA: Polity, 2017), 28–29.
2. Here I'm adding a little Charles Taylor to Foucault. I affirm Foucault's attention to power. But at times it seems to go too far. I don't think the whole of human agency can be defined or understood through power, but human agency is never devoid of power dynamics.

The dispositif describes the central or dominant way of being, but there are always other ways of being operating on the fringes of any historical time. These competing collections of cultural and societal artifacts and activities are of this period of time as well. Small groups of people take on these minority ways of being. But these minority ways of being do not encompass or define a time in the way that a dispositif does. They are present in a given time, on the edges, but do not frame and shape a period of time. The dominant dispositif gives a time its shape. There are always other tributaries (practices, artifacts, and networks) flowing along in time as well, but these side flows do not form the imagination, activity, and emotions of most people.

No dispositif arrives to shape its historical time *ex nihilo* or from nowhere. Every dispositif starts as a minority way of being, a smaller stream that pulls into it a few practices, artifacts, and discourses that are oppositional or counter to *the* dispositif. Eventually this stream widens, building momentum and pulling in other disparate practices, values, and social fields into a network of knowledge large enough to redirect the river, itself becoming the new dispositif.

The emergence of a new dispositif happens mainly without us noticing. We just get swept up in the momentum of a new way of being. The dispositif even gives us new ways of feeling (which connects Foucault with Illouz's thought on the sociology of emotions and the search for the real self, which we explored in the previous chapter).[3] Because a dispositif is felt as a switch in the disparate momentum of many practices, imaginations, desires, and more, we often can't know for sure when a stream's current builds strong enough to redirect the river and become the dispositif. Because a dispositif does not encompass a singular thing, it's hard to know when we've shifted from one to another. A dispositif is like a river in that it has no real center, though it does have a shared coordinating momentum.

We can wonder whether a Supreme Court decision, change in music style, new social media site, decrease in religious practice, tragedy, disease, or new technology may signal a fundamental change to a society's way of being. But we can never really know until after we're already in the new dispositif. Even when you're in it, though, a dispositif doesn't reveal itself in any straightforward manner. We always feel like we have a slippery grip on the time we're

---

3. Andreas Reckwitz critiques, while following, Foucault for not clearly enough seeing how emotions (feelings) play into a dispositif. Reckwitz, *Invention of Creativity*, 30.

in, able to feel it more than name it. Identities, values, artifacts, and practices sharing the same dispositif may directly conflict. They might conflict because one practice is from a minority way of being, hidden within the dispositif. The only way to know what historical time you are in is to take the aerial view of the river and its tributaries, looking at the dispositif's family tree. Foucault's work traces the genealogy of dispositifs. He examines the present dispositif by tracing its historical pathways, showing where and how it branched off, merged, and built up to become dominant as *the* dispositif. The process of describing what makes up a dispositif, in philosophy, is called "genealogy."

The Creative Dispositif

Andreas Reckwitz builds off Foucault, and his strange talk of dispositifs, to pinpoint a dispositif switch. Reckwitz believes that we entered a different time in the 1980s—a new dispositif dawned. Sometime in the middle 1980s (and building momentum into the early twenty-first century), a minority dispositif became the dominant dispositif. This new dispositif, he explains, was the dawning of a kind of creativity.

In his book *The Invention of Creativity*, Reckwitz shows that we're now in an expressive creativity dispositif. As we saw in chapter 2, it has become nearly unthinkable that creativity could be anything but good. It is now nearly unimaginable that some person, institution, business, or profession would not want to be creative—as an end in itself, as the instrument to find meaning, victory, and purpose. Our discourse (or way of talking) reveals that being labeled as creative is always a compliment, a rich value. Reckwitz's point is that now expressive creativity itself holds together many different cultural realities. Expressive creativity is the current that holds together divergent artifacts, practices, and identities. What does a server business, YouTube star, politician, drag queen, petroleum company, new downtown apartment complex, advertising for car insurance, airport gate, middle-class teenager, and a city bus all have in common? They're all in one way or another shaped and judged by the measure of expressive creativity. What gives them importance or value (or simply coherence in this time) is their aim and desire for creativity.

Applebee's Boy has a near disdain for Bearded Brown Turtleneck because Bearded Brown admits that he doesn't want to be creative. That seems crazy, almost immoral! It sounds to Applebee's Boy's ears like someone saying they wish to be evil. The fact that Bearded Brown thinks creativity has little to do with pastoral ministry is repulsive to Applebee's Boy. And that's because Applebee's Boy is fully a man of his dispositif. Bearded Brown is not. He swims against the current while Applebee's Boy goes with the flow. Of course, Bearded Brown is still tossed about by the current, but he resists as much as he can. It hurts to be tossed against the rocks. Bearded Brown is uncomfortable; he's aware the river has branched off, recalling former lost dispositifs and wishing they were again dominant. This gives him a hard edge as he feels like (even wishes to be) a man from another time.

But according to Reckwitz, there is no other time. Our time is a creative one. The desire and drive for expressive creativity shape and mobilize our dispositif. Expressive creativity is now our dispositif. The winners in this dispositif are not noble, loyal, courageous, holy, or dutiful. Having such traits may have been the best way of being in past dispositifs. But in our time the best way to be is to be creative. To live well in this dispositif means all those other ways of being must be filed under the higher way of being creative. Only those who express their creativity thrive. True, other times and other dispositifs had creativity. But in no other dominant dispositif was expression of creativity the momentum that held together all other practices, artifacts, values, and social fields. The creative outputs of the paintings and sculptures of the Renaissance, as we said in chapter 2, were not made for the purpose of expressive creativity, but to reflect the beauty of God, the beauty of the human form, or the glory of the patron (not the unique creativity of the artist). The objective was to touch something transcendent and be a conduit for something beyond you, to be swept up into the event of creation, not to represent and express yourself as a creative force.

Fiona is LeBron, the star of the team, because she's the *most* creative.[4] Reckwitz's point is that everything in this dispositif is held together by the drive for expressive creativity. The momentum and unifying force of this dispositif is creativity itself. Our imaginations, practices, artifacts, and values are infused with an aestheticization. Nearly every part of our globalized culture is now

4. Actually, LeBron has become LeBron because he's creative. Very few people want to be shy Tim "the Big Fundamental" Duncan when they can be creative King James or Air Jordan with cool shoes sold through aesthetic commercials. Michael Jordan is a good case in point here. Watching the docuseries *The Last Dance* gives us a clear picture of Jordan's greatness, which was inseparable from his creativity. He was the greatest because he willed to win at all costs, but to always win with style, with the aesthetic of the cutting edge of the new creative dispositif. Jordan, in sports, must be named as one of the agents who brings the new creative dispositif into dominance.

overcome by this dispositif, seeking an expressive, creative aesthetic. Reckwitz explains that creativity now "encompasses . . . everyday techniques, from . . . work processes to private fashion decisions . . . , as well as truth discourses from psychology and . . . notions of the ideal creative person." He continues, "The creativity dispositif incorporates typical sets of artifacts, ranging from digital data streams to gentrified suburbs and corresponding forms of subjectivation for creative workers and global city tourists." Relevant to our discussion, connecting us back to the previous chapter and Illouz's discussion of the true self found through the reworking of emotion as you work on a project with a team, Reckwitz explains that this creativity dispositif even "develops its own affective structure, cultivating the sense [the emotion] of novelty, the fascination for the creative subject's perfect body, enthusiasm for creative teamwork and constant creative activity."[5]

Church and denominational leaders, like Synod Executive Guy, feel that the church is falling behind. How exactly it's falling behind they can't quite name, but they can feel it. They can sense, maybe rightly, that the church is slipping out of its time. Foucault and Reckwitz help us see that the church is falling behind the dispositif. The church is not in tune with the dispositif. Leaders worry that the church is disconnected and losing ground inside this expressive creativity dispositif. The assumption is that the church can survive only if it catches up to creativity. Because of our own boundedness in this creativity dispositif, we assume that only expressive creativity will allow the church to catch up. Church and denominational leaders often can't name it, but this dispositif is directly why the language of innovation and the practices of entrepreneurship seem so appealing.

Innovation and entrepreneurship can have such a deep and broad cultural value only inside an expressive creativity dispositif. No one glorified innovation or entrepreneurship in the time of Keynesianism, because the dispositif that enveloped Keynesianism was not creative. Concern for creativity and an authenticity of aestheticization was a minority way of being located in enclaves in New York, Weimar, London, and Paris. Only when this minority way of being became *the* dispositif, redirecting the river and making such enclaves mainstream, could the drive for expressive creativity be assumed to be the best way to live. And only then could expressive creativity be understood as the best way to work. Innovation and entrepreneurship are venerated when

5. Reckwitz, *Invention of Creativity*, 30.

the core value judgment of our practices or artifacts (even our person) is to be creative. Only in a dispositif that glorifies expressive creativity can disruption and insecurity (over routine and security) be embraced as a better way of being. Workers can accept the anxieties and tensions of disruption and insecurity because they're implicitly, but profoundly, promised creativity. The company gets permanent innovation; the worker is given the permission, even the demand, to be creative (even if the completed work isn't). To be creative is to be squarely in your time, to be authentic, to be developing and finding a truly valuable self. In turn, it is the way to have a sustainable, growing business.

The Aesthetic Economy

If we were to find Max Weber frozen in carbonite, à la Han Solo, and we freed him and took him to Times Square, Silicon Valley, Champs-Élysées, or the Shibuya Crossing in Tokyo, he would be shocked. At the people, at the speed, at all the lights. But he'd also be amazed that capitalism was playing a major part in pushing forth creativity. He'd be shocked that capitalism was one of the forces (if not *the* major force) behind the momentum of the expressive creativity dispositif.

When Weber died in the 1920s, he assumed that the functions of capitalism largely stood in opposition to creativity. Capitalism was about regularity and standardization, a hard ground where creativity as an aim couldn't survive. The avant-garde from the late nineteenth century to the mid-twentieth opposed capitalism by seeking creativity through bohemianism (capitalism was the enemy for the creative enclave of the Beats in 1950s New York). To be creative was to stand in opposition to the bourgeois and their capitalist commitments. Neither Weber nor these avant-garde could ever have imagined that creativity would become the central thrust of capitalism.

To make this point further, think about technology. Technology, inside our dispositif, is now nearly synonymous with expressive creativity. Technology, thanks to design firms, has been melded almost completely with the aesthetic. The workspaces of the new forms of work birthed by digital technology firms in Silicon Valley feel like art studios and college dorm floors. Weber would have been stunned by the fact that technology has been aestheticized and become a catalyst for expressive creativity. Technology before our present dispositif was intended to be the opposite of creativity. The technological breakthrough of Fordism, for instance, sought to rationalize systems.

It did not turn workers into creative team members who pour the energy of their truest self into a project. Rather, it turned workers into functions that were small, automated parts of a much larger machine—for the sake of standardization and therefore the elimination of creativity. It may have taken ingenuity to create technological systems like Ford's assembly line, but these systems were all for the sake of standardization—that's how modern capitalism worked. At the time of Weber's death in 1920, this was the heart of capitalism. Weber would be confused as to how the great capitalist victors of late modernity could organize their businesses around innovation and creativity. He would have wondered how the great winners of capital, like Steve Jobs, Elon Musk, Bill Gates, and Mark Zuckerberg, could be lauded as creative geniuses. Weber might ask, How does a focus on innovation and creativity not undermine capitalism?

That question is worth considering. Permanent innovation is possible for companies, and not a poison pill for capitalism, only because we find ourselves in this expressive creativity dispositif. The economy itself amalgamated to match this dispositif. This is capitalism's genius. Capitalism helped to bring forth this dispositif, but it didn't create it alone. A dispositif is always the combination of many disparate realities. On their own, neoliberal owners, bosses, executives, and even managers could not have run their companies in a state of permanent innovation. Workers needed to understand themselves inside an expressive creativity dispositif—believing that the self (to find its truest self) needed to develop its own creative output, seeking its own authenticity. Otherwise, capitalism would have stuck with rationalization and efficiency to produce its slower (but steadier) growth (the extra).

The Designer Wears the Crown

Reckwitz demonstrates, as he sketches out the invention of creativity in late modernity, that for permanent innovation to become a way of being (for companies and workers), it must correlate to and therefore have direct coherence within the expressive creativity dispositif. Permanent innovation must be justified as a form, asset, and even privilege of finding the workers' true self through creativity. But to make this all operate, the economy itself must be made aesthetic. Neoliberalism, to its credit, had an intuitive sense of the coming dispositif. It therefore was willing to oblige it, moving us from an organized capitalism to an aesthetic capitalism.

This switch from an organized capitalism to an aesthetic capitalism led to design being so venerated in our time. No one cared about design in organized capitalism. Well, I suppose designers did! Only the designer or the design department cared about design in organized capitalism. Design ended with the task of designing the product. Design was just one element, one cog in the machine of the functional and rationalized systems of production. But inside the expressive creativity dispositif and its different kind of aesthetic capitalism, design needs to be at the heart of everything. Inside the capitalism of the creativity dispositif, *everything* is now design. The economy from top to bottom is design. Design is the lifeblood of the aesthetic economy. When things aren't working, for whatever reason, for whatever institution, collective, individual, or business, the solution is design. It's assumed that a better design will save us. In the creativity dispositif, this assumption has been as true for commercial as noncommercial entities.[6]

Across our institutions, including the church, we have this sense that design thinking is the truest catalyst for real change. Design thinking importantly raises the need for listening, even calling the designer to have empathy for the end user. This is all good. But it shouldn't be missed that the objective of listening and having empathy is still instrumental: make something useful or design an aesthetic expression of creativity that will be accepted, bought, or followed. Ultimately, the church is lured into thinking that if we redesign what seems to be falling behind, such as the congregation's life, giving it an injection of the aesthetic through design, it will magically catch up. Inside the creativity dispositif, it is believed that the challenge for the church is not to find a way to encounter the living God inside an immanent frame but to find a new design. Following the creativity dispositif in this immanent frame, we assume that design can save us.

And why wouldn't we assume so? Why wouldn't sinking budgets and even spiritual apathy be solved by design? We imagine that divergent things like budget shortfalls and spiritual apathy can be solved by design because we are people of our dispositif. Design heralds that all the issues we face are a crisis of expressive creativity, an absence of a true, authentic aesthetic. Inside an aesthetic economy, everything (the product, building, marketing, desks, even the dress code) is to be designed and therefore creative. Design answers all

6. Andreas Reckwitz adds, "Design, which always has to be considered in discussions of culture and materiality, seems to serve as the model for cultural production as a whole." Reckwitz, *The Society of Singularities* (London: Polity, 2020), 137.

problems because design is an expressive, creative process that renews (or, better, brings a *new*) creativity.[7] Design is your best hope, because design infuses your lacking product or culture with expressive creativity. Design functions as a kind of spirituality without a god, an empathy[8] for people's product use without the necessity of encountering their spirit or being responsible for their soul. The temptation inside the expressive creativity dispositif of the aesthetic economy is to see the best pastors as essentially designers. They are the best not because they can interpret revelation and wait for God but because they are able to infuse every element of the church with an aesthetic that signals to creative people that they can find in the congregation an emotional space to find (maybe God, but more directly) their truest self. When the organized Keynesian economy is replaced by the aesthetic economy of neoliberalism, design escapes the walls of the department and becomes the solution for everything.[9]

7. Reckwitz adds, "Design can be applied to individual artifacts as well as to services, to electronic bearers of signs, and to whole spatial and virtual environments. The organizational form that provides the supporting framework for this kind of activity is aesthetic management. The important consequence of this is that the aesthetic economy is more than a symbolic economy or an economy of signs. Signs and symbols are indeed the elementary constituents of the aesthetic economy, but their prime function is to stimulate the senses and the emotion rather than merely to convey meaning." Reckwitz, *Invention of Creativity*, 124.

8. Tim Brown, the great design guru, says, "Our real goal, then, is not so much fulfilling manifest needs by creating a speedier printer or a more ergonomic keyboard; that's the job of designers. It is helping people to articulate the latent needs they may not even know they have, and this is the challenge of design thinkers. How should we approach it? What tools do we have that can lead us from modest incremental changes to the leaps of insight that will redraw the map? In this chapter I'd like to focus upon three mutually reinforcing elements of any successful design program. I'll call them insight, observation, and empathy." Brown, *Change by Design: How Design Thinking Transforms Organizations and Inspires Innovation* (New York: Harper Business, 2009), 40. Byung-Chul Han says this about empathy: "The neoliberal regime isolates people while at the same time invoking empathy. Because it is a resonant body, however, ritual community does not require empathy. The demand for empathy can be heard in particular in atomized societies. The present hype surrounding the concept has primarily economic causes: empathy is used as an efficient means of production; it serves the purpose of emotionally influencing and directing people. Under the neoliberal regime, a person is not only exploited during working hours; rather, the whole person is exploited. In this context, emotional management turns out to be more effective than rational management. The former reaches deeper into a person than does the latter. Neoliberal psycho-politics attempts to elicit positive emotions and to exploit them. In the final analysis, it is freedom itself that is here being exploited. In this respect, neoliberal psycho-politics differs from the biopolitics of industrial modernity, which operates through disciplinary compulsion and command." Han, *The Disappearance of Ritual* (Cambridge: Polity, 2020), 12.

9. This interesting combination needs more development than I have space to explore. But there is a kind of Gramscian counterrevolution here. Neoliberalism is able to take avant-garde and progressive positions into its more conservative disposition by the adaptation of the aesthetic.

The Shape of the Aesthetic Economy

What might surprise Weber most—and what would be an outright shock to Karl Marx if we were to unfreeze him with Weber in Jabba the Hutt's lair—is that capitalism has been so durable. Marx thought capitalism was a weak, evil invention that would inevitably attack itself, eat itself, and disappear. When Marx died in London (not Tatooine) in 1883, he figured capitalism would soon follow him to the grave, which was not a completely unjustified assessment. Karl Polanyi taught us (in chap. 3) that the end of the nineteenth century was starting to produce economic problems that would lead to the bloodiest century in human history. But ultimately Marx was wrong. Capitalism was far more resilient than he figured. Weber never saw capitalism as the existential or even pseudoreligious evil threat that Marx did. Nevertheless, Weber, coming out of his carbonite freeze, would be surprised at how adaptive capitalism has been.

The capitalism that Weber wrote about, and that came to mobilize the organized Keynesian economy, was at its core rational and cognitive. For the sake of rationalized functionalism, it was sturdy and dependable but stiff and cold. Weber couldn't see capitalism any other way. His imagination was framed by his bourgeois and organized dispositif. What would surprise Weber, and shock Marx, is that capitalism has been quite successful in altering itself, showing its impressive dexterity, so that it can be part of (even central to) a much different dispositif. Weber would never have imagined that capitalism could be driven by anything other than rational, cognitive pursuits. It was assumed that if capitalism were to lose the rational and cognitive, it would be buried next to Marx in London.

But as the new expressive creativity dispositif started to coalesce around a new ethic of authenticity and a new economic theory of deregulation, capitalism was able to trade its organizational thrust for an embrace of the aesthetic. It exchanged its rational and cognitive focus for an attention to (even obsession with) the sensuous and affective. Weber would be shocked to see that in the dawning aesthetic economy, capitalism began to operate primarily out of emotions. How could you sell emotions? By the late 1960s some of the only artists embedded deeply in the Keynesian organized economy (the admen!) were finding a way.[10] This way would play a major part in moving

10. For more on this, see Thomas Frank, *The Conquest of Cool: Business Culture, Counterculture, and the Rise of Hip Consumerism* (Chicago: University of Chicago Press, 1998).

the expressive creativity dispositif from the fringe to the center. The Viennese worm inadvertently prepared the ground for this kind of capitalism and for its worker/buyer to take an emotional turn. Weber would be shocked that capitalism could be centered on feelings. Here it was running on a fuel Weber believed it wasn't built for: sensations and sentiments.

Ultimately, the capitalist centrality of feelings was fixated on novelty. Capitalism takes an aesthetic turn because it discovers the best way to grow extra capital in a consumer society is to get people to desire, want, and deeply feel a need for the sensation of something new. The driving force of the aesthetic economy is the production and desire for the new. The sensation of consumers and workers chasing something new moves the aesthetic toward growth. Buying something new feels like working on the self. Working on something new (e.g., a new project for permanent innovation) feels creative. The production of desire makes the self an entrepreneurial self who becomes a new self through the energy of its own expressive creativity. The aesthetic toward growth is to feel, from top to bottom, a sensation of newness. Reckwitz says, "The aesthetic economy shifts capitalism's orientation towards the production of novel goods away from its fixation on technical invention."[11]

The cultural contradiction of Keynesianism asserted that companies and workers functioned as rational and cognitive agents. They were not to feel—at least, not until after work and a shot of whiskey. Only outside of work were they to feel their desires for novelty. Post-WWII Keynesianism needed a society filled with consuming families. But in its rational and cognitive form, it wanted this buying to be embedded in duty. Those admen, and with them a few designers, who operated at the rhythms of an expressive creativity dispositif in a time in which that dispositif was the minority dispositif, found duty and responsibility (and any other rationalized and cognitive forms) as no way to meet the objectives of further growth and the selling of novel products and services. Now in a consumer economy, it was clear to marketers and designers that the rational and cognitive way of working and consuming had its limits (and therefore needed to meet its demise). From watching the young people revolt, seeing them grab hold of (buy!) the avant-garde's creative practices, these marketers and designers realized that buying, that seeking something new again and again, could be an emotional (even pseudospiritual) pursuit.[12]

11. Reckwitz, *Invention of Creativity*, 89.
12. I've discussed this history in depth in Andrew Root, *Faith Formation in a Secular Age* (Grand Rapids: Baker Academic, 2017), part 1.

By following the young expressivists, capitalism could become creative. Creative capitalism could grow by tapping into the emotions (the expressive), moving at the level of sensations and sentiments.

Aesthetic capitalism played a major part in putting the spotlight on the self. The expressive creativity dispositif was a time to find yourself, be yourself, and never stop re-creating yourself into something that feels true by always seeking novelty. Inside the expressive creativity dispositif, it appears coherent, even obvious, to assume that the true self is unearthed by consuming sensations of novelty. When you feel something new, you are closer to touching that elusive true self.

Weber would be shocked that the aesthetic economy of the expressive creativity dispositif isn't centered on creating stuff (of course, it does create stuff, but that isn't its spirit), as it was in the organized capitalism of Keynesianism. Rather, the aesthetic economy of neoliberalism specializes in creating feelings. Apple creates phones, but even more so it creates a feeling, a sensation of what it's like to have one of Apple's phones. Apple spends so much energy on the design of the phone, and just as much on the design of the packaging of the phone. Opening a new phone must bring an overwhelming feeling of pleasure. It must provide a sense that you are unleashing a tool that will help you uncover your truer self.

By focusing on emotions and selling feelings, the neoliberal aesthetic economy gains coherence and importance inside the expressive creativity dispositif. When the aesthetic economy is humming inside a dominant expressive creativity dispositif, then an obsession with the self also rises vigorously to the surface of our culture. Through the unique creativity of the self, feelings of novelty become the way to be a self. All other moral visions, all other confessions of what makes a self, are eclipsed by the individualized drive for creative expression and recognition, for more and more feelings of the new.[13]

13. Reckwitz adds about novelty, "The creativity dispositive contains a contradictory source of dissatisfaction. It seems there is at once too much and not enough novelty. The sense that there are too many offers of aesthetic perception can be experienced as overly taxing. At the same time, one starts to suspect that the sea of apparent novelty no longer really conceals anything new and original. The possibilities for creating something new in the arts, in design, in partnership, etc., have been exhausted and individual aesthetic events lack intensity. Complementary to these symptoms of depression and exhaustion, which can be read as a reaction to the demand to achieve and heighten, is the so-called attention deficiency syndrome. In some cases, ADS develops into a compulsive search for new perceptions for their own sake. It can therefore also be interpreted as a further, typical, contemporary sickness brought about by the creativity dispositive." Reckwitz, *Invention of Creativity*, 226.

The self must be uniquely creative to find itself. But finding a true self, finding a creative way of being a self, is substantiated by contradictory measures. In one way, you'll know your true self because you'll feel it. An aesthetic capitalism teaches you to know the self through individually feeling and fully embracing novelty. You'll find your true self when your unique creativity unveils your singularly unique self. This feeling of your own uniqueness, not a community or a creed, will tell you who you really are. No one else can tell you who you really are because only you can feel yourself, and what you feel is what you are. Only you know when the emotions of being something new feel right.

Yet in a second, somewhat contradictory way, it's assumed you'll know your true self, and feel sure your new emotions about your new self are not deceiving you (as the Viennese worm tells you they so easily can), only by the recognition of others. If finding your true self is dependent on expressive, creative acts that excavate the true self, then it demands an audience, like all creative acts.[14] We'll see in the following section that creativity is performative, and performances require an audience. Inside the expressive creativity dispositif, it's assumed that you'll know that you've found your true self when you have admirers and fans (fans are essentially devoted customers, social media heightening exponentially the sense that our own self is a company and others are our customers). When you feel the emotions of others' admiration—when your own way of being a self comes about through your own expressive creativity for an audience that experiences your creativity as an emotion of novelty—then you're sure of your true self. No wonder so many twelve-year-olds want to be YouTube stars and sixteen-year-olds long to be Instagram influencers. These are forms of expressive creativity bound fully and completely in the self. They don't even necessitate an object like a

14. Roberto Verganti discusses the importance of the audience. Verganti follows a leading business professional named Alessi as he embraces the move to call the consumer the "audience." Notice also how the artist is central to his imagination. He says, "To reinforce this idea, Alessi often refers not to users but to the 'audience': 'There is a way of doing design that is giving people what they ask, which is never something innovative. And there is a way of doing design that is more artistic and poetic. It is like commercial art ("commercial" because it needs to be approved by the audience; eventually people need to love it). . . . When Picasso painted, he never thought about a target audience. He didn't have a target segment of users in mind. But eventually he was not only a great artist. Those who discovered him made also a great business. There is an enormous (and unexploited) business potential also in this type of innovation.'" Verganti, *Design-Driven Innovation: Changing the Rules of Competition by Radically Innovating What Things Mean* (Boston: Harvard Business School Press, 2009), 48.

painting or a song (they are an aesthetic absent art). The self is now the canvas of creativity—as long as it gets enough recognition from an audience in likes and follows.[15] Digitization of the neoliberal economy (the availability of social media sites and creative tools) deeply imposes this expressive creativity dispositif and does so by making an audience available to everyone with an internet connection.[16]

The Audience and the Star System

Inside the expressive creativity dispositif and the aesthetic economy, a star system is born. Of course, a star system of celebrities was present throughout the whole twentieth century.[17] Even in an organized dispositif of a Keynesian economy there were stars, particularly movie stars and sports heroes. The mid-twentieth century wouldn't be the mid-twentieth century without Mickey Mantle, Grace Kelly, and Frank Sinatra. But emblematic of the bold line that separated work and home, the mid-century star was locked on the movie screen or in the game of the week. The star had her or his place, and there was little sense, especially once you were grown up (moving past your major league dreams), that somehow you could become a star yourself. You might still find yourself with some fame, but this fame was embedded in offices, as historians have shown has been the case for thousands of years. The monarch's or owner's office, not their personality and creativity, made them famous in their domain or company (often passed on through blood, not talent). There was fame in the office, not the personality.[18]

15. Ulrich Bröckling calls creativity a religion. He says powerfully, "Like all religions, creativity is easy to uncover as ideology—for example, as a response to the compulsion to innovate inherent in capitalist modernization or, more generally, as a reaction to economic necessities. However, the fact that creativity fulfills a function explains neither why it is so unquestionably accepted, nor how it comes about and how it can be awakened. Like all religions, the religion of creativity consists, in addition to articles of faith, of social practices and adepts announcing its works and guiding the laity. The general call for creativity expresses not only a 'necessarily false consciousness' but also a way of exerting influence upon yourself and others. In other words, creativity is a programme of governing, a means of governing the self and others." Bröckling, *The Entrepreneurial Self: Fabricating a New Type of Subject* (Los Angeles: SAGE, 2016), 101–2.

16. Andreas Reckwitz goes into depth on the digital impact on creativity and the self's drive for singularity. See *Society of Singularities*, part 4.

17. We simply don't have space to get into it, but there's something about the way the mass media functions that it creates stars.

18. This is no longer true. The final barrier came in presidential politics, where personality, through expressive creativity, became more important, even more powerful, than the office itself. This has a long history that goes through the twentieth century. It started with JFK and the

In the expressive creativity dispositif and the neoliberal aesthetic economy, the star system, like the rest of the economy, becomes more fluid. Creativity becomes central, and the self seeks its own unique way to broadcast itself, receiving recognition through the positive or negative emotions of an audience. The star system bleeds into everything.

We find this in our language. For example, particularly in the UK, "legend" describes anyone who's done something even somewhat creative, who has won even the most niched sense of admiration or acclaim. Even one night at the pub, with one hot streak on the dartboard and a few moments worthy of Facebook posts, can win the label of "legend." The person is introduced as a star: "This is my friend Ed. He's a real legend in this pub." You don't need to narrate why he's a legend. Telling your friends that Ed is a legend simply but profoundly relays that Ed is someone to watch. He is performing an expressive, creative self worth noticing. To say Ed is a legend is to say, "Keep your eye on Ed tonight. You'll see some creative, entertaining stuff!" It's to say, "Watch Ed! He's someone who can give you emotions of novelty. He's an expressive, creative self that can inspire you to be your own expressive, creative self." He may even make it so that you flip quickly from audience to performer (the star system makes the line between audience and performer ever permeable). The fact that you don't really know what Ed did to win him the label of "legend" communicates to you all the more that you, too, with an expressive, creative performance of your own self tonight, could leave this pub a legend. At least for this night, your self can impose enough emotions of novelty on others who are watching you (maybe for only a few hours, but immortalized on social media) that you too could be a star.

Inside the disruption and insecurity of permanent innovation, the star system becomes essential at work. The star system reaches deep into our society, playing a major part in the knowledge system that builds the momentum of the expressive creativity dispositif. Innovation is appealing in the expressive creativity dispositif, where the aesthetic economy becomes a place to work on the self. Work can be a place to work on the self only if it is made into

---

first televised presidential debates, and moved into Bill Clinton and Barack Obama, who were 'celebrity presidents.' But this movement came home to roost in a terrible way in 2016, when a celebrity reality TV star was elected to the office of president. Not surprisingly, Trump cared little (if at all) about the office. He was a celebrity star and therefore demanded that everyone love him, and if not love him, then bow to his star by hating him. He wanted nothing in between because he did not care about the office. He cared only about the shine of his star.

a place to perform the self. Work, as a place to perform the self, becomes a fundamental part of the star system.

Innovation and entrepreneurship are appealing—even as they impose disruption and insecurity on workers—because they are a direct way to perform the self for an audience. Innovation and entrepreneurship are direct ways to become a star or legend. They allow you to be overcome with meaning as the label of "star" delivers the feelings of novelty, assuring you that you have found your true self (at least for a time).

The environment of the star system is particularly present inside team-based project work. If your team is going to win in this project-by-project environment, it needs to be made up of stars (call Fiona first!). Your team needs to make stars. If your team wins often enough, you as an individual could be known as a star. Other teams working on other projects will want to recruit you, telling stories about you, believing they could have a winning project if you were on their team. You'll be a star when you're wanted on other teams for other projects. Inside the permanent innovation of the aesthetic economy, the star system is the way to procure security. Only the stars are safe in a neoliberal economy of an expressive creativity dispositif. That's good for business because it keeps workers driving for an epic innovation, working excessive hours so that they can be a star. Then they can continue performing the self on other teams in other projects. And eventually they can walk into a conference and have people whisper, "There's Lavon. He designed and coded CrashMedia's app in two weeks. Supposedly he slept at his desk for like four hours total. That dude is a legend. If we had him on our team, we couldn't lose. It'd be epic."

It's deeply advantageous to be known as a star, because the brightest stars are always given the most opportunities to shine even brighter. Labeled a star, you'll be given more opportunities to perform and build your legend, which gives you more chances to experience the emotions of novelty and therefore discover your true self as you broadcast your creative self. The stars are the winners of the expressive creativity dispositif and the aesthetic economy. The whole world, whether at the pub or at work, is a stage that you're asked to perform on. Reckwitz says, "The star becomes the template of an ideal self because her achievements as an expressive individual consist in the public attention she receives, her attainment of a higher degree of social recognition."[19]

19. Reckwitz, *Invention of Creativity*, 155. Reckwitz continues, "If modern society is typified by the widespread growth of an audience function in a variety of social fields, then the aesthetically interested audience is one outgrowth of this development. Further, if the audience is an

The Inflating Self

Russ's grant team was experiencing an exodus. To the grant leaders' credit, they intuitively recognized the expressive creativity dispositif. They sensed that the church needed a creativity transfusion. What was wrong with that? What harm could that do? Unless you are stuffy Bearded Brown Turtleneck, who doesn't want more creativity? *There's something exciting, even full and good, about creativity.* As with happiness, no one should be against creativity. But we need to recognize where creativity (like happiness) sits inside a late-modern secular age.[20] Expressive creativity, and therefore innovation, is not free of other cultural realities. Some of these cultural realities that accompany expressive creativity corrode the faith life of the Christian confession. They become problematic for faith formation.

The grant's assumption was that young adults were somehow more deeply at home in this expressive creativity dispositif; their status as digital natives seemed to prove this. It was exciting for the first year or so as each team got to know each other and bathe deeply in the expressive creativity dispositif by learning about exemplar innovators. But the teams had to shift from being solely creative voyeurs. They became directly engaged in the practices and processes of the capitalist aesthetic economy, using these design practices in a noncommercial setting. When that switch happened, something much heavier arrived: the obsessive pursuit and performance of a true self. Here came the pinch of the star system.

The grant leaders at the seminary didn't intend for this to happen. But by focusing on innovation, they were asking these young adults to enter (even at low grade) a competition to find a new sensation for the self that would be substantiated by their performance. What neither Russ nor the grant leaders at the seminary realized was that to ask young adults (or anyone) to innovate was to ask them *to justify that they were indeed a truly singular and unique self.* Was their innovation creative enough to reveal a self they could feel good about by receiving recognition for their expressive creativity? Eventually, the

important precondition for the emergence of the creativity-dispositive, then the mass media clearly assume a function of pacemaker for the development of the dispositive. From their very beginnings, the mass media are placed in a structurally analogous position to the social field of art, with which they are also interconnected, in that both fields address human beings primarily as recipients. The star as the object of admiration presupposes the emergence and expansion of this observer position of the audience" (157).

20. For a discussion of happiness, see Andrew Root, *The End of Youth Ministry?* (Grand Rapids: Baker Academic, 2020), chap. 8.

entirety of Russ's team quit. The process became too demanding. Expressive creativity felt too existential. They feared that their ideas weren't creative or effective enough. Russ had the sense that if their ideas had been better, if they had broken through and felt like stars, they would have stayed. But no one wants to perform a bad script. No expressive, creative self, like Fiona, wants to receive a bland or negative form of recognition that threatens to bury a true self under a pile of self-doubt. She doesn't want to deal with the possibility that their idea is dumb and therefore worthy of negative recognition. She doesn't want that dumb idea to communicate that she doesn't really know her self because her expressive creativity didn't induce emotions of novelty in her own self. She knew the idea didn't meet the threshold of creative because it didn't induce others to sense her creativity and label her a star.

It might be true that the Protestant ecclesial turn to innovation can offer an infusion of creativity into flat congregations and denominations falling behind in an expressive creativity dispositif. But if it is not carefully gauged, with many other (theological and formative) precautions, then the encouragement to innovate will overinflate the self. The creativity and aestheticization of the expressive creativity dispositif, operationalized through innovation and entrepreneurship, overinflates the self.[21] It claims that the self is itself not when it is lost in Christ but instead when it is found in and through its own expressive, creative performances, and the feeling it receives from an audience. *The self is justified by the works of its creativity.* Such an approach will lead to a much different theological anthropology and the practical shape of congregational life that will eventually explode or peter out. The grant team will leak members, or the project will fail, or the people involved will be malformed. Innovation may be worth doing, but never flippantly. It needs far more theological reflection than we've given. Innovation is too deeply

---

21. The aesthetic does not necessarily always overinflate the self. For instance, Hans Urs von Balthasar has developed the aesthetic in a rich theological direction (making it particularly interesting inside Reckwitz's argument). Kevin Mongrain explains Balthasar's position, and the reader will see its distinction from aestheticization: "Aesthetics in the classical sense, therefore, leads to the veneration and worship of some specific object that is other than the self, but Kantian-Romantic aesthetics leads to veneration and worship of the creative self; classical aesthetics celebrates nature and the gods, but Kantian-Romantic aesthetics celebrates the self who is capable of celebrating nature and the gods. Therefore in his effort to construct a theological aesthetics he takes classical aesthetics as his primary dialogue partner. For von Balthasar the religiosity of pagan devotion to a particular god is analogically related to Christianity's devotion to the image of God's glory in Christ." Mongrain, *The Systematic Thought of Hans Urs von Balthasar* (New York: Herder & Herder, 2002), 62.

embedded in a secular age of immanence and its economic systems for us to not pay closer attention to its hidden goods.

***

Russ now needed to face the question of whether involving Fiona in innovation was bad for her faith formation.

8

Why You're Not That Special but Feel the Need to Be

Singularity and the Self

Neither Russ nor the leaders of the grant at the seminary would have thought that innovation could negatively affect anyone's faith formation. The idea was that innovation would benefit the church by infusing both creativity and young adult investment. For Russ, though, it seemed to do the opposite. But even in the tension of his entire team quitting, Russ still couldn't imagine that innovation was having a negative impact on faith formation. It took the departure of his star, Fiona, to open him to this possibility. Yet Russ couldn't be blamed for being slow in seeing this connection. His inability to see it only shows how deeply we're all locked inside an expressive creativity dispositif. We're so waterlogged in the stream of this dispositif that we can't recognize that the shape of creativity in late modernity may risk overinflating the self. We fail to recognize that linking arms with innovation inside neoliberal capitalism, if not taken through a cruciform process, can overinflate the self and work against the formation where the self is lost (and then refound and transformed) in Christ.

Russ was now scrambling to refill his team. Like the Cleveland Cavaliers after LeBron left, Russ had to admit that the prospects for victory (whatever that meant) were low. The team's best idea was mundane and basic. Russ wanted to be okay with that, but for some reason he wasn't. He didn't want to admit it to himself, but he was running out the clock. Russ just needed a team to get him to the finish line of the grant.

To Russ's credit, he didn't want to leave it there. His pastoral concerns led him to follow up with everyone who quit. Coffee and a chat seemed the best way to get at why the team so easily split. Russ met individually with each person. Everyone said basically the same thing. They all mentioned feeling bad about leaving, but in the end, they each just got too busy. Russ sensed that what they meant was that the investment of time and energy wasn't recouped in the expressive creativity of the grant.

Yet there was something else. While no one said it was the reason they left, they all communicated in one way or another that they got spooked when Fiona's confidence waned. Even those in lay leadership looked to Fiona. She was the team's star after all. When she had her doubts, repeating over and over that she feared the idea was dumb, the rest of the team lost nerve. Lacking confidence, they all found it easier to find a way out. The reasoning was sound: if Fiona couldn't perform the self inside the team's idea, clearly they couldn't.

Russ chose to meet with Fiona last. They had a good, long conversation over cheesesteaks. Any tension dissipated. As Fiona discussed why she quit, two statements stuck with Russ. First, Fiona, though apologetic for leaving the team, repeated a few times, with the slightest tone of defiance, "I have so much on my plate. I can only give energy to the things that are clearly going somewhere. As an entrepreneur, I can't use up my time and creativity if I'm not convinced something is a winner."

Russ wanted to remind her that this team was about something bigger than any single idea or project. It was about the church and our life together before God. But it was clear to Russ that inside the drive for innovation, this "something bigger" seemed incoherent. Or it at least seemed to be eclipsed by the singular drive for expressive creativity and what this kind of creativity meant to the self. Fiona, for good or ill, recognized that there was a real limit to the team's and the project's creativity. It was time to cut bait and bail.

Second, Fiona said jokingly with a laugh, but still with an air of seriousness, "I'm not basic. Never typical." She confessed to Russ that she was "basic and typical" in high school, that she had hid her real self inside basic conventions. She promised herself that she'd never do that again, because that wasn't who she was. Being basic or typical was the worst thing she could think of being. She didn't say it, but Russ knew she meant that the team's project relayed a warning signal to her very self that the idea was too basic. If she gave herself to something basic, it would form her into something typical. Being perceived (receiving negative recognition) as basic and typical would make her feel that her self *was* basic and typical, lacking novelty. It would sweep her back to her high school self. Fiona said to Russ, "I'd rather be *extra* or *over-the-top* than *basic*. I can live with being extra, but not basic."

Into the Singular

In the previous chapter, we leaned into Andreas Reckwitz's *The Invention of Creativity*. He helped us see how innovation and entrepreneurship became part of an expressive creativity dispositif, even coherent and laudable inside this dispositif. From inside this presentation, we began to see what this does to our conception of the self. In a later book, Reckwitz articulates the deeper ramifications of this dispositif. In that acclaimed text, *The Society of Singularities*, Reckwitz shows that we now live in societies driven by singularity. An expressive creativity dispositif leads to a society of singularities. From a society of singularities, we get selves who fear being basic and yearn to be extra.[1]

In this second book, Reckwitz sketches out how, inside the expressive creativity dispositif, what is important, good, and celebrated shifts from the general to the particular. The particular, or particularity, becomes the goal or even obsession. "Rather than being directed toward anything standardized or regular, the hopes, interests, and efforts of institutions and individuals are pinned on the unique and singular."[2] Nearly everyone and every institution across our capitalist societies are looking for their own singularity. They want singular vacation experiences, singular consumer goods that no one else has, a singular personality that is far from typical. In late modernity, to find your true self is to find, even construct, your singularity. Companies share this drive for singularity. To survive in the unregulated Darwinian world of neoliberalism,

---

1. Reckwitz explains, "Late-modern society—that is, the form of modernity that has been developing since the 1970s or 1980s—is a society of singularities to the extent that its predominant logic is the social logic of the particular. It is also—and this cannot be stressed enough—the first society in which this is true in a comprehensive sense. In fact, the social logic of the particular governs all dimensions of the social: things and objects as well as subjects, collectives, spaces, and temporalities. 'Singularity' and 'singularization' are cross-sectional concepts, and they designate a cross-sectional phenomenon that pervades all of society." Reckwitz, *The Society of Singularities* (London: Polity, 2020), 5.

2. Reckwitz, *Society of Singularities*, 1.

each company needs to find its singularity. Each company is desperate to find what differentiates it in the market. The innovation has to be ongoing because success is dependent on singularity.

Consultants make big money helping companies (even churches) find and then hone their unique singularity. "What makes you different?" appears to be the most important question (or at least the first question). This question has a tangible importance for the company as well as the individual worker. Only those who are *different* survive inside an expressive creativity dispositif and an aesthetic economy.

It's exactly the opposite in an organized dispositif and a Keynesian economy. In Keynesianism, uniqueness and singularity were dangerous. Mid-twentieth-century companies and individuals were assumed to thrive inside standardization and an overall sense of conformity. In the cultural break of the late 1960s and the arrival of an age of authenticity, conformity was swiftly transformed from a virtue to an evil vice.[3] Since the late 1960s, no individual wants to be known as typical or regular. Since the mid-1980s, no company wants to be known as standardized or regimented (even the military in the 1980s had to change its marketing campaign to "Be all you can be," fronting the search for a unique self, to match this move away from the regimented to the singular).

The swift change from conformity to singularity happened because inside neoliberal capitalism, differentiation is most important. Differentiation in the market becomes the key to survive and thrive in the aesthetic economy. If you don't know what makes you different, you can't capitalize on that difference. In neoliberalism, difference gives you a runway; in Keynesianism, it was standardized conformity that promised longevity. Inside the aesthetic economy of neoliberalism, difference becomes a very high good. Without permanent innovation, the company cannot discover and embrace its differentiation at the level of both product and culture. Innovation's ability to produce differentiation and release from standardization is one of innovation's major appeals to church leaders.

3. I sketch out this point further in *Faith Formation in a Secular Age* (Grand Rapids: Baker Academic, 2017), part 1. Many of the social thinkers who were teaching the new generation were survivors of National Socialism. They saw German cultural conformity as a major reason for the Holocaust. Therefore, they taught a generation to worry about and even oppose conformity. Hannah Arendt's famous piece on the banality of evil points to the problematic nature of conformity. See Arendt, *Human Condition* (Chicago: University of Chicago Press, 1998).

Release for Denominational Standardization

Church leaders, like Synod Executive Guy, enthusiastically embrace innovation because innovation promises to pry the church loose from its old, standardized denominational forms. Innovation is appealing because it's a direct way for denominations to bury their old functions, operations, and, maybe most importantly, culture. No wonder Bearded Brown Turtleneck is angry! Innovation becomes a way for the denomination to exorcise its old ghosts and update itself for an expressive creativity dispositif.

Just like with companies, the congregations that seem to be surviving (even thriving) have differentiated themselves in the religious market. The congregations that have (purposefully or by happenstance) distinguished themselves from the denominational mold seem to be doing best. The congregations that have adapted to an expressive creativity dispositif have often taken distinct steps away from the denomination. The denomination usually needs such congregations more than those congregations need the denomination (often creating tension). What a significant switch from fifty years ago.

Mainline denominational Christianity, and the denomination itself, did quite well inside Keynesianism and the organized dispositif. There are many reasons for this,[4] but one reason relevant to this discussion is that, like the franchisee and the corporate franchise, the congregation would thrive if it followed the standardized forms of the denomination (using its hymnal, curriculum, publishing house, magazines, life insurance, seminaries, etc.). Everything was standardized, which was deeply appreciated inside an organized dispositif.

Standardization and organization couldn't happen solo. With standardization, no congregation could go rogue and survive. Inside the organized dispositif of the Keynesian economy, the hierarchy imposed standardized forms. Those who conformed to the headquarters got its goods (they were understood as good congregations). The standardization from headquarters allowed each congregation to receive what it couldn't produce on its own: an organized and rationalized way of doing things that raised the tide and therefore lifted all the boats of the conforming congregations.

This standardization gave each denominational church a similar feel, even a similar shared culture that was quite intricate. If you were on vacation, for

---

4. I've unpacked many of the reasons for this throughout my other writings. See particularly Andrew Root, *The Congregation in a Secular Age* (Grand Rapids: Baker Academic, 2021), chap. 8.

instance, away from your local American Lutheran Church (ALC), you could look up and find another ALC church in your vacation town. That other ALC church would feel similar and operate nearly the same as your congregation back home. It would have the same hymnal, same pledge forms in the pew, and same style of preaching (because the two pastors went to the same seminary and most likely knew each other). The standardization would create a general shared experience across the denominational congregations. The embracing of standardization made differentiation, uniqueness, and even originality unimportant (for some, they were even unwanted or dangerous).

The denominational headquarters was the center of gravity inside an organized dispositif. It was the organizing force. When each congregation happily conformed to the denomination's standardized forms, the denomination was essential. Inside the organized dispositif of Keynesianism, the best and brightest worked at church headquarters. Their impact was extensive because everything and everyone was following the standardized forms the denominational headquarters oversaw.

But today the situation is all quite the opposite. Inside an expressive creativity dispositif that now affirms differentiation and ultimately singularity instead of conformity, the "best" congregations are understood as the most original and unique. They are not those most in step with the denomination, but often those most out of step—dancing to the beat of their own drum. Those doing new things outside the denominational standardization (those who write their own curriculum, don't use a hymnal, train their own pastors, and draw from networks across traditions) are the exemplars. The last thing you want is for your congregation to feel like every other Presbyterian church (especially those that still have a trace of denominational standardization). The congregations are most lauded that build cultures where the denominational standardization can't even be smelled. Inside a creativity dispositif of a neoliberal aesthetic economy, the denomination is sprayed with a stink because standardization and conformity have been overcome by differentiation, originality, and uniqueness. The best congregations are not those conforming to the denominational standards but those doing something original. The congregations that have differentiated themselves in the religious market, particularly from their own denomination, are seen as best. They are "thriving" because those congregations are singular. They are one of a kind.

It wasn't until the early and mid-1980s that nondenominational (or hidden denominational) congregations came to thrive. Their "success" was embedded in their ability to differentiate themselves from other denominational congregations, promising people a uniquely singular church. They promised this by first avoiding any standardized signals, even in the congregation's name. "Willow Creek Church" or "Bear Path Community Church" or "Pine Falls Faith Community" (and eventually "The Well," "Oasis," or "The Gathering") replaced "Culver City United Methodist" or "Knox Presbyterian" or "Lutheran Church of the Incarnation." To be a "successful" congregation was to never conform to the standardization of the denomination, to differentiate yourself and signal your uniqueness in programs, worship style, and culture. Conferences were offered to pastors to help them find and curate their congregation's singular uniqueness (never mind that those programs often had more than a hint of standardization to them). Ultimately, the objective of leading a good congregation was to seek its singularity. As with a company, innovation was the mechanism the congregation could use to find and broadcast its singularity.

Into our time, this all goes a step further. This unthought need for differentiation and singularity has come to be adopted by the denomination itself. Deep inside an expressive creativity dispositif, innovation and entrepreneurship are embraced by ambitious pastors and also denominational officials. These officials, like Synod Executive Guy, embrace innovation as the direct way to (like in the old organized dispositif of standardization) provide direction to congregations. But innovation is in tune with an expressive creativity dispositif and the aesthetic economy. The denomination can no longer provide direction in standardization, moving all of its congregations into a general pattern. Rather, now each congregation needs to be singularly unique. This uniqueness needs to be found within the congregation itself. The congregation, not the denomination, needs to determine what makes the congregation different from all other churches.

The denominational leaders can't overstep and impose on the congregation's form, treading on the pastor's creativity, as it once might have. Now, instead of being held on to as a relic or being subjugated to heavy (uncreative) administrative roles, the denomination can become a resource for innovation. This new role infuses the denominational leadership with a new purpose! Leading congregations into innovation (giving them a process to find their unique differentiation and even singularity) leads the denomination to return to some expertise, but without the standardization or hierarchy. And it can all be done in a way that fits an expressive creativity dispositif. Innovation allows the denomination to affirm and invite each congregation's unique self, embracing its own creative singularity. Innovation allows the denomination to assist the congregation in finding its singularity. The denomination can coach the congregation in its pursuit to escape being basic.

That's not entirely bad; it may even be good. But it means that what holds clergy and congregations together is not a shared denominational identity but just an individual choice to use the resources and processes the denomination offers. For pastors, it means the theological commitments and traditions (of doctrine and practice) that the denomination once stewarded become much less important. But these losses are rarely grieved in light of the felt gains.

Yet these legitimate gains come with a danger. Reckwitz wants us to see that even these gains do something to the self. And this is what becomes perilous to faith formation.

The Singular Self

The expressive creativity dispositif and neoliberal aesthetic economy witness an overall societal move from the general to the particular, so it shouldn't surprise us that individual subjects embrace this same move. To be a self (of any value or esteem) is to be different, unique, and ultimately singular. The self welcomes particularity over the general. Inside an expressive creativity dispositif and an age of authenticity, no one wants to be just a face in the crowd. We admire those who swim against the current, those who have unique, creative selves. Being unique and swimming against the current is deeply embedded in us. We forget that not long ago (and still in small towns and non-Western locales) uniqueness was not celebrated. In such times and places, being general (being basic!), falling in line and taking on the standardized form, was valued more than expressing your own uniqueness (e.g., see the movie *The Boy Who Harnessed the Wind*).[5]

Not expressing your own uniqueness is an ethical problem, because our ethic is one of authenticity. We believe that it's best (even a must) that every human being has the *right* to define and express their own unique way of being human. This leads us to judge as dangerous collectivist views of the

---

5. Thanks to Blair Bertrand for pointing this out.

self (the idea that we're only a self inside a community) and the way these views often drive conformity. Collectivist views *do* run this risk of being dangerous. There are real gains to embracing each person's particularity. There is something deeply humanizing and theologically significant about giving space and encouragement for each distinct person to speak of their own particular experience. But this view of the self has its own dangers and excesses. The ethic of authenticity and the affirmation of the particularity of the self rightly check the oppressive overreach of collectives. But they also run the risk of turning these very collectives into enemies of the self.

In late modernity, to one degree or another, we all assume that being part of a family, country, or neighborhood can no longer forge our primary identity (which is forged in the myth of the innovative and entrepreneurial self, imposed by a neoliberal capitalism). But the real danger is assuming that those collectives actually hold you back because they're simply too general. The true self is too particular to be caged by them. The true self is always working to stand out, to throw off the typical, to be unique and singular, not to be part of a general collective. We still want collectives such as family, country, and neighborhood. But instead of the self being expected to conform to the generalized pattern, we expect the collective to accept us in our particularity. We want the family, country, or neighborhood to accept and affirm us in our uniqueness.[6] We even want these collectives to help us be our true, singular self. We particularly want our family to be (a good family is even defined as) a hub of support for each individual self's pursuit of their own singular uniqueness.

The assumption that collectives should *affirm* the self more than they should directly *form* the self means, for example, that what is defined as "bravery," "courage," and "vulnerability" shifts. Inside a dispositif where the general is more important than the particular, bravery, courage, and vulnerability mean sacrificing for something outside yourself. It means service for the good of a collective of which you're only a small part. It's brave and courageous to put this collective's survival above your own. "For God, family, and country!" or "For Queen and country!" are the shouts of the brave

6. This is especially clear at the level of the country. This is what Taylor means by "politics of recognition." The politics of recognition is the idea that each self needs to be recognized for its unique way of being. It is politics because it becomes important that the institutions that run the country recognize such groups of identities. See Charles Taylor, *Multiculturalism*, ed. Amy Gutmann (Princeton: Princeton University Press, 1994).

passions of another time. Those shouts are imbued with a different understanding of bravery and courage, because they come from a much different sense of the self.

When the scales tilt from the general to the particular, then bravery, courage, and vulnerability are reimagined. What is brave and courageous, and therefore an act of vulnerability, is to risk a bold presentation of your unique self. State your mind, show the world your talent, express your true self to an audience. Being brave enough to be you, to broadcast your unique self and stop being typical, conformist, and just another basic self, is celebrated as courageous and true. The collective is eclipsed. The family has no direct forming impact on the self. But the family can support (emotionally and financially) each person's individual drive to find and express their unique singularity. (Of course, when one feels dissatisfied with the self, the family gets blamed for malforming the self by its lack of support.)

Having vulnerability risks overexposing yourself as you broadcast your own felt singularity (which makes Brené Brown so powerful inside our expressive creativity dispositif of neoliberalism). You have to accept vulnerability, not as an existential or ontological reality, but as an expressive and creative one. The vulnerability that Brown discusses—which so resonates with her audience that it's made her *the* thought leader of our time—is *not* the vulnerability of facing your finitude and death. Rather, this vulnerability risks the dangers of rejection, misunderstanding, and being overlooked that could come with expressing your own inherently felt singularity. Will anyone recognize your true self as you wish to be known? You must risk living with the burden that your unique acts failed to give you the assurance that your singular self is valuable. Even in such moments of disappointment and overexposure, Brown reminds us that we've done something good for our singular selves. We may not have the rewards, but the fact that we were brave, exposing ourselves and reaching for our uniqueness, promises us that at some point we'll find that true self. Having been vulnerable makes us one step closer to finding our true singularity. We need to be encouraged again—pushed to have courage once more. We shouldn't fear vulnerability but should try again for a creative expression that unveils our singularity. We have to, really. We'll only ever know our self (thanks again to the Viennese worm—which says we can't trust that we know our true selves) when we uniquely express our selves and receive the recognition that confirms that our self has surpassed the basic.

Becoming Unexpendable

As our society moves from the general to the particular, accepting vulnerability becomes important for another reason. We have to accept vulnerability, because the way we work (which is the primary stage and audience for the recognition of the self) is fundamentally vulnerable. Permanent innovation imposes constant disruption and insecurity onto workers. The worker in neoliberalism is always vulnerable. The open markets cannot protect workers from being trampled. Tomorrow could bring downsizing or a corporate merger. The seeming whims of a new innovation could upend your project and make you expendable overnight.

The label of expendability is death for a worker, because the only mechanism for loyalty in the aesthetic economy of neoliberalism is to be indispensable to the company. Neoliberal companies are *always* looking to cut expendable costs. If you can somehow make yourself (i.e., make your *self*) indispensable, you'll have security, and the constant disruption will become meaningful or at least thrilling. (It will keep you from being bored and therefore from facing the question of whether your self is dull and your life vapid. Constant disruption keeps you from wondering whether novelty can really take the place of transcendence.)

Inside this reality, every worker has to explicitly or implicitly face a question: What produces indispensability? The great prize for the worker in neoliberalism is to be labeled as indispensable. But how do you achieve this label? Deep inside the aesthetic economy of the expressive creativity dispositif, it is *expressive creativity itself* that makes you indispensable. Hard workers, even experienced workers, are often downgraded in the aesthetic economy of neoliberalism and its drive for permanent innovation. Hard work in workers can be produced from other management mechanisms. And experience, though nice, is nowhere near as valuable as creativity. Most companies will take creativity over experience ten times out of ten. After all, experienced workers are expensive and, double whammy, often assumed to be stuck in their uncreative ways (adding nothing to the corporate culture of fresh novelty). Sure, a company organized around teams working on projects can benefit from experience. But without creativity, the teams, the projects, and therefore the whole business will die a bloody death on the battlefield of a neoliberal economy. When you're creative, you're indispensable.

But "being creative" is tricky and often confounding to certain workers. Expressive creativity is a slippery reality, making it an essential but enigmatic label to achieve. True creativity (which is deeper than expressivism and moves closer to something theological), like that of the craftsman, often looks nothing like what we romanticize it as being. Day to day, it's plodding, ordered, dull, and slow. Mixing a song or painting a portrait or making a wooden chair is tedious and meticulous. Companies racing for market share, fighting for their life, needing another innovation to stay alive, can rarely give the space, security, and independence for their workers to be creative in the craftsman kind of way. This kind of creativity, as we'll see in the final chapter, is dependent on an epiphany—and no neoliberal company racing for innovation has much time to wait, let alone surrender to the event of an epiphany. Usually the craftsman used by a team in its project is an independent contractor. The craftsman can't work under the watching pressure of the manager, and the executives don't want to commit a budget line for the salary and benefits of someone who, day to day, seems to be wasting more time waiting for an epiphany than producing in the time the company is paying for.

The kind of creativity valued by neoliberal companies isn't bound in the skill of the hands but in optimizing the self (being fully expressive!). It's not necessarily what the hands create that labels the worker as creative and therefore indispensable. Rather, it is the self. The perception of the worker's self signals whether the worker is creative or not.

The worker is indispensable when their coworkers and bosses perceive them as a creative, expressive self: this is achieved when the worker is able to cross a threshold and be seen as a unique, even singular, self. They are creative because they know as much as they do (they even know instead of do). For instance, they know about and consume singular realities. Their clothes, technology, vacations, friends, clubs, and parties are all singular.[7] They are creative because they have secret knowledge of singular things. These things they know about are different, new, always unique. They are creative because they are cutting edge, and they are cutting edge because they know how to position themselves within the reach of singularities, which gives their own self the perception of being singular. They are creative not because they make something but because they know what is singular. They are creatures

7. Bill Hader and John Mulaney were pointing out this drive for singularity in all its absurdity in their Saturday Night Live Weekend Update character Stefon, who was singular and creative, not because he made something but because he knew the most singular clubs in New York City.

of singularity. Their ability to curate and consume the singular makes them creative, though not in act but in style.

Such singular creatives aren't simply scamming the company. Inside an expressive creativity dispositif of an aesthetic economy, the company—no matter its business—will be judged by its feel of singularity. Why else would insurance companies spend billions on funny commercials fronted by pitch persons who are singularly quirky selves? These commercials show that being offbeat has now become cool; it shows a self who is unique, who is simply different without trying to be. The indispensable worker is the worker who is an expressive, creative self. The creative self is judged by their ability in all ways to transcend the general and be unique.

This sense that the self is creative not in action but in style, broadcasting a uniqueness and never being basic, moves throughout our society thanks in no small part to the shape of work. Expressive creativity is now equated with singularization. What the company sees as indispensable is not craftsmanship but the singularization of its innovations. The kind of workers it needs are skilled not with their hands but with their self-optimization.[8] Creativity is a performance of the self.

But this performative creativity, Reckwitz believes, imposes on us a stabbing "paradoxical social expectation."[9]

You've Got to Be Exceptional

When creativity is embedded in craftsmanship (or in an epiphany), the practice of creation regulates the self, rather than inflating it. The master craftsman knows that she is working somewhat at the will of materials, conditions, ritualized repetition, and mysterious inspiration.[10] Her self is relativized, even shrinks, in the shadow of the awe and epiphany of her participation in a creation. The deeper she gets into her craft, the more the art form becomes exceptional. Her own self doesn't become more exceptional.[11]

8. This is one reason Wozniak left Apple before Jobs, and why, when Apple struggled, they asked Jobs (not Wozniak) to return. Wozniak's genius was expendable; Jobs's singularity was not, as history has shown. (Apple's rate of innovation and singular creativity has not continued—at least in perception—at the same rate as when Jobs was alive and running the company.)

9. Reckwitz, *Society of Singularities*, 3.

10. See Matthew B. Crawford, *Shop Class as Soulcraft: An Inquiry into the Value of Work* (New York: Penguin, 2009).

11. It can impose a sense of humility.

But this all becomes flipped when creativity is not *what you do* but *what you know* (even *who you know*), when creativity is not an act but a style. When creativity is a performance of the self, the self is inflated as it rushes for singularity. There is no craft or mystery to relativize the self, to subjugate the self under something bigger than itself.[12] When this happens, the need for the exceptional escapes the realm of the practice and lands squarely on the shoulders of the optimizing knowledge and style of the self. The drive for the self to be singular, especially inside the expressive creativity dispositif of neoliberalism, demands that the self bear the weight of the exceptional squarely on its own shoulders.

To Be Special and Reality TV Fights

To be told you're special has become the highest statement of value in a late-modern aesthetic economy. It's a statement of elite, undeniable recognition. To be exceptional is to be a star, to be part of the star system (even in its broadest form). Even romance is renewed in the post-1960s culture by the affirmation that romance seeks intimacy and sexual union with *special* selves. In movies and in songs, a lover's heart melts when another special self declares one's own self as special. For a lover to declare that you are like no other, singularly special, brings ecstasy.

No wonder breakups after such confessions are so painful. They renege on the confession of singular, exceptional specialness. The brokenhearted wonder how their ex could have said such things to them and yet now love someone else.

To see this in action, just watch reality TV. It doesn't take long for the heartbroken to be sent into rage over the ex's new lover. Even if the couple was together only a few days (an episode), hearing that a new lover received the same words about being special will demand attack. The jilted one attacks the new partner instead of the ex-lover, usually because the jilted partner no longer feels special. On reality TV, it often has nothing to do with the former lover; it's about the perception of being exceptionally singular and therefore special. The jilted lover is so angry because they fear they've been punked. Were they mocked and called special just to be manipulated? Interestingly, the conflict is usually only squashed when the ex-lover assures the heartbroken ex that even though they're

12. For a similar argument showing how work has lost this essence of craft, see Richard Sennett, *The Craftsman* (New York: Penguin, 2009).

no longer together, the jilted is still special, still exceptional. The ex makes assurances that their feelings for the former lover's exceptionality were *real*, even if short-lived. Almost always, that's enough to assure the brokenhearted that they are indeed special and therefore can let go of their indignation.

But before this can happen, the jilted, heartbroken ex must have it out with the new partner. The new partner needs to be belittled because they think they're the special one now. The new lover's very presence seems to degrade the specialness of the self of the heartbroken. When the ex-lover told the heartbroken that they were special, the confessed specialness ("you're like no one else in this house") precipitated the hookup in the first place. To win the lover's affection was proof of their singular uniqueness. It made them (if only for an episode) the exceptional one in the contestant house.

It becomes a voyeuristic watch-fest to see the battle between who is more special as the heartbroken and the new lover face off like rams in a field. In this conflict, both the new lover and the heartbroken flaunt their uniqueness, waving hands in each other's faces, calling each other bland and basic, asserting that the other is not exceptional enough to win this label of specialness. "Don't get it twisted, you've got nothing on me! You're just basic!" they shout. All of this is done in front of two audiences. That's why it goes down with such venom in the first place. There is the audience of the roommates and fellow contestants—their participation as observers is essential as judges of specialness. These fights almost never happen without others watching; the battle for singularity is always performative, as we've said. And then there is the audience behind the screen, watching and tweeting. Both audiences are directly involved in evaluation, making our pick of who is indeed more exceptional, deciding which self is more unique.

The new lover and the heartbroken ex fight each other, butting heads back and forth while the deceiving dopy dude seems to skate. He slides into being one of the crowd in the audience, winning his bro points for being the singular self in the house who hooked up with two contestants. He skates, in part,[13] because what the new lover and the heartbroken ex want is not *him* (he's usually the most vapid of people) but the recognition of their own exceptional and singular selves. They want to be the star of the house.

Even outside the exaggerated space of reality TV, the pain of the ex-lover is clear. If you said I was exceptionally special, like none of the others, then

13. The other part is the double standard that stretches far back into our sexist societies.

how can you be back with one of the others? This is just what Alanis Moris-
sette and Taylor Swift reveal in their classic break-up songs.

Onto the Paradoxical Path

This talk of lovers and specialness indicates that the self is now the beacon
of exceptionality, and therefore bears that weight. It is not an art form or creation (not mystery or epiphany) that holds the weight of exceptionality, but
only the self. Inside a society of singularities, where selves are made indispensable not by doing things but by curating independent optimized selves, the
supposed free self must race to cross a line and be known as an exceptional
lover, worker, and even friend. Exceptionality makes her indispensable as a
worker (or lover or friend) in a neoliberal aesthetic economy.

Reckwitz calls all of this paradoxical. I'd call it impossible. Why? *Expectation*. Expectation makes this drive for exceptionality paradoxical. There
is an expectation that lovers, children, and workers (even companies) be exceptional. Somehow the normal, expected way of being inside the expressive
creativity dispositif of cutthroat neoliberalism is to be an exceptional self.
Everyone must be exceptional to not be a loser! Therein lies the impossible
paradox. How can exceptional even mean exceptional if *everyone* is exceptional, if we expect exceptionality from everyone? It's not just a paradox but a
sharp contradiction. Exceptional, after all, means you're the exception to the
rest. To be special is to have some quality almost no one else possesses. But if
exceptionality is expected from every lover, child, or worker in an expressive
creativity dispositif, how can there be anything like exceptionality? It will
take a constant state of permanent innovation at the deepest level of the self
to find and maintain this expected exceptionality.

Just as companies are expected to stay exceptional by taking on a state
of permanent innovation to survive in neoliberalism, so too is the self. This
creates an odd marriage in our time, which leads to never-ending quarrels.
Both sides in this rocky marriage are united over the centrality of permanent innovation and the expectation of exceptionality. On one side, some
think this permanent innovation must be lodged in unregulated markets.
Others see permanent innovation as necessary in identity constructions. The
unregulated-market advocates and the identity-construction activists couldn't
live without the other, though they violently fight. The commitment to permanent innovation, in different forms, keeps them contentiously together. The

unregulated-market advocates tend to hate the idea of identity fluidity. The identity activists despise the corporate overreach for profits. But both accept that some form of permanent innovation is necessary inside this expressive creativity dispositif.

Nonetheless, the issue of the paradox of exceptionality remains, no matter which side you identify with in this tense marriage. How can we expect every lover, child, and worker to be exceptional?

The Subjective Expectation of Exceptionality

Expecting a broad-reaching exceptionality, I suppose, is possible at the subjective level by sidestepping the harsh paradox and turning inward. Subjectively, we can expect each person to consider themselves to be exceptional. With enough self-esteem and a dogmatic ethic of authenticity, we can drive for each individual to embrace their own self as exceptional. This is often what it means in late modernity to love yourself. It doesn't mean accepting that there is indeed a reality outside of you that claims and cherishes you. It means accepting that your self is exceptional, if only to you. You love yourself because you accept your self. And if you're singularly exceptional—if you truly believe that your self is exceptional, esteeming your self—only then can you believe you deserve love.

This logic opens up a whole genre of books (memoirs), podcasts, bloggers, and Twitter threads of exceptional people telling their followers to be gentle with themselves, to accept their selves, and to recognize that their own self is uniquely exceptional (though never as exceptional as the personality with all the followers who's telling you to love your self). Your self is assumed to be the ground of its own being, so much so that your self can affirm itself as exceptional enough to deserve love from your self. It's a dizzying circle.

We often find ourselves trapped, with no clear way out of the back-and-forth spin. We continue to assume that exceptionality (not grace or mercy from another being, from the great divine other) is the impetus for love and acceptance. The trick in a society of singularities is *not* to reach for something transcendent or other that could upend the tyranny of the arms race for exceptionality. Instead, the goal is to somehow, with only the power of the self, subjectively accept your self as exceptional. Which creates an odd, backward kind of understanding of acceptance and love. This understanding traps many of us in its illogic. But somehow it's coherent enough that the shadow of this society of singularities, this neoliberal aesthetic economy, and this expressive creativity dispositif reaches so far that we can't see beyond the edges of its shade.

To escape this trap and step out beyond its shadow, we would have to admit that we never accomplished this utopian world of subjectively maintained exceptionality. While we yearn for every self to subjectively embrace itself as exceptional, it has not been achieved.[14] Schools have tried by affirming that each individual student is unique and singular. Each student has their own way of being who they feel like they are (bullying is zero tolerance, and some schools even allow grading to be done by the student). In a society of singularities, being super odd or weird can be a valuable strategy to cover for a lack of talent. Or maybe it is a talent. But it's a talent with no substance other than the ability to claim exceptionality by a bold expression of singular uniqueness. Similarly, for generations now, every player in little league or U7 soccer gets a trophy and a ribbon. We want no child to feel badly that they are not exceptional and therefore stop dreaming of being a singular star.

We have asked these societal structures to affirm the subjective affirmation of everyone's exceptionality. We've implanted in schools and sports programs the assumption that as long as the individual is affirmed in their uniqueness, they can at least subjectively embrace that they are one of a kind, knowing their true self. But still so many people feel stuck, not sure if they have done enough to love themselves, not sure they truly feel exceptional, insecure in their specialness.

The Necessity of the Social, Where the Subjective Goes to Die

This universal exceptionality (hear again the biting contradiction) of all subjective individuals is theoretically considered to be possible (e.g., if each person lives their uniqueness to its fullest), but it has never been accomplished in actuality. Despite efforts to embed such an imagination in our children through schools and sports, we have not lowered depression, anxiety, self-harm, mental illness, or medication use; rather, rates have actually increased.

14. There is something deep within the Christian tradition that claims that all human beings are special, or have value. But what determines this is not the self's own exceptionalness (in many traditions, the self is caught in the paradox of its own sin) but the special found outside the self. The self is special not because of what it does or can do but because God loves all selves, saving all selves, and meeting all selves in love and acceptance. What makes a self exceptional is the transcendent reality of a personal God who acts outside the self to save the self.

In practice, this idea of universal exceptionality has not produced a greater sense of self-acceptance and confidence in society. The feeling of exceptionality is not a reality that can be produced only subjectively. I'd argue that no emotions are constituted purely subjectively or even completely internally. But even if some emotions, such as contentment, could be internally produced, exceptionality is not one. You cannot *feel* exceptional without being in discourse with a larger community or collective. Exceptionality (to be exceptional) can have coherence only socially. Exceptional people are labeled such because they exceed the talent, depth, wisdom, or expression of others in their society. The label "exceptional" demands comparison; it works only over and against something else. Competition against something or someone outside the self is an inherent component.

Reckwitz wants us to see the heart of this biting contradiction. Inside a society of singularities, we glorify exceptionality because it is the sure sign that a self has crossed the threshold into singularity (we love our stars!). But we value exceptionality so much we've come to expect it not only from our own self but also from our children, lovers, and, most importantly for our argument, workers. Remember, it is through work, and workers, that this backwash is carried into the church.

Reckwitz explains that this drive for exceptionality inside an expressive creativity dispositif actually becomes the shape of the new middle class. A society of singularities doesn't eliminate class strife; it actually adds an intense new dimension to it. Reckwitz says, "By now, we have gradually come to realize that the . . . singularization of late-modern society [has] brought about not the end, but rather the beginning, of a new class society."[15] Inside a society of singularities and its necessity to be exceptional, the middle class itself flips from being what Reckwitz calls *leveled* to *cultural*. Whereas Keynesianism produced and supported a leveled middle class, a society of singularities inside neoliberalism creates a culturalized middle class, thereby shrinking the size of the middle class.

Exceptionality and the Middle Class: Welcome to the Culture War

In a society that drives toward the general over the particular, the middle class can grow and expand, as it did under Eisenhower and Johnson. The middle class expanded because economic opportunities, housing options, and

15. Reckwitz, *Society of Singularities*, 200.

access to loans and health care were generalized (for most people, notably white people, with the exclusion of African Americans). Rationalization and standardization made these realities *generally* available to a large swath of the public (the GI Bill, for instance, generalized higher education). The barriers that kept people from flowing into the middle class were leveled. Such a focus on *generalization* and *leveling* in the 1950s and 1960s allowed the middle class to grow exponentially.

But since the mid-1980s, the middle class has been shrinking. The middle class contracts inside the neoliberalism of an expressive creativity dispositif because leveling is attacked and framed as an affront on freedom (the freedom to be singular). It's not just corporate greed that attacks this leveling and shrinks the middle class. What also plays a major part is the imposed cultural-ization (the idea that you must walk, talk, and dress the right way and like the right things), which creates insatiable drives for singularity. In other words, in addition to profit mongering, the middle class's own acceptance of a certain view of the good life bound in a view of a singular self also contributes to the shrinking of the middle class (I'll circle back to this in the next section).

Inside a society of singularities, people oppose the general so they can seek the exceptional. They stand against generalization and therefore will not support most of the leveling strategies used in Keynesianism to expo-nentially expand the middle class. *The new middle class is constituted not by structural access but by a cultural ethos.* Being middle class is no longer correlated with your line of work but with the ways you express your self and its drive for singularity culturally. The new middle class is constituted by its approximation to singularity.

Therefore, the new middle class, unlike the middle class of the 1950s and 1960s, is now completely a *cultured* class. In the mid-twentieth century (and before), only aristocrats were fundamentally bound as a cultural class. Not so now. The new middle class is fully culturalized.[16] Those in the new middle class seek to live in exclusive and singular neighborhoods, own unique things, travel to original places, signal the right virtues, and overall embrace the marks of exceptionality. Inside this deep competition, what is important is not

16. Reckwitz adds, "In conjunction with this, the new middle class has also turned food, homes, travel, bodies, and the upbringing of children into objects of singularization. The mem-bers of this class now desire and expect a unique eating experience, a unique neighborhood, unique physical experience, and unique children who attend unique schools. This, too, has given rise to conflicting dynamics of singularization and standardization." Reckwitz, *Society of Singularities*, 224.

expanding access to add to the middle class but a drive to shrink the middle class by guarding middle-class boundaries using culturalized measures. The competition in the suburbs is real! It's hard for those left out of this shrinking middle-class space to *not* feel the sharp cultural derision of exclusion.

If the middle class has become culturalized, there should be little surprise that our politics have become culturalized. Since the mid-twentieth century, the middle-class vote has been the coveted vote. Yet inside a culture of singularity, politics is no longer about who can level or provide access but rather who affirms and recognizes your singularity. Which politician affirms your self by bearing the marks of your culturalization? When the middle class becomes culturalized by the drive for singularity and leveling becomes unwanted, politics becomes fully emotional and completely felt.[17] You vote for who represents not your general interest but your own sense of culturalization. You vote not for policies but for exceptional, singular personalities who mirror, in one way or another, your own sense (or grievance) of singularity.[18]

For example, you vote against Hillary Clinton even if her policies would level things for you. You vote against her because you feel hatred toward her. She represents the new middle class that excludes by culturally deriding your self (the deplorables!). Hillary's way of being her singular self (the way she expresses her supposed exceptionality) reminds you of all those elite, culturalized middle-class excluders who look down on you, like your sister-in-law. Inside this new shrinking middle class, it's not the ultra-rich who you despise but those new middle-class haters. Those latte-drinking, NPR-listening jerks who act like they're better than you, always telling you you're just basic and ignorant.[19] They tell you that your own culturalization is generic. In response,

17. For more on this, see Jonathan Haidt, *The Righteous Mind: Why Good People Are Divided by Politics and Religion* (New York: Vintage, 2012).

18. Reckwitz says further, "First, in the society of singularities, the 'grand narrative' of political progress has in many respects been replaced by the 'minor narratives' of (private) success and of the (private) good life. Paradigmatic of this is the lifestyle model of the new middle class, which, as we have seen in detail, is oriented toward successful self-actualization—here, to some extent, normative ideals are realized on the level of the particular and not on that of the general. Second, the temporal structure of late-modern society, as regards both its social fields and its ways of life, is fundamentally oriented toward the present, so that systematic future processing, which is characteristic of progress-oriented societies, is no longer as prevalent. Late modernity is governed by a radical regime of novelty, which is concerned with the present moment; it is not oriented toward long-term innovation and revolution, but rather toward the affectivity of the here and now." Reckwitz, *Society of Singularities*, 312.

19. Back in 1995, Christopher Lasch pointed to this coming reality in his book *The Revolt of the Elites and the Betrayal of Democracy* (New York: Norton, 1995).

you wrap yourself in the Americana they are too good for, embracing as yours all the discarded cultural forms that the new middle class despises. You drive a gas-guzzling truck, accessorize with the flag, and oppose all the high-minded ways the new middle class and their media talk.[20] You cross every politically correct boundary because those are the coded ways they've used to determine who is culturalized enough to be open to exceptional singularity and therefore part of the new middle class. And thus the culture war goes hot, fought on the very ground of the boundaries of the middle class.

What better candidate than Donald Trump for those pushed out of, and therefore despising, the new middle class? He was perfect because he was anything but part of the new middle class (even if he was rich). Even better, Trump violated all the cultural sensibilities of those new middle-class snobs who were happy to call the excluded ignorant, bland, and painfully basic. To watch Trump crash through every line of the new middle class's culturalization was too delicious to not vote for. Few who voted for him really cared whether Trump and his party wanted to return to the leveling that would benefit them. They didn't care because in a society of singularities, the war is not fought at the structural level but the cultural level (which explains why conservative evangelicals stayed loyal to him).

But I suppose this conversation is getting too intense. So let's pivot.

The Need to Be Exceptional

To not miss the forest for the trees, let's swivel away from the theater of politics. We can actually see this culturalization most poignantly by looking at educational opportunities. The cutthroat competition around the education of children reveals the new culturalization of the middle class and its tacit desire to shrink, not expand. Inside the new culturalized middle class, it is anathema

---

20. Reckwitz provides texture, saying, "In late modernity as a whole, the underclass seems like a locus of 'bad' culture that has no value but is instead problematic or even threatening, on account of its lack of education and cultural competencies; its bad eating habits and health; its bad parenting, neighborhoods, and schools; its difficult youth; its backward notions of masculinity and femininity; and, finally, its problematic political views. Culturalization means, above all, aestheticization and ethicization, and although the negative culturalization of the underclass certainly takes place in an aesthetic register (in the sense that the tastes of the underclass are perceived as insignificant or vulgar), it occurs all the more prominently on the level of ethics: seemingly lacking the features of a *good* life, the underclass's way of life is regarded as a composite of *bad* characteristics, from its eating habits and parenting style to its politics." Reckwitz, *Society of Singularities*, 258–59.

to level educational opportunities *if* it risks your own child's opportunity to make it into an elite university and therefore wear the marks of exceptional singularity. Boundary-keeping is intense in this new culturalized middle class.

This imagination, coupled with the deregulation of neoliberalism, works in tandem to shrink the middle class. The shrinking middle class is often blamed on the corporate greed of the controllers of neoliberalism. There is perhaps deserved blame here. But the shrinking middle class is also caused by the more progressive acceptance that the self is an individualized project that can be accomplished only by finding the recognition of exceptionality. This, too, does its part in making the leveled structures of a growing middle class seem morally repulsive.[21] When you're trying to cultivate your child's singularity, you can't support things that might level educational opportunities. (For example, if the public schools in your neighborhood ranked poorly, you would put your child in a private school, even though you support the idea of public education. Or, if the school wants to expand bussing and bring in students from outside your neighborhood, you are concerned about what that will do to test scores and class sizes and your child's education.) You are behind universal public school education as an idea—that's what good culturalized middle-class people do—but *not* as an actuality if it threatens your child's shot at exceptionality.[22]

21. In my mind, a true recovery of socialism, or something like socialism in health care and educational opportunity, social safety net, and so on, will need a spiritual revolution as much as an economic one. The culturalization that the left supports undercuts its desire to see the change they hope for. Their own idealizing of the self ends up opposing their economic and structural hopes. The self will need transformation, being freed from its drive for exceptionality and its fetishizing of singularity, if we are ever to return to a growing middle class. It's little surprise that the middle class shrinks when mainline faith traditions trade in a theological conception of the self for the dominant culturalized idea of singularity.

22. Reckwitz pushes this further, saying, "The field of educational sociology has shown that, since the 1980s, the new middle class has developed a demanding parenting style that can be described as 'intensive parenthood.' Despite the fact that these are often dual-income families, they have become child-centric to a historically unprecedented extent. The idea is that the uniqueness of individual children should be promoted as much as possible. Beyond fostering their children's emotional, social linguistic, and cognitive-argumentative competencies, parents in the new middle class are also expected to provide them with a number of diverse inspirations. Annette Lareau has referred to this educational strategy as 'concerted cultivation.' We read to our children, take them to museums, go on faraway trips with them, teach them how to interact in socially 'appropriate' ways, and introduce them to art, music, foreign languages, and nature." *Society of Singularities*, 239. Reckwitz continues, saying, "Children have therefore become prominent objects of post-bourgeois status investment. In order for them to achieve status in the society of singularities, formal education is, of course, a necessary and indispensable condition. At the same time, as we have already seen, it is not enough in itself to guarantee success

Ultimately, these parents of the new culturalized middle class demand that teachers, coaches, and tutors recognize, cultivate, and hone their child's singular, exceptional self. They have to demand this, because they sense that it's *the* way to assure their child's security and meaning inside a shrinking middle class and an economy of cutthroat permanent innovation. If only the indispensable worker can survive a state of permanent disruption and insecurity, then only the exceptional child can turn into the indispensable worker. Therefore, even a five-year-old child needs to be extra (extra talented, extra interesting, extra confident) so they can avoid the death mark of being basic inside the aesthetic economy of neoliberalism. Only the exceptional selves survive. If we want what's best for our children, if the new middle-class parents want them to thrive in an aesthetic economy, we must *expect* exceptionality, demanding that schools and teams include only fellow exceptionality-seekers.

No wonder anxiety and depression are spiking at lower and lower ages. The paradoxical expectation of exceptionality is hard to cope with. It's hard to be in a state of permanent innovation as a seven-year-old, seeking exceptional singularity for your self.

Evaluation and the Cancer of Innovation

The anxiety for fifty-five-year-olds or five-year-olds in late modernity is real. The anxiety is tangible because in a society of singularities, where there is a demanding expectation that everyone is to be exceptional, evaluation becomes ubiquitous. Who can avoid anxiety when you're in a constant state of assessment? When your self is always performing for an audience, even an audience of your own self? In a society of singularities where exceptionality is expected, you're always checking in with your self, wondering, doubting, and testing if your self really is exceptional or special enough to receive love and acceptance, even from your own self. Evaluation is so pervasive that it moves at a frenzy both internally and externally, imposing constant appraisal on both your self and on everyone and everything you encounter. A society of singularities born from an expressive creativity dispositif and its neoliberal aesthetic

---

in the volatile knowledge and culture economy, so that informal cultural capital has become essential as well. The latter is conveyed above all through one's family background, and thus it follows that early-childhood personal development has become such a crucial asset in today's portfolios of human capital." *Society of Singularities*, 240.

economy equates *evaluation as the very shape of life itself*. Particularly in the new middle class, inside the drive for singularity, selves evaluate nonstop.

It has become essential to evaluate everything all the time according to the measure of singularity. Everything in a neoliberal aesthetic economy is measured by its exceptional singularity. There becomes a demand on every self to sift through loads and loads of things, people, places, and ideas, evaluating them for their approximation to singularity. "That's stupid!" "She's so unoriginal!" "I hate the colors of this place!" "Who would go to Cancun? That's so high school!" "I don't know . . . he's just . . . ew." "This shop is so weird, it's awesome." "Did you get that app? It's so clunky." "Who wears a shirt like that to a place like this?" "Look at them; ugh, they're so superficial." Eye roll. Eye roll. And more eye rolls. The eye roll (and its digital friend, the emoji) is now the shortcut evaluation needed in the accelerating pace to be a singular self through your constant assessment and adjustment.[23]

With all of this in mind, it is no wonder *Queer Eye* is a hit show. It takes the masters of evaluation and uses their powers on behalf of basic selves. The evaluation superheroes help each self on the show find their singular style by turning the self's wardrobe, haircut, and home from bland to fabulous. They help the individual remake the self by erasing the points that attract negative valuation (often equated as a spiritual cleansing). Those points that so clearly scream unexceptional are exorcised. Those areas couldn't help but attract negative valuation, but the guys from *Queer Eye* can cast them out. Inside a society of singularities where evaluation is a must and an always (even becoming a sport), the compliment becomes the highest (and at times most vapid) form of social discourse. Observe how friends, even acquaintances, greet each other: "Oh my gosh, you look amazing!" "I love that top!" "Oh, you're so cute!" "Dude, you look fit; great to see you." "You ready to go to this place? It's the best, and no one knows about it." The examples could go on.

To take us back to the beginning of the chapter, think about the expectation of exceptionality and the evaluation in light of Fiona. Fiona is the most creative person that Russ knows. Not just because she creates stuff but even

23. Reckwitz continues, "Cultural goods frequently have a narrative and hermeneutic quality in that they take the form of narratives that are meaningful to their recipients. That is, cultural goods often tell stories—and this cannot be stressed enough. A narrative can become a good directly—in the form of a novel, a film, or a journalistic article. Or a complex web of storytelling can be spun around a good (whether driven by marketing or not): the story of design style or a designer associated with a certain object, or the multifaceted story of a city that can be experienced during a visit to it." Reckwitz, *Society of Singularities*, 88.

more so because she has a keen eye and skilled way of evaluating. She's a thought leader, a creative juggernaut, because her skills of evaluation are sharp. She's so good at evaluating what does and doesn't cross the threshold of being unique and exceptional. She can quickly and articulately evaluate a person, shop, website, and much more for its exceptional singularity.

Evaluation is both why she quit and why it hurt so badly when she did. Fiona quit because she assessed that the team's innovation would never meet her own standard of singularity. The team wasn't near the level of exceptional. She didn't want—she couldn't allow her own singular self—to associate with something she herself valued so lowly. Who would she be if she did? How would others, also in a constant state of evaluation, think of her and evaluate her own creative self? (Exceptionality can *never* stay within the boundaries of the subjective.) Her departure from Russ's team was a double blow, because it was a clear act of evaluation. Anyone who stayed needed to admit, and therefore bear, the negative evaluation of the group's idea, but even more so, of the group itself.

Reckwitz explains that the company needs to be particular, even singular, in what it sells and even more so in how it feels (its culture). If workers are to stay committed to the firm, the company's culture as much as its products must cross some threshold of uniqueness. Russ had to admit that Fiona quit not simply because the innovative idea (the product) was lacking. She quit because of the culture. The team itself wasn't unique or singular enough to keep Fiona from worrying that her investment on the team was staining her with the mark of being basic (i.e., general, regular, standardized).

The grant leaders at the seminary didn't recognize that inviting the church and its teams into innovation unknowingly pushed the church further into the trappings of singularity. It forced on the young adults yet another locale where they would need to be evaluated. Innovation simply can't be done without evaluation. Innovation is culturally coherent (and lauded) because of the centrality of evaluation, which is ignited by innovation's search for the holy grail of singular exceptionality.

Innovation is a process of making corporate cultures and product lines exceptional. Inside an expressive creativity dispositif and its aesthetic economy, only those cultures and products evaluated as singularly exceptional thrive. And innovation manifests these exceptional singularities and can receive the high capital of evaluation. The high capital of evaluation promises the capital of money in an aesthetic economy. The church may need an infusion of creativity. But we've failed to see that the kind of creativity embedded in the drive for singularity idolizes the self. While it may drive the church to new ideas and initiative, it will also give it a theological and formative cancer.

The cancer is aggressive, because inside an expressive creativity dispositif and a neoliberal aesthetic economy, the primary source of the self is the self's own uniqueness. This is the chemical by-product of embracing innovation and entrepreneurship across the whole of our lives. While it allows for a direct way to infuse our institutions, congregations, and selves with purpose, it nevertheless induces an unhealthy concern for the performance of the self, a competitive drive (mixed with anxiety) that the self be uniquely singular. Innovation and entrepreneurship, unless deeply and directly theologically judged and brought back to life, impose and even demand a creativity-induced *incurvatus in se* (turning in on oneself).[24]

An expressive creativity dispositif and aesthetic economy produce admiration for subjects who are overly obsessed with themselves. Inside this dispositif and its economy, we somehow come to think it is admirable to be overly attentive to our style, manner, and received recognition. We now believe that this self-obsession is the core mark of creativity. The danger of innovation for the church is that it becomes very hard to disconnect innovation from the drives to perform an exceptional self. It's hard to disconnect innovation and entrepreneurship from being about giving all your energy to finding your meaning in curating a self that is performing its singularity exceptionally.

Russ felt embarrassed. As the teams from each congregation of the grant gathered at the seminary to present their innovations and complete their projects, Russ sat at an empty table. It was just Russ and one other young adult who represented their congregation. Everyone else had quit or had a conflict on the day of the presentation. Russ swallowed his pride and made it through. He felt neither creative nor singularly unique as he presented their idea. It was fine, but not special. The idea didn't make him or anyone on his team or the congregation admirable and therefore singular. Worse, Russ felt like through it all he was missing something. He felt misdirected in regard to

24. This is Luther's very definition of sin.

ministry. Somehow the process had produced the opposite of what he wished for Fiona and his other young adults. But all he could do now was sit with his discontent.

Yet, while doing so, a strange sensation came over him.

As the presentations were coming to an end, having listened to a dozen ways of bringing innovation and entrepreneurship into the church, Russ had the temptation to strip himself naked and throw his money out the window.

9

Standing Naked against Money

Russ resisted the temptation. A police escort off the seminary property and a psych evaluation didn't seem like the best way to end the day. But still Russ couldn't stop thinking about Francis. It was in a classroom down the hall that he had first learned about Francis's naked money throwing. The class Russ took his final year of seminary on Francis of Assisi was one of his favorites. Even well into his first years in ministry, Russ had no idea what practical relevance the course had for his ministry. But now, sitting inside the crater of the discontent of innovation and entrepreneurship, there seemed to be something to learn from Francis and his naked, money-throwing ways.

If we can take a step back, we may be able to leap forward. By examining the very period when money arrived, and exploring its spiritual impact, we might spot some ways to respond to the inflation of the self in our own time. Following the wisdom from this medieval period can help us respond to the ways innovation and entrepreneurship, inside an expressive creativity dispositif and a neoliberal aesthetic economy, apotheosize the self. To step back in order to leap forward and respond to the self's obsession with singularity, we'll start with Francis and then spend most of our time with those mystical Dominicans who cleared the ground for Martin Luther.

Naked Francis

Francis of Assisi was born in the thirteenth century into a moneyed family. His father was a cloth dealer. As a young adult, Francis himself began in the trade. But while learning the trade and helping his father build his fortune, Francis was overcome with dreams and visions. Soon he was spending most of his free time praying in a cave. In that cave, he was wrestling. His first biographer, Thomas of Celano, explains that he would come out of that cave exhausted from an intense tussle.[1] Francis appears to have been wrestling with the call of two gods: the God of the Bible and the god of money.

One day Francis hooked a cart full of fine cloth to a horse and traveled ten miles to Foligno. There he sold all the cloth, and then the horse and the cart. Francis walked back to Assisi with a pouch filled with coins. On the outskirts of town, he entered a small church. He begged the priest to take the money and allow him to stay. The priest refused the money but invited Francis to stay as long as he wished. Upon the priest's refusal, Francis took the great deal of money and threw it out the window.

Francis's father couldn't find him or, worse, the money for a month. When he finally found Francis, he wasn't attached to the money. His father, along with many others in Assisi, figured that Francis had gone mad. His father took him home and locked him in chains. Eventually, Francis's parents relented and said if he returned the money and went to visit the bishop, they would allow him to follow whatever path was before him.

Francis found the money where it had landed in the shrubbery beneath the church window, and with his father he went to visit the bishop. Maybe as an ultimatum, maybe as a way to scare Francis straight, Francis's father explained to the bishop that they stood before him so that Francis could renounce his inheritance and any rights to his father's money. This was the moment for Francis to equivocate, recant, and return to his father and his money—his father's ultimate wish. Instead, Francis stripped himself completely naked, releasing himself from even the cloth on his back. Francis chose to be in the world naked with God, rather than follow the money.

The Invention of Money

The use of money had been building in the West, but it didn't arrive in full until the twelfth century. At that point, the West entered a fully moneyed world. Other societies like the Romans and Babylonians had coins much earlier.[2]

1. Thomas of Celano, *Francis Trilogy: The Life of Saint Francis, The Remembrance of the Desire of a Soul, The Treatise on the Miracles of Saint Francis* (New City Press, 2004).
2. Lester Little gives some context, saying, "The first silver coin minted that was larger than the penny was the *grossus denarius*, equivalent usually to twelve pennies and variously

But in the West, it took until the middle of the medieval period for the whole of European society to run on money. The West was still centuries away from a capitalism that makes it a spiritual calling to gain extra. Nevertheless, the economic structures of society had shifted from a gift economy to a money economy (this would be the first move that would someday lead to capitalism).

Lester Little begins his fabulous book *Religious Poverty and the Profit Economy in Medieval Europe* with two stories of found gold. He uses these two stories to illustrate the shift from a gift economy to a profit economy in the medieval period. He explains that in the sixth century, King Gunthram of the Burgundians had a dream in which he was informed where a treasure of gold was hidden. He ordered his servants to dig exactly where the dream had foretold. Sure enough, he found gold, and more than he could have imagined. The king used all the gold to make a huge, opulent altar canopy that he gave as a gift to the sepulchre in Jerusalem. Little's point is that the treasure was used for the sake of a gift. The gift was how the king would bring glory to his own name. He had no thought to exchange it for services or goods, just for the glory of receiving and giving gifts. The gold's power was bound in what kind of gift it could be made into, to give and to obligate others who received the gift to give in return. The gold represented no other exchange value than the gift it could be forged into.

However, four centuries later—moving us closer to Francis's time and his moneyed father—Bishop Arnoul of Orleans took on the task of reconstructing the Cathedral of the Holy Cross. A devastating fire had ruined the cathedral and the whole town with it. As the masons were preparing the new foundation of the cathedral, they uncovered a huge cachet of gold. They took it to the bishop and, unlike King Gunthram, Bishop Arnoul never considered turning it into a gift. Instead, the bishop liquidated the gold into money, using the profits of the gold to finance the reconstruction—not to directly win favor of God, kings, or tribal leaders. The gold brought money, and money bought labor and material. Unlike the gift of King Gunthram, the gold, now turned into money, could represent many things it wasn't. The liquidation was so successful in producing profits that the gold paid not only for the reconstruction of the Holy Cross but also for "several other churches in need of repair."[3]

---

designated as groat, grooten, groschen, gros, grosso, ducat, solidus, or shilling. Venice issued the first grosso (but worth twenty-four pennies) in the year 1202. The launching of this coin was probably stimulated by the payment of 51,000 marks of silver to the Venetians by the knights of the Fourth Crusade, who convened at Venice in 1201." Little, *Religious Poverty and the Profit Economy in Medieval Europe* (Ithaca, NY: Cornell University Press, 1978), 16.

3. Little, *Religious Poverty and the Profit Economy*, 3.

We use the same logic of this second story when we think about innovation in the church. Russ got the sense that innovation was our new gold. We hope to find an innovation like the booty of Bishop Arnoul. We seek to liquidate it for profits that can fund our under-resourced programs, buildings, staffs, and initiatives. Nowadays we don't hope workers find gold (though that'd be awesome!) as much as we hope to stumble upon a creative idea that could be parlayed into money (or its substitute) to fund our projects.

Lester Little explains the importance of these two stories of King Gunthram and Bishop Arnoul, saying, "In the first [story], the reconversion of treasure into yet another form of treasure is typical of the gift economy that flourished in the centuries following the Germanic migrations. The exchange of treasure for building materials and labour in the second [story], however, signals new modes of thought and behavior upon the very threshold of the eleventh century."[4] Starting in the eleventh century and building momentum through the twelfth and thirteenth centuries, the West arrives at an economy of money.

Yet something interesting happened. In the wake of this arrival of a new money economy came a building beckoning for reform. New voices arose calling for a return to God and renewed faithfulness. Particularly in Francis's thirteenth century and after, when the money economy was present throughout all of Europe, calls for reform began to vibrate at high frequency. These humming tremors for religious and spiritual reform became a mainstay of Latin Christendom.[5] And they've never left us.

At first glance, money and reform seem unconnected. But they can't be. The more that money soaked into Western society, the louder the voices of reform became. In the early thirteenth century, Francis got naked, tossing money out the window as an act of reform. Yet most of these reforming voices, even Francis himself, wouldn't necessarily make money the direct target of their critique, though almost every reforming voice was concerned with usury (a way of profiting off the money-debt of others). What's clear is that with the arrival of money came a spirit of reform. This was happening long before the Reformation in the sixteenth century. The reforming voices hummed for more than two hundred years before Martin Luther. And after Luther, this buzz of reform has been continuous in the West, in one way or another.

4. Little, *Religious Poverty and the Profit Economy*, 3.
5. For a longer cultural history of the reforms, see Tom Holland, *Dominion: How the Christian Revolution Remade the World* (New York: Basic Books, 2019), chaps. 10–13.

Reform and Money

The reforming spirit of the Latin West (a spirit that the Eastern/Greek church never quite shared[6]) was present, in major part, because of money. The reforming spirit of the West came to the foreground when the money economy arrived. For example, without money and the shift to a profit economy, the reform movements coming out of monasteries, cathedral schools, universities, and even the creation of the new orders of friars (Franciscans, Dominicans, and Cistercians) would not have been possible. Money galvanized these reforming movements, with enough independence from the hierarchy of Rome or the crown to order themselves and speak their mind. The money of tuition fees, for instance, allowed both Franciscan and Dominican monks in Paris to become professors, accepting the money (coins) of tuition fees to probe Scripture and write essays on reform. Without money, the very functions and operations of the reforming spirit would have been much more difficult to come by.

But money did something more than just allow the reforming spirit to find its functional form in new orders, houses, and schools across the continent. Money also became the object or target of the reforming spirit itself. Many of these new orders, for example, renewed and radicalized vows of poverty. When Dominican friars traveled, they were not allowed to bring money or anything that could be sold. They traveled in poverty, surviving only on the gifts of other brothers and the faithful laity. The spirit of reform was ignited, in part, because the faithful sensed that money demanded sovereignty, devotion, continued contemplation, and even glory for itself. They sensed, like Francis, that they were being pulled between money and God. One of the two needed to be tossed out the nearest window.

Ultimately, they sensed that money called for things once given only to God. Money became a kind of sneaky rival god. Reform was needed because the people in a new moneyed economy could seek the coin with more devotion than they sought their God. Inside a gift economy, God was not rivaled by the exchange of gifts. God was the ultimate gift giver, exchanging or substituting one gift (God's crucified Son) for another (our forgiveness and devotion). Anselm (who died at the end of the gift economy in the beginning of the

6. I think one reason for this, which I'll explore more below, is how the mystical functions. The East has had more flush and consistent connection to mystical and apophatic elements of mystical tradition.

eleven century) reminded his people that God gave us God's own Son as a gift of substitution, for the sake of substituting exchange. This gift—like all gift exchanges—obligated us. Substitutionary atonement makes perfect sense inside a gift economy (much less so in a profit economy, hence the arrival of Abelard, and no sense at all inside the consumer economies of Keynesianism and the neoliberalism of modernity). For Anselm, we owed it to God, inside this gift substitution, to give God glory and obedience. Gift exchange as opposed to money (as the representation or stand-in for services, labor, and material goods) is easier to see as being ordered under God. When money becomes a representation for many things, bringing nearly anything (everything has a price!), then money has a way of rivaling God in our imaginations. At that point, constant reform appears necessary.

God and Money

Philip Goodchild shows how money can rival God in his insightful book *Theology of Money*.[7] Goodchild's argument is far too intricate to rehearse in detail here.[8] It will need to suffice to draw out just a few points on how money takes a godlike shape.

Goodchild explains that it's important to point out that money, unlike a gift, seems to be self-animating. Like God, particularly for the thirteenth-century person, money seems to move beyond and outside human volition. For a gift to animate a response and have coherence, it must represent, even reveal, the person behind the gift. Even the gift of a Secret Santa has its significance in the fact that some unknown person has given you something that has its value in being a gift from this hidden person. What makes Secret Santa fun is not the exchange value of the gift (usually the gift is capped at $20). Rather, the fun is in guessing who the person is behind the gift. A gift is not a gift without persons who give and receive the gift. Ultimately, a gift cannot be without personal volition animating the exchange.

7. Philip Goodchild, *Theology of Money* (Durham, NC: Duke University Press, 2009). Eugene McCarraher makes a similar point in his long cultural history of the metaphysic of money in American capitalism. See McCarraher, *The Enchantments of Mammon: How Capitalism Became the Religion of Modernity* (Cambridge, MA: Belknap, 2019).

8. For the classic text on money, see Georg Simmel, *The Philosophy of Money* (1900; repr., London: Routledge, 2011). For a little, more contemporary book on money, see Geoffrey Ingham, *Money* (London: Polity, 2020).

But money seems to do the impossible. Money has an exchange power that appears to exist outside and even beyond the human power to will significance. Money has what Goodchild calls a "spectral" (i.e., ghostly or even supernatural) power to it.[9] Money does its work, animating itself, seemingly without (or at least beyond) any human willing. Prices are set by invisible hands (to point to Adam Smith's language in the eighteenth century[10]). Money, unlike a gift, is self-propelling. Money has a power beyond personal wills. Money seems to do something only God could do before money's arrival.[11]

I suppose that's not completely true. Natural phenomena like lightning storms, floods, and comets were animated forces far beyond human wills. But even so, it was assumed that such phenomena rested squarely within the animating will of God (or the devil). Plus, such natural phenomena, even if far outside of human wills, had little to no access to the deepest elements of our human personal will. A lightning storm may shake us to our core, leading us to plead with God to save us. But even such natural phenomena didn't seem to adapt to or even shape our deepest internal desires (storms and rain didn't seem to know or shape the heart and soul).

Money, on the other hand, like God, does just this. Money has a direct way of getting deeply within us. It seems to exist—animating itself—beyond our will, and in turn it seems to possess the power to get so deeply inside our will that money can take the shape of our will, becoming our will and directly forming our desires. Money, like only God or the devil, can overtake our desire, even over and against our will.[12] Augustine, *the* patron saint of the Western Latin

9. Goodchild explains, "It is easy to observe how this shift naturally leads to secularization and a direct opposition between God and money. Where God promises eternity, money promises the world. Where God offers a delayed reward, money offers a reward in advance. Where God offers himself as grace, money offers itself as a loan. Where God offers spiritual benefits, money offers tangible benefits. Where God accepts all repentant sinners who truly believe, money may be accepted by all who are willing to trust in its value. Where God requires conversion of the soul, money empowers the existing desires and plans of the soul. Money has the advantages of immediacy, universality, tangibility, and utility. Money promises freedom and gives a down payment on the promise of prosperity." Goodchild, *Theology of Money*, 12.

10. For a helpful overview of the epoch-making thinker, see Craig Smith, *Adam Smith* (London: Polity, 2020).

11. Only God could do this before because in that time, à la Charles Taylor, they lived not in a universe but in a cosmos, meaning all natural phenomena were understood as being under God's control. See Taylor, *A Secular Age* (Cambridge, MA: Belknap, 2007), 25–38.

12. Little says sharply, "Attitudes towards money did not shift abruptly from one of awe before precious treasure to one of habitual acceptance of it as a practical, everyday tool. In something of an intervening stage, money was seen as an instrument of exchange that had devil-like, magical powers of luring people and then of corrupting them. The traditional theological

Church (who was having a revival in the middle of the medieval period), taught all the reforming voices of the thirteenth and fourteenth centuries (particularly the Dominicans) that desire was essential. Lightning may impose on us a desire to live, but money has a way of taking the shape of the will, forming our deepest desires. Money becomes inextricable from, even the catalyst for, security, purpose, meaning, power, love, and hate. Money, like God, can uniquely get into the heart or soul (pointing to another significant Augustinian theme).[13] Before the arrival of money, only God or the devil could do this.[14] This made the fourteenth century in the West particularly a time to become aware of and contemplate the inner self. The theologians who did so—inspiring Luther and the Reformation—will have something important to teach us as we confront the ways late-modern work inflates the self in the pursuit of singularity.

But before we can get there, we must further examine money's unique godlike character. Because money can impose itself on my will, shifting, framing, and forming my desires, it calls me—unlike a gift—to contemplate money continually. With a gift, I contemplate the person who has given or who promises the gift. Yet with money, my mind (heart or soul) is only on money. This is why some grandparents hate giving grandkids straight cash or even gift cards for birthdays or Christmas. Such transactions, which give American currency or Amazon dollars, seem to strip the personhood from the gift giver. When money is the gift, money (not the giver) floods the soul of the receiver. Unlike a gift, money demands that it be contemplated and reflected on over and against the person. For instance, when you're given straight cash, you rarely contemplate the gift of the person, rarely feel drawn to another by the object of the gift, but instead find your mind squarely on the money. You now need to think hard and long about what that money can get *you*. You need to put your mind on your money and consider how best to spend it, contemplating all the things it can conjure for you. In this small but powerful way, money makes you think more and more about money.

---

programme of the virtues and vices invested in avarice some of these same powers. The major sources of our knowledge about attitudes towards money include the writings about and representations of avarice, and an abundant satirical literature of the twelfth century complements these quasi-official viewpoints." Little, *Religious Poverty and the Profit Economy*, 35.

13. This sense of inwardness, so central to Augustine, is not as present in the East, which is another reason the reforming obsession wasn't shared beyond the West.

14. And often did. Taylor calls this assumption that something can get deeply inside of us, even touching our essence, the porous self (*Secular Age*, 38–40). My point is that in the medieval imagination money now has the power to get to the soul. And, honestly, it does for us as well.

Money can reach into us and shape our desires, but it is also self-animating outside of us. It's very powerful in that way. I find myself thinking about it without ceasing, as it imposes itself on my desires. And even if I wanted to *not* have my mind on money, I have to keep my eye on it, because while money imposes on the heart of my desires, it also moves beyond me. Therefore, I have to keep thinking about it, anticipating its spectral will and movement. I don't want to waste the opportunities (missing the sales and investments) that money gives me.

Money, suddenly and assuredly, gets me to worship it. I worship what I can't take my mind off. For what my mind is on is what my heart longs for (Matt. 6:21). Money demands, as Snoop Dogg saw long ago in Long Beach, that I have my mind on my money and my money on my mind. Inside this circle, my self, in turn, is inflated. My self becomes my own center, because money doesn't ask me to lose myself, but to make my self and its pursuits of more money essential to my being. My self, and how my self can win value in the money-induced arena of competition, becomes all that matters. I find myself wanting more money and more money. For what purpose? I'm not sure, but my mind is always on my money, and money is always on my mind. This means my own self, and what it can acquire, becomes the height of my desire. Money and a world based on money turns me in on my self. A profit economy always threatens to cause me to curve in on myself. It threatens to overinflate myself as my mind is on my money and money is on my mind. It tempts me to make myself everything and the only thing that matters.

Money and Its Spectral Ability to Inflate the Self

These are major claims about money's significance. It may help to take it one step further and peer directly at what specific dynamics allow money to have this spectral or pseudosupernatural power, and how this power leads to an inflation of the self. There are six dynamics to money worth exploring.[15] The first three impose the spectral nature on money. The last three do their work to inflate the self.

The first dynamic is that the value of money has a kind of transcendence to it.[16] Money's value is bound in an imagined assurance. The value of money

15. See Goodchild, *Theology of Money*, 12–13.
16. Goodchild, *Theology of Money*, 12.

(toward the end of the gift economy) was in its fine metals. The money had value because the gold that the coin was made of had value. I gave you a shovel because its value (in material and time) was judged to be concurrent with the gold or silver in the coin. But soon the coin and what it invisibly represented, not its fine metal, held the value. Your neighbor could give you ten silver shillings for a cow. As pure silver, the cow was worth much more. But you're not selling the cow for pure silver, but for the invisible value the money possesses. Though the pure silver that the money is made out of is not valuable enough to buy a cow, the transcendent/invisible worth of money is. You discern that the money's invisible value, which transcends the silver, is far more valuable than the cow; it could buy you a wagon or protection. It's a good deal for you! You can buy a lot of pure silver with the minimal silver of ten shillings.

For money to work, we must place our faith in its invisible value. Its invisible value is in what it can deliver. It takes a leap of faith to trust that coins received for a cow can give you something more valuable than the cow and its milk. The money can directly conjure up more than the cow and more than the materials that make up the coin. *Money takes faith*. Money's worth is related to the faith that people have in its invisible value. If people lose faith in money, it loses its value and prices inflate. It might then take twenty or even two hundred silver shillings to buy the same cow. It's perhaps little surprise that in the sixteenth century, Luther made faith the very location for encounter with God. People had lived nearly three hundred years having a kind of faith in money. But this faith, which Luther's father (like Francis's) ambitiously pursued and wanted his son to do the same, curved the self in on itself. Money has a transcendent value.

This moves us to the second dynamic of money. Money gives all things a universal value. Our example of the cow shows that "money is both a means of payment and a measure of prices."[17] The buyer of the cow must give (pay) the shillings. But what I pay for the cow is determined by the seller measuring the worth of the cow next to money. Money through its markets directly values everything next to itself.

In a moneyed economy, everything has a price. Money universally and completely has a say on all things, valuing their worth. This universal sense of value became radicalized exponentially in neoliberalism. Everything has

17. Goodchild, *Theology of Money*, 12.

a money value now, and everything is always and continually for sale (like public transport or health care or even people's debt!).

To acknowledge this shouldn't prevent us from recognizing something good here. Money's drive to universally measure the value of everything by its price in turn means its only discrimination is money. Money doesn't see anything else but money. Anyone from anywhere can buy anything (like all the top English football clubs) as long as they have the money. This is why racial justice and economic equality are so closely connected.[18] In a moneyed economy where everything can be bought, racist systems work hard to keep the people they oppress from having money (which is the very reason money was *the* longing and desire in the lyrics of Snoop Dogg and other early rap artists coming out of Reagan's America). Money's ability to measure the value of all things gives it a universal, nearly omnipresent, even omnipotent reach.

Because money has a transcendent value that universally measures payment and price, it is always in motion.[19] Your money must constantly be on your mind and your mind on your money, because money is always in motion. Money and its value move. It appears to act on its own—outside of human wills, as we've said. It's stressful to decide if you should pay those ten shillings for that cow, because sometime soon money will move the price. The value of the cow could go to seven shillings, or it could jump to seventy, but more than likely it will not stay the same price or value. Your job is to (you're winning if you) get the cow at a low enough price that it becomes an asset in the growth of your own money. If its value—again measured by money—goes up, you did well. If you can sell that cow or its calves for much more than you paid for it, you've successfully ridden the wave of money's constant motion. Money measures everything against itself and is therefore universal.

But now comes the third dynamic of money. Money demands anticipation of a coming future that never arrives. Money demands hope, expectation, and trust. Money has an "eschatological" orientation without rupture or

---

18. This is what Isabel Wilkerson is getting at so poignantly in her excellent book *Caste: The Origins of Our Discontent* (New York: Random House, 2020). She sees that the issues of America are better framed within the conception of caste (i.e., Black Americans placed in a low caste). It helps the reader understand structure and move away from subjective feelings.

19. Goodchild says further, "All other ends must be suspended until sufficient money is obtained for their realization. Money thus posits itself as the supreme being, the focus of attention and desire, the principle for the realization of capital projects. Money posits itself as God, the principle of all creation. Its hold over attention is the worship it demands. As long as the world is regarded from the perspective of exchange, the power of money is absolute." Goodchild, *Theology of Money*, 106.

apocalypse (if that's possible). It demands we look eagerly to the future, but it's a future that has no consummation or completion. Money's spectral (pseudosupernatural) nature directs us toward a future that we ultimately can never reach. We just remain in a state of constant innovation to run down money's spectral motion. We come into a future only to find that it now jumps us into another new future we need to race to catch up to.

Money never rests. Financial advising companies promise that they never rest because money never does. They make your restless money work for you. The ramification is that if your money never rests, neither should you. You need to race to grab hold of money's slippery value. You need to make sure you're the kind of self who can keep up with it. Money keeps us actively pursuing a future that will never arrive.

These three dynamics (money's transcendence, universality, and constant motion toward a moving goal) give money its spectral/pseudosupernatural power. They also do something to the self. These dynamics demand that the self have faith in the value of money, evaluating the world (and particularly the self) next to the value of exchange, and the race to keep up with the momentum of money, by keeping our mind (heart and soul) always on money. But with these three dynamics of money that give it a pseudosupernatural quality come three more dynamics to money that inflate the self by curving the self in on itself.

The fourth dynamic of money is that to possess a lot of money is to directly achieve power. The self with money is given a hit of power, able to influence and even manipulate structures and persons, because everything has its price. If everything has its price and if you have the means of meeting all those prices, your self feels like it has access to all things. That's a strong hit to inflate the self. No wonder twentysomething Silicon Valley billionaires and millionaires think they can solve any of the world's problems. Money has a way (if we're not careful) of opposing humility and despising magnanimity. The self can become petty as it sees all things as commodities, calculating their exchange value (it's for this same reason that Silicon Valley whiz-kid billionaires take expressivist spiritual turns, trying to have their cake and eat it twice). Money gives the self power and the illusion that the self is independently and uniquely powerful.

This brings us to the fifth dynamic of money. It instrumentalizes all relationships and connections.[20] It threatens to make the self a constant calculator

20. Daniel M. Bell (not the Daniel Bell of *The Cultural Contradictions of Capitalism*) says, "Under capitalism people exist for one another in an instrumental fashion; capitalism encourages us to view others in terms of how they can serve our self-interested projects. In the worst

of exchange value, always wondering, What am I getting out of this? This bleeds into all parts of society and culture, even the church. Our relationships become instrumentalized and therefore stripped of their true transcendent and revelatory possibility.[21] Money makes all things instrumental, measurable, and transactional.

The final dynamic of money is its imposing of debt. Because money's value transcends the coin, providing a universal value that is constantly in motion and producing power by the force of commodifying and instrumentalizing everything, it necessitates debt. Nearly everyone must bear debt in a moneyed economy. Some benefit from debt and others are trapped in it. But because of these other dynamics to money, debt becomes a necessity. The presence of debt demands that money be worshiped (no wonder the reforming voices speak against usury). When I've profited from another person's debt or find myself in debt (and even those profiting from debt are usually in debt to someone else), I can't help but keep my mind on money and money on my mind. I become hyperaware that I'm a self in debt. Inside debt, to keep my money on my mind and my mind on my money means keeping my mind always on my self. In debt my self yearns to make something out of itself, becoming overly concerned with my self. This outlook is necessary because it will be my self that frees my self from the debt that lays a weight on my self. Debt makes the weight of my lack of money pierce straight into my self. Debt prices the self, communicating a direct message of value. A self in debt is a self thirsting for salvation from the hand of money. If the self could squirm itself loose from its debt, it could, it is imagined, finally be a self that feels (or even is) free. (It

___

case, people are reified and so become commodities themselves—mere bodies to be exploited or consumed and then discarded; think of slavery, organ mining, or the sex trade, for example. In a less extreme case, we stand before one another merely as representations or owners of commodities that we seek to acquire. The capitalist market is nothing less than a Darwinian calculus of human lives, with the highly productive regarded as more valuable than others, who are esteemed less and hence may be sacrificed or abandoned. In a world dominated by commodities, persons come to be valued by the same criteria as commodities—marketability, profitability, and consumability." Bell, *The Economy of Desire: Christianity and Capitalism in a Postmodern World* (Grand Rapids: Baker Academic, 2012), 106.

21. Goodchild adds, "Yet money does not provide a source for social cohesion until it brings with it an obligation: the obligation of debt. If in religious life people renounce enjoyment to achieve spiritual goals, then in modern economic life people renounce their property, labor, and time in the pursuit of money. Modern secular life is ascetic like religious life, even if it has its moments of hedonism. Human flourishing is still ensured by a detour. A preoccupation with the conditions of one's life is now a preoccupation with money. Through its use in structuring everyday life and practice, money lends its shape to the categories of modern life and thought." Goodchild, *Theology of Money*, xv.

was inside of this kind of logic that Charles Hodge, in the nineteenth century, updated Anselm's substitutionary atonement to a concept of being in debt to God by sin, which shaped how most supporters think about it today.) Maybe you could even become a self free of debt to be the kind of self that is obsessed with the self as it makes money off the debt of other selves. Money makes debt necessary, and debt means my focus is always on my self.

In addition to money's so-called transcendence, universality and motion toward a future that never arrives are the way money turns us back to the self by giving power and the illusion of power, instrumentalizing all relationships, and through debt necessitating constant attention to the self. To illustrate how this all coalesces, Lester Little explains that the rise of anti-Semitism in Europe can be traced back directly to the arrival of the moneyed economy.[22] He explains that there is little evidence of scapegoating Jews until money arrives. But once it does—once Jews particularly become involved in banking in the new urban centers, giving loans and recording debts—hatred toward Jews escalates.[23] Money, and particularly debt, works to turn the self in on itself, leading us to hate other selves. Money and debt can lead to vicious, violent attacks on other selves in and through a deep awareness of the moneyed profit of these other selves. As money and debt turn the self in on itself, the self is tempted to hate otherness (we see this clearly in our own culture wars). It becomes easy to scapegoat others for putting our own self in debt and discontent. The arrival of the money economy brings a new awareness (and temptation) for the self, and one that reverberates all the way to Russ and his group.

Back to the Reforms

We can now return to the reforming movements of the Latin West in the thirteenth and fourteenth centuries. Having made our way through the dynamics of money, we can see more clearly why these reforming movements arose. The arrival of money did allow such groups to functionally operate. They needed money to receive tuition fees and support itinerant preachers. But while money assisted reform movements functionally, money also brought a theological and ministerial crisis. Money seemed to capture human desire

22. Little, Religious Poverty and the Profit Economy, 42–54.
23. This is also discussed in Lauren Winner, The Dangers of Christian Practice: On Wayward Gifts, Characteristic Damage, and Sin (New Haven: Yale University Press, 2018), 20–28.

and therefore inflate the self, particularly in the new urban centers. All the more reason, then, to push all the harder, *not* for a money economy to be destroyed (that was never going away) but for hearts and minds to return to God. People, and the church itself, needed to be taught, inside this moneyed economy, how to turn their hearts to God.[24]

The new reforming movements of the thirteenth century did this in their own ways. Following Francis, the Franciscans accepted poverty and simplicity. The Dominicans, too, embraced practices of poverty. But their ultimate mission wasn't simplicity but preaching. Accepting some poverty, they followed the streams of commerce into the new urban centers to preach. Preaching was the impetus for reform. Needing schools to prepare preachers, the Dominicans ended up birthing an intellectual theological revolution, seen most clearly in the Scholasticism of Thomas Aquinas.

The Dominicans are an interesting case for us as we seek to respond to singularity and recognize how innovation imposes an aesthetic of self-interest on workers. The Dominicans of the thirteenth and fourteenth centuries, like us, accepted the moneyed economy. They saw no reason (nor should we) for destroying it. Both Thomas and his teacher Albert the Great wrote in favor of private property, for instance. These great Dominican thinkers seemed to recognize the benefits, as well as the perils, of money.[25] Their reading of Aristotle assured them of both money's possibilities and its problems.

Yet, even with this acceptance, it was another of Albert's students, one of his last, who saw the necessity of following a different path. This young student and friar from Thuringia, Germany, recognized the great temptation to inflate the self inside a moneyed world. Money can impose an instrumentalizing of the whole world by pricing it and giving off the perception that it is all attainable for the self. To confront this temptation, this friar from Thuringia did what neither Albert nor Thomas did before him—he embraced fully and completely the mystical path. The mystical path, even inside a moneyed world, became the way to keep the self from curving in on itself, stripping money

24. Eventually, at its most corrupt, it became advantageous to simply use money, with the selling of indulgences, to return hearts and souls to God and add to the balance sheet of Rome.

25. For example, Little says, "Albert the Great and Thomas brought about the emancipation of Christian merchants. Other writers, such as Hugh of Saint-Cher and a follower of the Franciscan theologian and prelate Eudes Rigaud, had established the crucial distinction between honest and deceitful merchants. The honest merchant, for all these writers, was a man deserving of the profit he made, for they considered it as payment for his labour (*quasi stipendium laboris*)." Little, *Religious Poverty and the Profit Economy*, 178.

of its divinizing dreams and therefore its ability to overcome our desires and to inhabit our minds.

This young friar became known as Meister Eckhart. Meister Eckhart welcomed his own students on this mystical path. Notably, the late medieval preacher John Tauler, whose sermons Martin Luther so loved, was a follower of Eckhart. And from the inspiration of Eckhart and Tauler appeared a mysterious text called the *Theologia Germanica*, written by an unknown Teutonic priest from Frankfurt. The *Theologia Germanica* is a little book Luther placed behind only the Bible and the church fathers in importance.[26] These three mystical thinkers (Meister Eckhart, John Tauler, and the Mysterious Frankfurter of the *Theologia Germanica*) may give those of us standing in late modernity some insights into how we should respond to our own temptation to inflate the self, which is so endemic in an expressive creativity dispositif and its aesthetic, neoliberal hypermoneyed economy.

In the next chapter, we'll turn to the wisdom of these three pilgrims and their mystical path. We'll see what difference the mystical path they beckon us onto might have had for Russ and his young adults, as well as for Synod Executive Guy and the synod.

26. Luther says, "And, if I may speak with biblical foolishness: Next to the Bible and Saint Augustine no other book has come to my attention from which I have learned—and desire to learn—more concerning God, Christ, man, and what all things are." Frankfurter, *The Theologia Germanica of Martin Luther*, trans. Bengt Hoffman (New York: Paulist Press, 1980), 54.

10

The Three Amigos of the Mystical Path

How the Self Is Freed from Singularity

Zoom was choppy that day. Everyone in my house was eating up the band-width. All four of us were in some online meeting or class. This was life in month six of a global pandemic. I launched Zoom already fatigued with Zoom but ready to enter a conversation with four denominational leaders, one of whom was Synod Executive Guy. I hadn't seen or talked with him since the pandemic shut down the world. I wondered two things immediately as I saw him. My first thought was: I wonder how his synod is doing. And how are Applebee's Boy and Bearded Brown Turtleneck getting along? But I have to admit that thought was very quickly eclipsed by another: I wonder what Netflix documentaries he's watching? He must have pounded through some good ones during lockdown. I'd just finished *Secrets of the Saqqara Tomb*. I almost asked him if he'd seen it. But something stopped me. It wasn't just my fuzzy connection. It was clear that Synod Executive Guy was listless. I didn't know what to make of it. My connection couldn't reveal if the listlessness had its source in contentment or defeat. Regardless, he had none of the easy, welcoming energy that flowed in our other meetings. I soon found out why.

Synod Executive Guy explained that since late summer and then into the first months of the fall, he'd lost twelve pastors from the roster of his synod. And four others (that he knew of) had severe enough mental health issues that they needed to go on long-term leave. It was pure carnage. Before the pandemic, the momentum toward innovation had been expanding. There were major bumps in the road, of course, like Bearded Brown's opposition. But, still, they were moving in the right direction, so he thought. There were real spots of growth.

Even in the first month of the pandemic, the pastors and congregations in his synod rose to the occasion. Synod Executive Guy told the group, "The innovation was coming from everywhere! It was amazing. I thought to myself, this is what this has been for." Even Bearded Brown, I gathered, was responding to the crisis and constraints of the pandemic.

But all bursts of innovation need something to be measured by. They can't exist without it. Usually (particularly inside an expressive creativity dispositif of a neoliberal aesthetic economy) growth is the measure that validates, authenticates, and continues innovation's pursuits. Growth is like money (growth usually *is* money, or at least money sets the terms and framework for what counts as growth). Congregations, pastors, and synods often seek growth as their measure (a major part of the backwash from work into the church), meaning they invite the same logic into the practice of the church that Francis so vehemently rejected, stripping naked and hurling money out the window of a church. Inside the innovation that comes from the work world of neoliberalism, growth is the highest good. This logic imposes itself on congregations. The good congregation is the congregation that is growing in the logic of money. Synod Executive Guy had no other measure for a good congregation than growth. Therefore, innovation was left unchecked to inflate the self by seeking growth through singularity. Synod Executive Guy would have never crassly connected his understanding of growth with money, but they were inseparable. This all somehow held together, until the pandemic made this kind of money-logic of growth impossible. Innovation, without growth, started baring its teeth. If Synod Executive Guy hoped to hold to something like innovation, he would need to connect it to a higher good than growth and its hidden money-logic.

At the beginning of the pandemic, the crisis response worked to engender a kind of innovation that had a good beyond growth. At the beginning, something other than growth mobilized many for the synod's innovations—it was helping people stay connected, maintaining divine worship and the practice of church. Unfortunately no one saw how these innovations connected to something other than growth. Instead, they misinterpreted the crisis response of the pandemic as the synod's congregations building muscles *for* the growth (and victory) of innovation. They missed that the crisis, and the need for triage, allowed for a reprieve from the measuring stick of growth bound in money-logic. The return of the money-logic is what burned out many pastors, leading them to contemplate quitting.

Early in the pandemic the pastor didn't need to have growth on her mind and her mind on growth, because everything was on fire with the virus. Innovation demanded by the crisis of the pandemic was met by the drive for a higher good—at first. But as the pandemic droned on, the good—of bearing the fear and loss of being separated, of bringing the message of the gospel and the sacraments to people isolated at home—couldn't hold. The common measures of growth returned. Inside a pandemic, growth through money-logic was not even a possible goal. How could a congregation be growing in members, staff, programs, and energy if no one was gathering? If new buildings were empty and new staff furloughed? Without the measure of growth, but still the insatiable drive for it, congregations began turning on their pastors, pastors turned on one another, and the exhaustion of it all broke many.

Starting in late summer, one by one pastors left for new calls (assuming that'd be better!), left ministry altogether, or were so burned out that only a long-term leave with no return date would help. To my shock—though I'm not sure why I was shocked; it must have been his self-assuredness—Applebee's Boy was one of these. He took an extended leave and then left ministry altogether. Without the ability to speed toward growth as a direct measure of innovation, innovation's constant disruption and insecurity became too much, even for him, its apologist! Without the fetish of growth that takes the shape of the spectral-like quality of money that makes it shiny and exciting, the push for innovation became a torture chamber.

"What did you do?" one of the other participants asked Synod Executive Guy.

"At first I thought about resigning. I even drafted my resignation letter. But then I just let go." He continued, now more pensive but somehow assured, saying, "I've had to face that my best efforts have come to nothing. It's been painful. I've had to look at myself again. I'm still struggling with it all. But in a weird and painful way I've found something in this. An odd kind of gift. A strange kind of assurance. Or I guess I'd call it a presence. I'm still trying to make sense of it all, honestly."

The Three Amigos of the Mystical Road

It's often wrongly assumed that the path down the mystical road is an escape from the world. This couldn't be further from the truth for our three
fourteenth-century companions who will assist us in combating the inflation
of the self. Meister Eckhart, John Tauler, and the Mysterious Frankfurter
all enter the mystical path for the sake of embracing the world and finding
God squarely in it.[1] They all are searching for how the self encounters the
living God in a world where money rivals God and the self becomes inflated
in its own self-involvement. All three travel the mystical path because they
faced cultural challenges that are very similar to our own—although none
of the three can be confused for modern or even pseudomodern thinkers.
For instance, Eckhart is unmistakably a medieval monk, though in the early
nineteenth century he did become a hero to many of the German idealist
architects of modernity.[2] Eckhart, his German prose, and his probing of the
dark corners of human existence were an inspiration to the modern German
Romantic response to French rationalism.

All three journey down the mystical road because they recognize how
money inflates the self, curving in on itself. They seek ways to help others avoid the temptation to ceaselessly keep their minds on their money
and their money on their minds. Or maybe that's not quite right. Eckhart,
Tauler, and the Mysterious Frankfurter can't be confused for protoliberation
theologians. Rather, living and operating deeply inside a moneyed world
as preachers, these three give us a way to keep our minds off our singular
selves and our singular selves off our minds. By keeping our minds off our
selves, they help us avoid measuring our worth next to the logic of moneyed
growth, even when not dealing directly with money. Their mystical path is

1. Bengt Hägglund explains, "*Theologia Germanica* brings a positive message about the
earth and incarnated existence. Its dualism is a dualism between self-will and God's will,
not between nature and spirit. God's living presence here on earth is more important to the
Frankfurter than the idea that God's spirit stands over against the material world." Hägglund,
introduction to *The Theologia Germanica of Martin Luther*, trans. Bengt Hoffman (New York:
Paulist Press, 1980), 35.

2. Joel Harrington explains, "It was Baader who introduced Eckhart to the great Georg
Wilhelm Friedrich Hegel (1770–1831), who in turn incorporated the master into his 1824 lectures on the philosophy of religion. Hegel especially loved the master's famous words on divine
inter-subjectivity (The eye with which I see God is the same eye with which God sees me), which
the philosopher considered the supreme expression of self-consciousness without distinction
between subject and object." Harrington, *Dangerous Mystic: Meister Eckhart's Path to the God
Within* (New York: Penguin, 2018), 302.

a way to encounter the living God in a moneyed economy that sends the self into itself.

But these three companions are timely for us to explore for even more reasons. Inside the moneyed economy and its inflation of the self, they confront ecological fragility and the plague. In the early fourteenth century, just as Eckhart moved fully into ministry, a little ice age arrived in central Europe. For the next hundred years, summer would never arrive every few years. Like Game of Thrones, winter came, came and stayed, went, and came back. In the years it came, temperatures remained cold all year. Crops failed. Famine spread across the land, leading to great levels of economic inequality. Some lived in castles, others in utter squalor. As these mystics were writing and preaching, climate change was a major issue, taking distinct economic forms—as it does for us. The other connection to our time is the plague. After Eckhart's death, and while Tauler and the Mysterious Frankfurter were living, in the latter fourteenth century, the Black Death arrived.[3]

This ecological fragility and the plague were interconnected with the new arrival of a moneyed Europe. Money allowed inequality to fester in new ways when crops failed and food went scarce. As in our own time, their virus—which killed millions—was spread by travel due to commerce and trade (on the Silk Road) and the overall search for new moneyed markets. These factors played their part in tempting the self to turn in on itself. The challenges of this early moneyed world led to new contemplation on God's action in the world.

A Little Background

In 1516, the year before Luther nailed his Ninety-Five Theses, he stumbled upon a little book called the *Theologia Germanica*, written around 1350. It had no known author. Luther loved it, and he had it printed.[4] The year after nailing up his theses, Luther found a longer version of the *Theologia Germanica* in a monastic library. Luther had thought that John Tauler was the author of the smaller book. Luther had been enamored of Tauler's sermons. The *Theologia Germanica* seemed so Taulerian in its themes and style. But

3. Bernard McGinn discusses these issues in *The Harvest of Mysticism in Medieval Germany* (New York: Herder & Herder, 2005), 3–5.

4. Luther was on the cutting edge of the new world of printing. For a wonderfully helpful read on the context of printing and Luther's place in it, see Andrew Pettegree, *Brand Luther: How an Unheralded Monk Turned His Small Town into a Center of Publishing, Made Himself the Most Famous Man in Europe—and Started the Protestant Reformation* (New York: Penguin, 2015).

the longer version quoted Tauler, and the author, though not revealing his name, says that he's a priest from Frankfurt. This is all we know: a mysterious text written by a Mysterious Frankfurter greatly inspired the young Luther as he worked out his theology (particularly his theology of the cross and the need for faith to overcome sin, which causes us to curve in on the self). In the introduction to the printing of the longer version of the *Theologia Germanica*, Luther says that now all those who think that this new theology coming from Wittenberg is the invention of crazed lunatics can see that he and his friends stand on the shoulders of mystical German preachers who came before them.

Those shoulders were no squarer than John Tauler's. Tauler was born in 1300 in Strasburg. As a young man he entered the Dominican order, receiving a rigorous education. Tauler became one of the most important preachers of the fourteenth century. His sermons were filled with invitations and descriptions of the mystical path. Tauler, though no academic and having a certain disdain for professors, nevertheless learned of the mystical path (adding his own dimensions to it) from his teacher Meister Eckhart.

Eckhart was born around 1260, probably to a low-ranking knight in the Thuringia region of the Germanic nations. He entered the Dominican order as a teenager, residing in the monastery at Erfurt, the same city that two centuries later was the scene of Luther's education (as an Augustinian, not Dominican), before he entered the monastery.

Eckhart quickly went from teenage novice to leader. His intellect, which was particularly clear, led him to be sent without delay to the Rhineland to study in the faculty led by Albert the Great in Cologne. Eckhart separated himself further from his peers in Cologne. He was soon sent from Cologne to the university in Paris.

At the time, Paris was both the intellectual and the economic center of Europe. It was by far the largest city, its expanse fueled by commerce. Money was everywhere. As young Eckhart walked the left bank, following the narrow, twisted streets of the Latin Quarter, his senses were lit by the chattering of Latin and the ringing of coins in exchange.[5] All of this was done in the shadow of the rising cathedral of Notre Dame, still under construction. Eckhart was now following the footsteps of Albert's most renowned and gifted student, Thomas Aquinas. Both Thomas and Albert had been professors at Paris, and Eckhart would be soon (after returning to the German lands and

5. Harrington discusses Eckhart's world of money in *Dangerous Mystic*, 19–24.

then back again). Eckhart found himself placed in the same chair once oc-
cupied by Albert and Thomas.[6]

TOWARD THE MYSTICAL PATH

Both Albert and Thomas, in their unique ways, flirted with the mystical
path. But both were too focused on the implications of the rediscovery of
Aristotle to jump fully aboard. It's hard for us late moderns to imagine this,
but the legendary Aristotle had been almost completely lost. For more than
a thousand years, no one read or knew of him. The Latin West particularly
had no knowledge of the great philosopher. Not until Muslim scholars in
the thirteenth century rediscovered him and brought his books and ideas to
Spain did Aristotle reappear in the West.

Albert and his then protégé Thomas saw great implications for making
Aristotle a dialogue partner with Christian theology, exponentially deepening Scholasticism. Albert and Thomas spent large amounts of time and
energy not only understanding and connecting Aristotle to the tradition
but also explaining how a pagan thinker, brought to the church's attention
by Muslim blasphemers, could help in shaping the holy church's theology.
Albert and Thomas flirted with the mystical, but other concerns monopo-
lized their time.

Eckhart also worked on these problems, spending ample time reading Aristotle and doing theology in the cadence of Scholasticism. But in the latter
part of his life, when he taught John Tauler, he was back in the Germanic
nations again, closer to his roots, preaching and overseeing monastic life. Particularly, it was his charge to oversee a group of nuns, preaching regularly to a
congregation of women. It's in dialogue with them (more than with Aristotle)
that Eckhart's ideas are sharpest and his language most beautiful.[7] Tauler,
too, preached his most important sermons to nuns. The mystical thought of
Eckhart and Tauler is inextricable from the ministry of women.[8]

6. Harrington discusses Eckhart's relationship to Albert in *Dangerous Mystic*, 118–21.

7. Eckhart is often acknowledged as one of the first true masters of the German language,
one of Germany's first poets. Eckhart was one of the first to make German beautiful. The
beauty of his language became very important to early nineteenth-century German Romantics, who were living under the tyranny of France and French culture but took pride in the
Germanic. They found a great love for Eckhart and his ability to beautify a language that the
French mocked.

8. For a discussion of the place of women in Eckhart's life, see Oliver Davies, *Meister Eckhart: Mystical Theologian* (London: SPCK, 2011), 68–79.

Back in Germanic land and outside the thin air of the Scholastic debates in the Latin Quarter, Eckhart was more pastor than scholar. Helping these sisters encounter the living God was Eckhart's and Tauler's direct responsibility. Inside this responsibility, Eckhart (and Tauler and the Mysterious Frankfurter after him) walked fully on the mystical path, giving new depth and even a new way for the mystical to spill into the reforms of the Latin West. The pastoral focus directly beckoned Meister Eckhart onto this mystical journey.[9]

The shape of this mystical journey would become a piercing sliver embedded in Western theology. Eckhart's and Tauler's preaching to the sisters became an essential part of the branch of Luther's *theologia crucis* (theology of the cross). Eckhart's mystical path, as well as Tauler's and the Frankfurter's reflections, became the major branch of the tributary that's been called the "thin tradition." The thin tradition is a minority tradition in the West that has "never been much loved."[10] This tradition seeks God where God seems unable to be found. It claims, starting with the humble Eckhart, that God can be found only in the places that appear to be Godforsaken. All three claim that in Godforsakenness our *selves* are found by something outside of us that saves us, with no correlation to, or impetus in, what is within us. Only by meeting something outside of us, completely alien to the self as Tauler would herald, can the self be saved and made to flourish in the fullness of God's sole goodness. For the self to be freed from being curved in on itself and idolatrously believing the self can make something out of its own self (by the power of the self), the self must confront the void of its own impossibility. Tauler reminded his listeners that the self must recognize that it is bound in nothingness, sin, and tragic impossibility.

Eckhart's mystical path is not effervescent, bubbly spiritualism. Instead, it entails surrender to the dark, enveloping curtain of impossibility. The self is quite important for the Germanic mystics (thanks to Augustine), but never as singular, for nothingness and death surround the self. The self is always in need of something from outside, a power beyond, to save it. The *Theologia Germanica* insists upon this. The Mysterious Frankfurter claims that this saving power seems to always come in the opposite of might. The power that can uphold a self and yet keep the self from obsessively turning in on itself is

9. Admittedly, Eckhart was more than likely on the mystical path before this. But we have the most direct evidence of it from vernacular sermons he preached during this period. There are some connections in his Latin works, but more so in the German.

10. Jürgen Moltmann, *The Crucified God* (Minneapolis: Fortress, 1974), 1.

the power made known only through weakness. The weakness of God[11] in the crucified Christ (which the thin tradition claims) bears the ultimate power to bring the self from death to life. Because the self is covered in impossibility, God takes on impossibility by being crucified. The thin tradition, embedded in the reforms of the thirteenth century, contends that the true God can be known only in this backward way of weakness and nothingness.

Though seemingly heavy and foreboding, the thin tradition, for Eckhart, actually offers amazing hope and an invitation into the truest and fullest life. For the Frankfurter it is the way into ultimate goodness. In Godforsaken places (particularly the cross, and then the confessions of the impossibility of the poverty of the self), God promises to be found and present. Out of this impossibility, which God shares completely, God gives God's sure presence to minister directly to the self, giving to the self what the self cannot find within itself.[12] The self is given a direct and real encounter with the true God who comes into the weakness and impossibility of the self to redeem and save the self from its drive for singularity. The self is given true life not by curating itself but by receiving that which is bound outside the self but fully includes the self.[13]

The self must follow this thin and narrow path of Godforsakenness to find a God who is God. The self must follow this path to be given the gift of the self by something outside the self.[14] Tauler preaches that the self must humbly avoid seeking its own self-justifying singularity through its own creativity

11. This phrase echoes the title of John Caputo's book *The Weakness of God: A Theology of the Event* (Bloomington: Indiana University Press, 2006).

12. We can see the theology of the cross here: "Christ's soul had to visit hell before it came to heaven. This is also the path for man's soul. But note in what manner this occurs as far as we are concerned. When a person comes to know and see himself he discovers that he is wicked and unworthy of the goodness and comfort that he has received from God or from fellow beings. He then feels that he is damned and lost and unworthy even of that. Yes, he thinks that he is unworthy of the sufferings that he may undergo in his earthly life. He thinks that it is mete and right that all creatures should turn against him and cause him suffering and agony and that he is unworthy of this, too." Frankfurter, *Theologia Germanica of Martin Luther*, 72. The Frankfurter continues, "Now God does not leave man in this hell. No, He takes him to Himself and the result is that man does not ask for anything but the eternal Good alone and knows that the eternal Good is exceedingly precious. Yes, it becomes his ecstasy, his peace, his joy, his rest, his fullness" (73).

13. The Frankfurter says, "If the soul is to gaze or look into eternity, it must become chastened and empty of images and detached from all created things and, above all, from the claims of self." *Theologia Germanica of Martin Luther*, 68.

14. Again we hear in *The Theologia Germanica of Martin Luther*, "I answer: Man must put aside all 'selfdom' and concern with the 'self' so that he does not look out for himself at all, indeed as though he did not exist. In other words, he should be concerned with his own

and effort. The self must release all drives for valorization of the self's in-novations. The self must let go and bear its very impossibility, even its many deaths, to discover the God who is God, giving God's own self in Jesus Christ to our selves (making us Christ) by the impossibility of the self and the great possibility of the God who is the great minister, bringing life always and eternally out of death.

On the mystical path of Eckhart, Tauler, and the Mysterious Frankfurter, we encounter God not through the self's accomplishment and powers but instead by the confession of the self's impossibility (this calls for an existential and ontological confession of vulnerability, something different from how Brené Brown is often interpreted). On the mystical path the self escapes the trappings of itself to find itself met by a great ground of something outside itself. The self does not stand or fall by its own uniqueness or exceptional singularity. The creativity that saves the self is not from within but without. God's creative act brings life and fullness. This ecstatic creativity comes only on the ground (*Grunt* in German[15]) that is the God who becomes nothing so that nothingness and death might be the place the self is found—found in God.

These few paragraphs attempt to capture the essence of Eckhart, Tauler, and the Mysterious Frankfurter's thought. But to get a better handle on the thin tradition that they were developing, we need to further tease out their thought to spot its implications for us. It will help if we unpack each of the themes named in the above paragraphs. Knitting together Eckhart, Tauler, and the *Theologia Germanica* (though giving organizing preference to Eckhart), we'll explore the negative, nothingness, letting go, and the ground. Like stakes along a wilderness trail, these four themes mark the path of the mystical way

---

self as little and think about his own self and his own as little as though he did not exist; yes, he should take as little account of himself as though he were not" (76).

15. McGinn gives a good amount of attention to the ground. He explains it as such: "Consi-deration of Latin terms that refract aspects of the meaning of *grunt* casts light on how the new master metaphor both absorbed earlier themes at the same time that it exploded and recast them. *Grunt* was often applied to the 'innermost of the soul'. . . what Eckhart, Tauler, and others spoke of metaphorically as 'spark,' 'castle,' 'nobleman,' 'highest point,' 'seed,' and the like. Much effort has been devoted to studying how *grunt* and its related terms are connected to Latin expressions for the depth of the soul conceived of as imago Dei—expressions like *fundus animae*, *scintilla animae*, *apex mentis*, *abditum animae/mentis/cordis*, *principale cordis/mentis*, *supremum ani-mae*, *semen divinum*, *ratio superior*, *synderesis*, *abstrusior memoriae profunditas*, etc. These terms pertain to what has been called the mysticism of introversion whose great source in the West is Augustine of Hippo. Eckhart knew these terms and made use of many of them in his Latin works." McGinn, *Harvest of Mysticism in Medieval Germany*, 88. For more on *Grunt*, see McGinn, *The Mystical Thought of Meister Eckhart* (New York: Herder & Herder, 2001), 38–44.

of the thin tradition. We'll take them two at a time, examining the "negative way of nothingness" and "letting go to find the ground."

THE NEGATIVE WAY OF NOTHINGNESS

The mystical path that leads to a theology of the cross is fundamentally a negative path. Selves in pursuit of innovating their own identities through an internally bound, expressive creativity (seeking to present to the world their singularly exceptional self) hate the negative. They don't mind being negative toward others' performance. That's just part of the game of evaluation. But they hate when their own selves receive the negative (haters suck!). The best friends of selves seeking singularity are always positive friends. Such best friends always direct negativity toward the right people and never toward that friend's own self. That's the mark (even substance) of a good friendship in a society of singularities.

This disdain for the negative stretches into the work world as well. No one bearing the disruption and insecurity of permanent innovation can stomach the negative. You're too stretched, too exposed in your performance, to be anything but completely firewalled from the negative. Downers need not apply. A negative source (or self) on your team will kill your project. The negative source must be cut out so the negativity doesn't bring all the selves of the team down, preventing each self from becoming indispensable. It's hard to be on a winning team that feeds the exceptionality of your self when you've got a negative loser on it. The burden of disruption and the insecurity of permanent innovation in neoliberalism are only possible to bear if all workers (all selves!) can be positive. Positivity (just after expressive creativity) is a quality highly sought after in hiring. After all, positivity is how you win friends and influence people, as Dale Carnegie's bestselling book claimed long ago.[16]

Yet the only way onto the mystical path of Eckhart, Tauler, and the Mysterious Frankfurter is through the negative way, the *via negativa*.[17] Eckhart is

16. Dale Carnegie, *How to Win Friends and Influence People* (New York: Simon & Schuster, 1936).

17. Mark McIntosh discusses this turn to the apophatic in Eckhart in *Mystical Theology* (Malden, MA: Blackwell, 1998), 222–28. Peter Kline adds, discussing Eckhart and Kierkegaard, "The apophatic rule might go something like this: when speaking of God, do not speak as if you were supplying predicates to a divine being. Speak, rather, an event, a happening, one that names the happening of the divine as nothing, a nothing-ing." Kline, *Passion for Nothing: Kierkegaard's Apophatic Theology* (Minneapolis: Fortress, 2017), 66. He continues, "Such speech resists the temptation of speaking about God. God cannot be spoken about. 'God cannot be an object.'

recovering this negative way onto the mystical path from the ancient church father Dionysius. This negative way isn't necessarily tantamount to being a downer. It's not the way of Eeyore from Winnie the Pooh, endlessly complaining. Teams in an aesthetic economy understandably don't want such negative energy near their projects. Rather, the negative assumes—in direct opposition to the drive for singularity in an aesthetic economy—that there is nothing inherent within the self that allows the self to produce its own good. There is nothing in the self that permits the self to know, understand, and encounter a God who is truly God. Selves are not constituted to know either their own selves or the God who made them. A self who wants to know God must first embrace that they cannot know God (and cannot in turn know the self). This is the negative way.

For Eckhart and Tauler, the self must receive something from outside (even outside its own creativity) to know God and to flourish. For Tauler, the negative way asserts that there is nothing in the self that gives the self access to this God who is God.[18] This God is God beyond whom nothing greater can be known and therefore who can never be possessed by our works or ideas. The self cannot know the greatness of God. The self can only receive it as a gift from outside. This negative way forces the self to take its mind off itself if it ever wishes to find the God who is true God, the God who is unrivaled by money. Money, as the spectral god, demands that I think continually about myself, curving in on myself as I think about myself in relation to money's impersonal force. Money's allure is in its ability to be had. Money may be spectral, but it is not wholly other. Money cannot take me outside myself. It just drives me deeper into myself. Money therefore makes no demand that I enter the *via negativa* to encounter it (maybe that's what makes it more appealing to immanent-bound moderns).

God moves elusively in a saying that does not congeal into a said, or even into a silence, but in a saying that keeps itself in motion, withdrawing from any fixed position or naming, moving at a slant, with a swerve, like a dance" (67).

18. Steven Ozment explains, "Tauler draws a most severe portrait of man's fallen situation. Nature is poisoned by the original sin and so completely self-inverted in all things that man loves himself (his createdness) more than God, God's angels and all that God has ever made. The fault lies not with God's having made nature—a Thomistic thrust against Manichaeism. Nature is corrupted by the emaciating distortion it has incurred by turning away from God and to itself. Here a poisoning occurs and penetrates to the very ground of the soul, where it establishes a false ground in the spirit and in nature, a ground which becomes manifest when one thinks that he is completely God and that all he does is his own." Ozment, *Homo Spiritualis: A Comparative Study of the Anthropology of Johannes Tauler, Jean Gerson and Martin Luther in the Context of Their Theological Thought* (Leiden: Brill, 1969), 27.

But because the true God is fully beyond and other than our selves, we can come to encounter and know this God only by the backward way of *via negativa*.[19] To speak of this God who is true God, Eckhart teaches, we must first speak in the negative, speaking of what God is not and what my self cannot know. Money, however, makes no demand that I seek something to save me from outside myself, nor that I confess that my self is not constituted to possess and own what can save me. Rather, the spectral god of money sends me back into myself, judging my own singularity by my profits or debts.

Eckhart and Tauler wish to help their nuns encounter the God who is God, mystically finding themselves in union with this God who cannot be known. Yet the only access to such a union with such a God is through the confession that God is unknowable. We should be clear, though, that the negative way doesn't begin by turning in on and beating the self. This is only the other side of the same coin of self-obsession. It's no wonder that as we've heightened the drive for singularity in late modernity, demanding that all children be exceptional, some (many more than in generations past) tragically take up practices of self-mutilation. The burden of obsessive singularity can be quite heavy. It elevates the self in a manner that allows the self to quickly turn on itself and hate itself (a different kind of obsession). Idols that can be possessed outside the negative way are often despised as much as worshiped, because they're discovered to have no power to fulfill or save, and yet they retain their tyranny.

The *via negativa* isn't a masochistic way to beat up the self. It's the only way to accept and love the self. The self can be loved by embracing the self's limit, by confessing that the self has no power in itself to know God. The self is freely allowed to be a creature again (instead of an unrelenting creator of the self and its singularity). When the self acknowledges that it cannot know God, the path opens to receiving a true encounter with God, who is outside and beyond the self. God comes to the self; God reaches out to us. The negative way relativizes the self so that the self can be a creature able to receive the gift of the real presence of God.[20]

19. Eckhart discusses the *via negativa*, saying, "If you can understand anything about him [God], it in no way belongs to him, and insofar as you understand anything about him, that brings you into incomprehension, and from incomprehension you arrive at a brute's stupidity; for when created beings do not understand, they resemble the brutes." Eckhart, "Sermon 83," in *Meister Eckhart: The Essential Sermons, Commentaries, and Defense*, trans. Edmund Colledge and Bernard McGinn (New York: Paulist Press, 1981), 207.

20. Reiner Schürmann beautifully adds, "An existence that dwells in nothingness is one in which everything just begins. It abides in the origin of the Creator. In this preoriginary origin, says

Tauler and the Frankfurter's point is that the self, even with all its money, is in deep poverty when it lacks otherness, communion, and encounters with revelation. The self needs to encounter something outside of it to live fully in the good. Only in dwelling in the unknowability of God can the self be relativized enough to realize that there is simply no source in the self to save and give fullness to the self. If the mystical could be found in the self, and therefore somewhere other than the negative way, it wouldn't be the God who is God that we encounter. It would be the echo of our own self.[21]

The mystical way of Eckhart disempowers the self so that the self can be a creature able to be loved by the true God who comes to us from outside of us. The mystical path of the thin tradition starts by the self confessing that it has nothing within it that can save it (this is central to the thin tradition). The self must not perform its exceptional uniqueness, taking pride in its own creativity, but must instead come to confess that the self—in itself—is incomplete. This incompleteness is a nothingness that the self can never escape. This nothingness, Eckhart believes, shouldn't be feared but embraced, because the nothingness is shared directly (ontologically) by God. For Eckhart, God *is* nothingness.

The mystical path that Eckhart is teaching his nuns, Tauler, and the Frankfurter is a journey that brings the self into union with the being of God.[22] The negative way is a way into nothingness. But this nothingness is not pure existentialism. (Some, such as Jean-Paul Sartre, have misinterpreted it this way, leading them to laud Eckhart for the wrong reasons.) Rather, this nothingness, for Eckhart and his mystical way, is *the* way into the being of God.[23] As the

Meister Eckhart, only silence maintains itself." Schürmann, *Wandering Joy: Meister Eckhart's Mystical Philosophy* (Great Barrington, MA: Lindisfarne, 2001), 117.

21. Richard Woods adds nicely to this, saying, "In practical terms, then, but not in terms of 'practices,' Eckhart's spirituality can be described as a progressive 'stripping' of the self—physically, mentally and spiritually, that is, the purifying of knowledge and emotion, desire and imagination. Through such radical de-tachment (*Abgeschiedenheit*), God eventually comes to be born in us, but not until we have also become detached not only from whatever is not God, but even from God as well. Eckhart thus advises us to negate our ideas of God as well as creatures and the self. Thus he even prays that 'God will rid me of God.' As with his indirectly affirmative 'nihilism,' Eckhart's 'a-theism' must not be mistaken for the simple denial of God that constitutes the ultimate blindness in life. Again, Eckhart takes us to the opposite extreme from what to him would have seemed nonsense." Woods, *Meister Eckhart: Master of Mystics* (London: Continuum, 2011), 92.

22. Eckhart has a central place for deification or *theosis* in his thinking.

23. Buddhists love Eckhart for saying that nothingness leads to God. But Eckhart means this in a Christological way that he doesn't develop enough. C. F. Kelley explains Eckhart's meaning: "The only answer, then, to the question 'What is God?' is, as Eckhart says: 'God is!'

self is moved outside itself, recognizing that there is *nothing* within the self that can save the self, the self is redeemed. By embracing nothingness, the self discovers a presence (which is what Synod Executive Guy confessed on Zoom). It is an encounter with the One who enters the nothingness of the Israelites' slavery in Egypt and Jesus's dead body in a tomb. This one true God acts, and therefore makes himself known, in nothingness. For Tauler and the *Theologia Germanica*, God is always found in nothingness, birthing nothingness's opposite through nothingness.

Where there is nothingness—where the self is not performing its creative singularity but confessing its nothingness in loss, need, and limit—God is found. In human nothingness God's own creativity fully bears nothingness, so that perishing brought by nothingness is turned into a new possibility. The God who is God is found in nothingness itself.[24] This is why Eckhart can say God is nothingness. Strip away all things, and all that remains is God. The *is* of God is beyond all that is. If there were nothing, God is. In nothingness God is present, most concretely in the cosmic embracing of the nothingness of the cross. The cross is the central event of God's own being in the world.[25]

---

or rather 'God is nothing.' And in saying this he simply asserts that 'God is no-thing, not this, not that.' By stressing the unconditioned isness that God is and the isness of all that is known and knowable, he never for an instant doubts the reality of God or the relational reality of himself and all contingent beings." Kelley, *Meister Eckhart on Divine Knowledge* (New Haven: Yale University Press, 1977), 70.

24. Oliver Davies says of nothingness, "'Nothingness' is a theme which is intrinsic to Christianity, but it is one which has too often been neglected. It is present in the kenosis, or self-emptying of Christ, who 'came down from Heaven' and 'was born of the Virgin Mary,' as it is present in the reciprocal self-emptying of the Father and the Son in the Holy Spirit, which is the ground of the Trinity. We find it, too, in the self-emptying of the believing individual, who seeks to conform their life to Christ so that, with Paul, they can say: 'it is not I who live but Christ who lives in me' (Gal. 2.20), and it is the theme of a spiritual nothingness which animates much Marian piety, whereby she becomes a 'vessel' or a 'window' or an 'empty space.' 'Nothingness,' then, is not foreign to Christianity, rather the concept of negation, transparency or self-denial is fundamental both to its doctrinal truths and lived experience of faith." Davies, *Meister Eckhart*, 211. He continues, "When he says that we are 'nothing,' Eckhart does not, of course, believe that we do not exist in an empirical sense. His call to 'nothingness' must rather be seen in the light of his professed technique of holding before his audience the deepest truths of their natures. Before God, we are indeed nothing, and the life of faith is indeed, in a sense, an ever greater participation in the divine nothingness, which is the fertile life of the Trinity. Eckhart is right, then, to stress this theme time and again, and he does so with a clarity and a vigour which surpasses the efforts of those who came before him and those who have come after" (212).

25. McGinn places the cross in connection to the *Theologia Germanica*: "The [*Theologia Germanica*] explores the fundamental option of taking up the cross and following Christ in loving obedience in many ways, calling upon ideas and forms of language characteristic of late medieval German mysticism. The treatise does not organize these themes into any sequence, but sees them as correlative aspects of the Christic redirection of the will. Following Christ

The work the self must do to be on the mystical path is nothing—let go and enter nothingness. Which means that this nothing is actually something. It confesses that the self has nothing within itself to save it. The self is not exceptional; the self's own acts of singular creativity cannot save. The self as a creature—not a creative singularity—must be enough. The something of the mystical path demands that the self turn over its many experiences of nothingness to allow God, than whom nothing is greater, to minister fully and completely to the self. God takes the self into the nothingness of God. This nothingness transforms into a great fullness—the full and good union with the being of God. The being of humanity and the being of God are united through nothingness.

This unity with God through nothingness is what Synod Executive Guy discovered. Inside his confession of loss and fear, inside the realization that his best efforts of his self had come to nothingness, he found a gift, a presence. Not despite the nothingness but because his self confessed the nothingness. He found the redemptive ministerial life of God taking his self into God's own self through nothingness. This was a good unlike anything permanent innovation could offer.

In his nothingness, Synod Executive Guy was beginning to recognize that the good congregation is not the *growing* congregation but the *confessing* congregation.[26] The good congregation looks for creativity not inside itself (which is what the turn to innovation in the church has often called for) but from God, whose creativity comes to the congregation, making a new way out of the congregation's many experiences of nothingness. In his negative way into nothingness Eckhart sets the stage for Luther (after taking Eckhart through Tauler and the *Theologia Germanica*) to assert that it is the cross that rightly orders the self. The cross rightly orders each self and each congregation. The cross allows the self, through its confession, to find the God of love who embraces the self by entering nothingness fully and completely for the self.[27]

---

here means not so much to undertake a journey, as to realize the need for abandonment and annihilation of self-will. The dominant practices, if such they may be called, are internal, involving emptying the self through detachment, abandonment, poverty of spirit, essential humility . . . and the radical obedience that sums them all up." McGinn, *Harvest of Mysticism in Medieval Germany*, 398–99.

26. Douglas John Hall, a theologian of the thin tradition, makes a similar point in *Confessing the Faith* (Minneapolis: Fortress, 1998).

27. McGinn adds, "The single-mindedness of the [*Theologia Germanica*], especially with regard to destroying self-will, helps explain the work's polemical edge. In the view of the anonymous priest who composed the book, there was no greater error in the spiritual life than striving

LETTING GO TO FIND THE GROUND

This leads us to two of the most well-known themes in Eckhart and Tauler: detachment and the ground (*Grunt*).[28] For us to enter nothingness through confession and encounter the God who is nothing that we can possess, the self must practice detachment.

At first read Eckhart's call for detachment seems like self-help voodoo. It sounds like something a highly paid life coach would tell a rich client. Because their mind is always on their money (and therefore their selves) and because their money and selves are always on their mind, people with a lot of money or desires who have little space in their calendars need detachment. They need to say no to many distractions so their self can live their best, most singular life. In hyperconsumer societies of constant choice, there is a type of detachment that allows us more clarity in buying what's really important and being selves that are really exceptional.

This talk of detachment pops up in late-modern consumer societies because the spectral god of money never operates in the same way as the true God, who encounters us in nothingness. The spectral god of money binds us again and again to stuff (that's what idols do). Binding us to stuff forces our attention on ourselves as we manage, sell, pay off, and carry the overall burden of many attachments that the spectral god foists on us. It becomes big business to teach selves to be exceptional and singular by detaching and attaching to the right products, places, and perspectives (why else would you need the website Goop?). Fiona, in Russ's grant group, knew this deeply. It's what made her the most exceptional, creative self of the group. Her perceived creativity was in no small part connected to her ability to know just what products and perspectives to attach to and detach from. She needed to bail quickly on Russ's group because it became unexceptional, overtaken by a spirit of the basic, offering no value for the outworking of her own expressive, creative self.

---

to attain union with God on the basis of prideful self-will." McGinn, *Harvest of Mysticism in Medieval Germany*, 402.

28. Steven Ozment gives us a sense of Tauler's understanding of the ground, saying, "In a Christmas sermon on Isaiah 9:6, Tauler specifies the conditions and nature of man's becoming one with God. He speaks of the necessity of an 'entrance' . . . into the 'ground,' i.e., an assemblage of all the powers of the soul and their subjection to the highest power, the ground of the soul. From this activity follows a 'departure' . . . from all one's desires; a pure disposition to God is attained. And this forms the final preparatory stage for the birth of God in the soul. If you have emptied yourself, then God must fill the empty place: 'so much out, so much in.'" Ozment, *Homo Spiritualis*, 203.

Living in a new moneyed economy of the medieval age, Eckhart and Tauler anticipate this reality. They see how money foists many attachments on the soul. Eckhart's goal isn't to destroy money but to move the self to enter the mystical negative way by detaching from money's many sticky attachments and attentions. Ultimately this detachment espoused by Eckhart and Tauler has more to do with the self than with money proper. These German mystics are pushing not for money to be eliminated but for their nuns to escape money's drives to bend the self in on itself.

For Eckhart, the self enters the negative way of nothingness by letting go completely, not by curating a discerning self of attachments and detachments. As we said above, this is the very something we do as we enter the negative way of nothingness. The discipline needed on the negative way is not the effort to create something out of the self. It's not *doing* at all. It's letting go.

Joel Harrington, in his exceptional book *Dangerous Mystic: Meister Eckhart's Path to the God Within*, argues convincingly that it is better to think of Eckhart's detachment as letting go. The point isn't to become more discerning but to let go completely.[29] For overly connected late-modern people driving for singularity, letting go is hard (and it creates all sorts of mental health issues of anxiety and depression).

Letting go begins, however, not with the self. Rather, we first let go of all our preconceived conceptions about God. We can join the negative way into nothingness only by letting go of all the ways we've allowed God to be conceived in the image of the spectral god of money or as an accessory to the self's own curating drive.[30] We must let go of such images of God, instead

29. Kelley says, "Eckhart is fully aware of the passivity that is at the root of action. He is also aware that the 'axial eternal act' can be neither an act understood as action nor an act understood by the common analogy of action. 'When detachment attains its supreme perfection it becomes inactive, unknowing knowledge through Divine Knowledge.' Transcendence, which is the very essence of detachment, can only be by way of act as known in the order of inversion and thus 'by way of unrestricted isness in primal act, that is, by God himself.' Grace is essentially 'the uncreated act' of God, that is, the Holy Spirit itself. Or, to put it another way, 'grace is the indwelling of the soul in God.'" *Meister Eckhart on Divine Knowledge*, 234.

30. Eckhart says, "I have read many writings both by the pagan teachers and by the prophets and in the Old and the New Law, and I have inquired, carefully and most industriously, to find which is the greatest and best virtue with which man can most completely and closely conform himself to God, with which he can by grace become that which God is by nature, and with which man can come most of all to resemble that image which he was in God, and between which and God there was no distinction before ever God made created things. And as I scrutinize all these writings, so far as my reason can lead and instruct me, I find no other virtue better than a pure detachment from all things; because all other virtues have some regard for created things, but

contemplating only God's nothingness. Luther gave this more concrete shape by telling us that our images of God must be crucified so that the only God we know is the God made known in the love of the suffering of the cross. We must let go of any sense that anything else can save us.

Innovation—inside neoliberalism—tempts us into making it into a growth-imposing attachment machine. If we are not careful, innovation becomes the opposite of letting go. Innovation becomes a new way to stimulate the self to overattach to the possibility that the self's own creativity can save (in this case, adding a major layer of hubris with the theologically problematic idea that the self's own creativity can save the body of Christ we call the church). It is an odd thing to imagine that innovation can save the church, though this is the language often used around bringing innovation into the church. Such assertions completely reverse the order of saving that the thin tradition holds to.

Innovation (as a process that seeks to open up the creativity of the self to solve problems and win growth) does exactly what Jesus told Mary not to do in John 20:17. Jesus tells her to let go, to let him return to the Father. Mary Magdalene is the great disciple and lover of the church because she lets go. She obeys and lets go of possessing Jesus so that Jesus can return to the Father and take her and the whole church into participation in the cosmic life of God.

Yet innovation runs the risk of producing an overattachment to the church.[31] It seeks to offer new, creative ways to hold onto the body of Jesus. Innovation has a hidden way of encouraging the self in its own power to attach to what cannot be attached to, thinking the church itself is dependent on our own creativity. But Jesus tells Mary to let go of his body. Innovation without a direct practice of letting go (innovative processes without a way onto the mystical path) will nearly always succumb to the idolatry of the self.

Russ needed much more than to empower Fiona to unleash her creativity on the church. At its best, this could only produce an attachment to the church that leads to a disdain of or warped obsession with the church. It leads away from the crucified one who is head of the church and who can

---

detachment is free from all created things. That is why our Lord said to Martha: 'One thing is necessary' (Lk. 10:42), which is as much as to say: 'Martha, whoever wants to be free of care and to be pure must have one thing, and that is detachment.'" Eckhart, *On Detachment*, in *Meister Eckhart*, 285.

31. Innovation first reduces the church to an institution, forgetting its place in the cosmic economy of God.

be known only through nothingness and impossibility. Innovation processes run the risk of talking too much about the church and not enough about the church's relation to the act and being of God. Innovation runs the danger of curving the church in on itself, making the church the star of its own story.[32]

If Fiona is going to be invited into exploring innovations for the church, she needs, most importantly, to be taken into practices of letting go. First and foremost, she must let go of any drive to be a singular self through the power of her own expressive creativity. The mystical way reminds us that our own creativity cannot save our selves or the church. Only the true God is able to save.

The church does not need more creative selves. It needs only the very self of Jesus Christ, the God who is found in the nothingness of the cross. Only then would Fiona be able to let go of any attachment to the church, letting go of the church just as Mary does to Jesus's body, so that the Spirit might come and call her into ministry, not just a performance of expressive creativity (which is why she quit). The church does not need more innovators. It needs more ministers. It needs more people who participate in the ministry of God. For what will save the world through the church is not the expressive creativity of the self but the encounter with the living God who is ministering new life out of nothingness.

Denominational officials and pastors would be better off letting go of the church's perceived shortcomings than attaching to innovation processes. As Russ discovered, if we are not very careful, innovation imposes the reverse of what Eckhart and Tauler call their nuns to and what *Theologia Germanica* ignites in Luther. Without the dialectic of the negative calling us to let go to find the God of nothingness, innovation pushes pastors and leaders to go looking to themselves for solutions to the church's decline.[33] Innovation can convince us that the solutions to the church's problems do not come from

---

32. See Andrew Root, "The Church Is Not the Star of Its Own Story," in *Churches and the Crisis of Decline: A Hopeful, Practical Ecclesiology for a Secular Age* (Grand Rapids: Baker Academic, 2022), 83–91.

33. This dialectic looks something like how Bernard McGinn describes it, saying, "The negation of negation is Eckhart's dialectical way of subverting the standard Aristotelian divide (both a logical and an ontological one) between 'what is' and 'what is not.' God 'negates' everything that we know 'is'; but the negation of all that is (not just some particular form of existence) opens up vistas into a new world in which our distinctions between what is and what is not no longer pertain. God as negation *negationis* is simultaneously total emptiness and supreme fullness." McGinn, *Mystical Thought of Meister Eckhart*, 94.

God or are dependent on God's act alone. Instead, the church can be saved by the self's own expressive creativity. When such a perspective is assumed (and often tacitly so), the church and its leadership will again and again be attached to the spectral god of moneyed growth. We will be moved to judge the good church by the logic of growth, as Synod Executive Guy did before he was led to let go.

But by telling a group of nuns to let go of themselves, aren't Eckhart, Tauler, and the Mysterious Frankfurter simply revealing their medieval chauvinism? Eckhart and Tauler can easily let go because their own identities are assured as Dominican priors, and Eckhart even as a former professor. Aren't Eckhart and Tauler tone deaf to the identities of the women before them? Perhaps. But Eckhart and Tauler believe that letting go is not a complete departure from identity, nor a way of living beyond or above the importance of answering "Who am I?" We all need to wrestle with this question. The nothingness of the mystical way doesn't eliminate us, but it does move the answer to this question outside the self.

Eckhart believes that when we practice letting go, we find ourselves squarely on the ground (*Grunt*) of our most core identity. Eckhart and Tauler tell their nuns that the ground is a birthing place. When we let go, we find the ground beneath us that births the Word of God in our soul. When we let go, we find ourselves on the ground of being in Christ—and this alone is what saves the church.

On this ground we find that our identity, our very being, is in Christ. When the self is pulled out of itself, it is placed on the ground of its own being. On the ground of the self's being, it meets the being of Christ who exists outside the self but binds his own self with our self, taking us into Christ.

For Eckhart, Tauler, and the Mysterious Frankfurter, only on this ground can we truly discover Paul's words: "I [my self] no longer live [having entered the negative way of nothingness through letting go], but Christ [who has met us at the ground of being as we let go] lives in me" (Gal. 2:20). What will renew the church (what the fourteenth-century mystics think will reform it) are not the creative ideas of singularly exceptional selves imposing their innovations on the church. What renews the church is union with the once dead but now alive Christ.

If Fiona, Russ, and the other young adults are to do something creative for the church, they must learn to let go and instead cling to the backward power of the nothingness of the cross. They must let go by confession, being released from the drives for singularity and all the ways late-modern work in a neoliberal aesthetic economy curves the self in on itself by the torch of permanent innovation.

Only then can they, can we, participate in the creativity of God's own act, which is outside us but includes us in ministering new life to the world.

11

Aesthetic Epiphanies, Mad Poets, and
a Humble Example of What
This All Looks Like

What does creativity on the mystical path look like in concrete practice? A full view of the church formed for the theology of the cross is available in the final two chapters of *The Congregation in a Secular Age* and the whole of *Churches and the Crisis of Decline*.[1] Therefore, what's sketched below is something a little different.

To end this project, I'll share the story of a creative named Marksteen, who had an epiphany while working deeply in the aesthetic economy. By all measures, Marksteen was a raging success in the aesthetic economy—a true creative of the age of permanent innovation, creating ad campaigns for some of the most important global brands—but he had an epiphany that vibrated at the frequency of the mystical. This epiphany shook Marksteen loose from the expressivist drives to inflate the self. He felt drawn to help (to serve) the young people in his village by taking pictures and writing poetry. This was a move into the aesthetic, but more than that, it was shaped by the

---

1. Andrew Root, *The Congregation in a Secular Age: Keeping Sacred Time against the Speed of Modern Life* (Grand Rapids: Baker Academic, 2021), chaps. 16–17; Root, *Churches and the Crisis of Decline: A Hopeful, Practical Ecclesiology for a Secular Age* (Grand Rapids: Baker Academic, 2022).

cross. The pictures and poems gave these young people a different encounter with their own selves and others' selves. It led them into events of epiphany. Marksteen's initiative moved a small group of young people to encounters of seeing and naming the personhood of another, and thus to let go of the drive for expression.

This epiphany shifted Marksteen into a different kind of creativity that was fully cruciform to the self. Yet simultaneously, like the beginning of Luke and Matthew, it welcomed the arrival of personhood. The self meets the cross to be pulled into the event of epiphany. This epiphany of personhood calls us to follow the living Christ to the cross, to the *ground* as Eckhart would say, to find the true life of resurrection—a creativity bound fully in God's own being.

But before I can tell you the story of Marksteen and his epiphany, to appreciate its depth, we need to hear another tale of three friends who changed the world, seeding our expressivist imagination in ways that would eventually get us to an age of authenticity. Before concluding this project with Marksteen's story, we need to move from our three German amigos of the mystical way to three German seminary frat boys. These frat boys, coming out of the high-minded times of the new Enlightenment, sought to return to the mystical. But, at least for two of them, this return to the mystical could be done without concern for a personal or transcendent God. The third, however, who will become our sage, was different from his friends (and his contemporaries). Following Eckhart and giving himself fully to poetry, this third boy entered the mystical to find an encounter with a living god. Alas, this search for the mystical was wrapped up tightly with his sharp fall into madness.

When We All Hated Our Seminary

The year is 1790. Three talented young boys find themselves roommates at the Grand Evangelical Seminary in Tubingen. It's Animal House hundreds of years before *Animal House*. These three boys (two of them barely in their twenties, the third a young teenage prodigy) were brought together by their shared animosity for the seminary. Their friendship was fueled by a shared hatred. Nothing seems to bring students together like a mutual disdain for their school and its administration. As in *Animal House*, those who hated the administration and staff found each other and started revolting.

Yet these three didn't use kegs and house parties. Instead, they revolted by reading the new rock star Immanuel Kant and yearning for a new kind of poetry. They despised the seminary because they felt like they were living at the nadir of a great cultural and intellectual breakthrough. The Enlightenment was about to produce its next stage, a particularly German response. Yet the dumb seminary, with its old professors, didn't seem to notice or, worse, care.

From the seminary dorm room of these three roommates, the Western world changed forever. Everyone, including the three frat boys, assumed that if anything epic were to come from the rowdy room, it would come from the mind of the youngest, Friedrich Wilhelm Joseph Schelling. He seemed poised to break new ground. Schelling was no slouch, becoming the youngest professor ever at the University of Jena. But though he was the brightest star at the seminary, he ended up not shining the brightest of the three.

That honor went to the supposedly dumbest, Georg Wilhelm Friedrich Hegel. Hegel, much to Schelling's jealousy, became one of the greatest philosophical minds ever. He created one of the most interesting philosophical systems the Western world has ever known. Poor Schelling, to his dying day, believed that his once seminary roommate had stolen his ideas. But when embittered Schelling tried to show how, even after taking the deceased Hegel's chair in Berlin, no one could see it.[2] These two friends-turned-rivals sought a new kind of philosophy that completely embraced reason but also returned to something resembling the mystical. It was a mysticism that would have to be deeply reworked now that they found themselves on the other side of the Enlightenment. The mystical had to be stripped of personal transcendence, of any real, direct encounter with a personal God. For Hegel, history held together reason and a driving Romantic impulse for the mystical (particularly in nature). Spirit (*Geist*) was still in the world, but it was inextricably bound in the unfolding of history, *not* in transcendent otherness.

The third boy was Friedrich Hölderlin. He escaped all the tussles about who was the greatest philosopher. Though he was no philosophical simpleton,

2. In those lectures sat a young Søren Kierkegaard. Kierkegaard was excited to watch Schelling destroy Hegel. Kierkegaard shared with Schelling a similar annoyance with Hegel. But after a few lectures, Kierkegaard realized that whatever Schelling was saying was not refuting Hegel's genius. Kierkegaard remained frustrated with Hegel, but he would need to topple the giant himself, because Schelling was no help.

he went another direction. Sadly, he also eventually went mad. Hölderlin became the greatest German poet since Eckhart. Yet this poetic direction was not unrelated to philosophy. Poetry was the means, the portal, by which he would get at what the new enlightened philosophy, particularly from France, couldn't access. Poetry, Hölderlin believed, could glimpse and attain these mystical elements of consciousness that the French Enlightenment could not. These young Germans were reminding the world that our minds contained more than reason. Our consciousness, our reason, wants much more than mathematics and the new unaffected and disconnected science. The mind also yearns for, can actually never escape, the feelings of love, desire, mystery, beauty, and terror. No disconnected reason can escape such realities. The frat boys were not necessarily rejecting the Enlightenment wholesale, but they were heralding that the Enlightenment needed to add a Romantic, even mystical, impulse to it.

This added impulse became necessary because the French Enlightenment met a French imperialism that imposed a kind of second-class status on those in the German nations. It particularly belittled German culture. The frat boys, and others before them, recognized that there was a Romantic genius in the German culture—a genius that went back through Luther to our mystical three amigos. Its culture contained an impulse to wrestle with the deepest realities of suffering, love, beauty, and dying. Nature itself was specimen for study, by a living reality of mystery. The frat boys had read older philosophers, like Goethe and Herder, who argued that every culture contained genius. Goethe's novels and poetry touched on this reality. Reason could not recognize the unique cultural expressions, nor could it know how these cultural expressions touched a certain mystical depth. The world changed—the spirit of history arrived—not through reasoned experiment but in expressions of the strong will, drawing from a depth and imposing a new direction (a new spirit) on a culture and its history.

The three frat boys (but particularly Hegel) admired Napoleon Bonaparte. At the beginning, Napoleon was believed to be the great hope from outside Paris (and outside royal privilege) who, by sure expressive will (by his very personality), would impose a new cultural order on all of Europe. With Napoleon on the throne in Paris (a throne constructed from the new iron of reason *and* imposing his expressive will), all things seemed possible in Europe. Napoleon was a concrete example of what reason and romance could do together—the impossible!

Many young Germans, particularly our three frat boys, admired how from inner genius and drive, Napoleon could do what seemed impossible—completely take down the ancien régime and its ancient orders, bringing the dawn of a new history. It felt spiritual and deeply mystical. Until it didn't. Napoleon became not a hero but a tyrant. The young frat boys at first watched with awe, dreaming of what could be. But the dream became a nightmare. Napoleon failed to be what the boys and many others believed he could be. This was particularly depressing for poor Hegel.[3]

Yet what Napoleon did was assure these frat boys that whatever was coming out of the Enlightenment (in both affirmation and critique) needed to be cultural. Building off Kant but taking it in a new direction, a German Romanticism was produced as a response to French Empiricism. It wasn't enough to have science and observable laws; there were also other truths, more mystical in nature, that revealed deeper ways of being. The way to access these deeper ways, Goethe showed, was through art and, most fully, poetry.

The third boy, Hölderlin, did his philosophical work as a poet, becoming the greatest German language poet since Meister Eckhart, surpassing the great Goethe. It was young men like Hölderlin who returned to Eckhart, bringing him back into Western recollection. More than Eckhart's theology, these young thinkers drew from Eckhart's beautiful use of the German language to describe the depth of the soul and its longings. Eckhart's beautiful use of language helped produce the new outlook they called *idealism* and *Romanticism*.

Hölderlin and the Event of Epiphany

Hölderlin became *the* poet of (and he possessed much of the DNA that would eventually move us into) the age of authenticity—although we will see that Romanticism's drive for authenticity to fetishize uniqueness and singularity loses something essential to Hölderlin's vision. Nevertheless, the Romantics were necessary for us to arrive at an age of authenticity, and they also led us to the glorification of singularity and its apotheosizing of creativity and uniqueness. Even so, we shouldn't miss that there is indeed something beautiful and important about the Romantics. (I'm personally more of a Romantic

3. Arthur Schopenhauer (maybe the greatest of all Hegel haters) believed that Hegel's system was really just a way of coping with Hegel's disappointment with Napoleon. It seems too simple, but Schopenhauer thought Hegel was a simple arse.

than not.) This Romantic disposition reminds us of the depth of the soul and the spirit. It seeks beauty more than rational fact, believing beauty to be more truthful than the truth that reason can possess. Hölderlin's lines and meter show how.

Yet, by the early 1800s, Hölderlin's genius of expression was turning on him. He was losing his mind (which sadly only added to his Romantic credibility). Eventually, the greatest poet in German history could be found wandering in parks, sleeping on benches, talking to people who weren't there. Tourists came seeking him out, hoping to glimpse the mad genius lost in his own mind. After being committed against his will and then released from a mental institution in 1806, Hölderlin settled back in Tubingen. There the great poet was placed in the custody of a foster family, kept in the building that after his death was called Hölderlin's Tower. It, too, became a tourist site.

Hölderlin and his frat brothers all agreed that a sense of the mystical was necessary, but only Hölderlin believed that this vital mystical turn needed to be an epiphany with a living, encountering god.[4] Such a turn was necessary to keep the self from turning in on itself. Hölderlin more than anyone else knew how the self could become a prison, attacking itself. The two other frat boys—particularly Hegel—returned to a kind of mystical reality but laminated this mystical reality onto impersonal ideas. God was returned to, but God's personal action of arriving in the world, acting and speaking, was lost to the ideas of historical struggle.

Hölderlin could not abide this. He was like Eckhart, who so deeply sought to encounter the living God who acts in the world that he prayed to God to deliver him from all ideas of God so that he might encounter the true epiphany of God's arriving. Eckhart claimed that God was nothing, because the God who acts as epiphany is dependent on nothing—certainly not ideas, human wills, of historical occurrence. This God is fully and completely an epiphany.[5] Hölderlin, for his own reasons, followed this thinking.

4. Hölderlin's sense of transcendence is intricately argued in Thomas R. Spencer, "'Was ist Gott?' The Representation of the Divine in Friedrich Hölderlin" (PhD diss., University of North Carolina, Chapel Hill, 2008), https://cdr.lib.unc.edu/concern/dissertations/ng451j651.

5. Charles Taylor says of Hölderlin and being personally captivated by his work, "Not only does Hölderlin's poetry show us and convince us that everything is held together in the world, it also gives us the very strong impression of touching this mystery, of being fully incorporated in it. His art does more than reveal: it also creates a relationship that makes us partake in something." Taylor, *Avenues of Faith* (Waco: Baylor University Press, 2020).

Mind you, Hölderlin was no orthodox theologian! Far from it. Hölderlin exchanged the Christian God of Eckhart for Dionysus—the god of wine. Even so, Hölderlin believed that this god arrived as an epiphany. Like Eckhart,[6] Hölderlin moved past speculative metaphysics and believed a true god must act in the world. For Hölderlin, the God or the gods were *not* just an idea but an event of encounter. The other two frat boys also returned to the ancient Greek gods for inspiration. But only Hölderlin believed Dionysus truly and personally acted in the world. Hölderlin called him *der kommende Gott*, the "god who's to come."[7] This god is no mere idea: he arrives, acting in the world.

Not unlike Luther, who was seeded with such thoughts from Tauler and the Mysterious Frankfurter, it was word (the Word) that was inextricable from this eventual epiphany of arrival. The arrival becomes known in the depth of its encounter as it's testified to in proclamation, narrative story, and poem (the genres of the biblical text that the confessing church uses in its confession of nothingness and loss through prayer). "Hölderlin lived and breathed in his poems; in the world of their language he hoped to bring a durability and dependability to his epiphanic moments."[8]

Hölderlin teaches us, as he stands against the grain of a secular age of immanence, the importance of the epiphanic. As Hölderlin's mind turned on him, he yearned all the more for his expression to not inflate his self but for his self to be lost in rest with God, who was beyond and yet came near in God's beyondness. Hölderlin, like Eckhart, sought an aesthetic that awakens to the world, not by drawing us into our own expressive creativity but by opening us to an epiphany. Hölderlin's creative act names, interprets, and articulates in the feeble beauty of words and meter the soul encountering an epiphany of the transcendent mystery. His creative act is not just a means to express the self. Inside the event of epiphany—an encounter with something outside of you—the poem is prayer! Prayer, particularly the psalms, is poetry that seeks to articulate the presence and absence of the arriving God of epiphany. The creative act of a praying poet of epiphany is not a performance of the self; it intends to lose the self—and then find it again—inside the encounter with the event of epiphany.[9]

6. And Luther and Barth after him (and Eberhard Jüngel and Robert Jenson after Barth).

7. Rüdiger Safranski, *Romanticism: A German Affair* (Evanston, IL: Northwestern University Press, 2014), 105.

8. Safranski, *Romanticism*, 109.

9. This connection to prayer links with the final chapter of my book *The Pastor in a Secular Age* (Grand Rapids: Baker Academic, 2019). There I claim that the way of being a pastor in a secular age is to teach people to pray. Here I drive that claim deeper.

The thin tradition of the theology of the cross—which not surprisingly venerates the psalms—focuses on the cross but not *in spite of* the incarnation. It is not a substitutionary focus on the cross. Rather, it attends to the cross as the complete and full manifestation of the epiphany of God's incarnation in Jesus Christ (for Luther, the cross is the hermeneutic of divine action, not a mechanism or machine of atonement). The theology of the cross claims that God's ministering of life out of death starts and ends with epiphany. It starts and ends with the event of the baby in the manger in Bethlehem who is true God of true God. This epiphany, and our mystical call to contemplate it in silence and poetry, moves us to find ourselves by losing ourselves in the grand event of God's arriving in the world. We lose ourselves not in masochistic or pietist religious effort but inside the beauty and glory of the epiphany.

Back to Charles Taylor for the Last Time

We can rework the aesthetic by giving different ground to creativity than the misguided expressivism that inflates the self. It is inside encounter and participation in the creativity as epiphany (which doesn't inflate but relativizes the self, as Eckhart does) that the self is moved to let go so that the self can receive a gift from outside the self. This gift to the self is bound to, even abounds with, the encounter with the epiphany of a transcendent personhood.[10] Through this epiphanic encounter, we are drawn into an aesthetic that cannot be colonized by the economy (which, as we've seen, innovation has been). An epiphanic aesthetic is free of this colonization because it is not moneyed. It is pure gift. It is an event of being overtaken by a creativity that has its source not in our self but in something that arrives, in an event of encounter in the world.

Almost all craftspersons speak of something like this mystical creativity (Instagram influencers almost never do). Craftspersons speak of a creativity that fully includes the self but has its source far outside the self. It is a creativity like Mary's own epiphany in Luke 1. It completely includes her, unable to

10. I discuss Christos Yannaras in the final chapter of *The Congregation in a Secular Age*, exploring a creativity that escapes the subjective trap by focusing on personhood. Creativity is an *eros* that avoids idolatry only through personhood. See Yannaras, *Person and Eros* (Brookline, MA: Holy Cross Orthodox, 2007). Yannaras discusses poetry in his little book, *Variations on the Song of Songs* (Brookline, MA: Holy Cross Orthodox, 2005).

be disconnected from her body and being. But it does not come from her; the child in her womb has no source in her own creativity. This epiphanic arrival demands simply reception. Mary's response shows humility, not inflation of the self. "Who am I to receive this gift?" she asks (paraphrase of Luke 1:43). In receiving, she feels blessed, gifted.[11] She is blessed by this encounter that allows her to participate in God's fullest creative act to save the world by flooding the world with the beauty of God's own personhood in the baby in her womb. Mary is the great (the greatest!) poet of epiphany.[12] Her Magnificat is so beautifully haunting and stirring. Hölderlin and Eckhart pale in comparison. They do so because they are not blessed like Mary to receive the gift of this full epiphany; she is the favored one. Mary shows us that the faithful response to the gift of epiphany is to allow poetry to spill from your being in response to the epiphany.

Charles Taylor, at the end of *Sources of the Self*, suggests that this epiphanic aesthetic is needed as a medicine for late-modern overindulgence of the self. For Taylor, the epiphanic aesthetic can hold together the goods of the age of authenticity and the importance of creativity without allowing both to fall into the self-involved temptations of the aesthetic economy and drive for singularity, which we've named above. Scholar Brian Braman says that Taylor holds that "an epiphany is a manifestation which brings us into the presence of something which is otherwise inaccessible, and which is of the highest moral or spiritual significance. It is in poetry that Taylor finds the clearest expression of epiphanic events."[13] Taylor thinks poetry is so important because it can show "concern for the subject, without falling into a disordered subjectivity."[14]

Hölderlin-inspired (or, better, Mary-inspired) poetry that seeks or opens itself to epiphany allows the self and its creativity to matter. In turn, this epiphanic reality keeps creativity from falling into the excesses of the self that

11. I discuss giftedness further in chap. 11 and the conclusion of *Faith Formation in a Secular Age* (Grand Rapids: Baker Academic, 2017).

12. This connects to the final two chapters of my book *The Congregation in a Secular Age*. Children, being creative, do their creativity in an epiphanic way. Children do all sorts of creative things, but the drive is never money or singularity, but to feel connected to the world—for the sake of resonance. They do art because of the way the world unveils itself in the act. It is all about the epiphany.

13. Brian J. Braman, "Epiphany and Authenticity: The Aesthetic Vision of Charles Taylor," in *Beauty, Art, and the Polis*, ed. Alice Ramos (Washington, DC: Catholic University of America Press, 2000), 225, which I lean on heavily in this section.

14. Braman, "Epiphany and Authenticity," 225.

the aesthetic economy and the drive for singularity wishes. Taylor quotes the British poet Percy Shelley, "The poet strips the veil of familiarity from the world, and lays bare the naked and sleeping beauty which is the spirit of its form."[15]

Perhaps in our secular age of authenticity and the drive for singularity, what the church needs isn't innovators and entrepreneurs but poets who pray. We need more Eugene Petersons than Rick Warrens, more Kendrick Lamars than Mark Zuckerbergs. We need poets who seek the epiphanic, losing their self in the beauty of the event of God's arrival, recognizing that their poems are prayers. Their prayer is poetry. Can innovation be epiphanic? Maybe. But not as it's constituted now, not without its crucifixion, not without its release from an expressivist, Napoleon-like will to dominate by disruption. Innovation, without bearing the cross, is too bound in the logic of money. It is therefore obsessed with forming (schooling) not poets but entrepreneurs. As we've seen, innovation overindulges the subjectivity of creativity, glorifying not gift but performance.

So how do we find and form (school) these poets of epiphany who pray their poems and whose poems are prayers? We can never control the arrival of the epiphany. We just have to wait (something late capitalism hates). But while waiting, we can form ourselves, and be formed by others, to take on the practices of waiting and discovering the words needed to give testimony to the arrival of epiphany. The way we find these poets is through a form of catechesis. We forge a school of poets.

A small but dynamic expression of such a school—which wouldn't even see itself as a school—has already started in a village about a three-hour train ride away from London.

Concluding with the Story of Marksteen

Marksteen looks the part and has the résumé of a creative who can chase and has even captured singularity inside the aesthetic economy. His firm, which he owns with his brother-in-law, has run marketing campaigns for some of the top global brands. Marksteen's creative photography is what separates his firm. His own persona is a blend of Nordic noblemen in jeans, a trendy hat,

15. Shelley, *A Defence of Poetry* (London: Edward Moxon, Dover Street, 1840), quoted by Charles Taylor, *Sources of the Self: The Making of the Modern Identity* (Cambridge, MA: Harvard University Press, 1989), 377.

and a Patagonia jacket. The British accent and Nordic style are completely genuine, yet they clearly signal that Marksteen is a creative of the aesthetic economy from top to bottom.

One day while his mind should have been on a campaign to help another brand capture the market through finding their unique creativity, he was swept into an epiphany. He began to notice a group of young people in his village. He decided to talk with them. Quickly he realized they were in crisis. The cultural drives for expressive singularity, the push to be obsessed with the self, had turned on them. They were lonely, apathetic, and depressed. Encountering the epiphany of their personhood, Marksteen felt the call of ministry. He felt a need to pray for them, but even more to invite them to pray. Yet all he could think to do, as he watched them numbingly scroll through Instagram photos, was to ask, "Hey, do you want to learn to take great pictures? I can teach you."

Soon Marksteen was meeting with them, showing them how light worked and what it meant to take a portrait. Marksteen had been drawn to them through the epiphanic, and so he intuitively stayed there. He taught them that the key to taking a good portrait was to really encounter—as an epiphany—the personhood of the other. And that requires waiting attentively on the person. But also attending to the light. These practices of being attentive to the light as it encounters the face of another person forced the young people to truly see others, to stand inside the epiphany of their personhood. Marksteen taught them that a good portrait is like poetry. It opens you to an encounter; it opens the world by stripping away the veil of the familiar. Soon enough Marksteen was asking them to write poems—not about themselves but about this other that they were intently and caringly encountering as an epiphany of personhood. The slow experience of seeing the other and naming them in poetry thrust the young people into the epiphanic. Soon life was spilling into this little school as their minds and hearts were drawn away from their selves to another.

After a time, the catechesis (the schooling) evolved. Now in groups of three (one person minding the light, another the camera, and the third getting their picture taken), young people were writing poems about each other—and, with poem in hand, they moved to the portrait. The portrait and the poem served as the layers of the epiphanic, making the whole experience for each group of three an epiphany. This school opposed in every way the selfie culture of singularity and demanded that in words and in vision they see

the other as an epiphany of personhood. Writing a poem and the honor of
capturing something true of another in the poem opened the world to these
young people, spilling it over with transcendence. The poems and the pictures
became cruciform. The self was relativized as the other was attended to, most
often through their longings and losses. It drew them all beyond their self
while totally including their selves. The most powerful experience became the
unveiling of the poems and photos themselves. Placing the poems alongside
the photos on display became an event of unveiling, a revelation of beauty,
pathos, and life. It became testimony, a shared event of epiphany, a small but
sure reverberation of the Magnificat.

The young people, through this little school of poetry and pictures, became
ministers to one another. Through epiphany, they followed the way of the cross
and did the most profound thing that can be done in a world that inflates the
self by driving for singularity: they saw and named the personhood of each
other. They attended to the other as an epiphany that included their own
creativity, not for the sake of performance but for the sake of being pulled
deeper into life, into encounter, into the mystery of transcendence coming
through the longing eyes of another beckoning for the friendship of ministry.

The young poets were drawn deeply into the world by placing their young
minds on the event of encounter with personhood. The poem and its photo
opened the world. Inside its openness, through the dawning of personhood,
the self was relativized and yet embraced. The creativity sought not singularity but epiphany.

Marksteen can tell you story after story about how the ministry of the
poem and the photo brought new life out of death, new community out of
isolation, killing the inflated self as it was brought back to life. The whole
process feels like prayer (because it is).[16] It brings forth an event of encounter.
Marksteen calls this school of poets PEEL. It peels away the performance of
the self, allowing young people to lose their selves, to let go as they encounter

16. In his insightful book *Thinking Prayer*, Andrew Prevot draws on Heidegger and his
reading of Hölderlin, saying, "In such an apparently godforsaken age there is a great need
for the poet. The poet's task is 'to attend, singing, to the trace of the fugitive gods.' The poet
is called to speak of the gods, to receive them as they appear, to seek them as they flee, all in
preparation for a final coming of the truly divine God that has not yet been granted. In short,
poetry offers doxology as a response to modernity. Poetic dwelling implies a kind of prayerful
dwelling, a dwelling that seeks and praises both being and the godly figures that it hides and
manifests—and Heidegger argues that this is precisely what the modern world needs." Prevot,
Thinking Prayer: Theology and Spirituality amid the Crises of Modernity (South Bend, IN:
Notre Dame University Press, 2015), 56.

the event of the epiphany of another, giving word and vision to another not as a service for their self but as a proclamation of this other's value—not as singular but as a gift loved by the God who arrives. This small example of a way forward testifies that it may be necessary for us in the church to pivot from innovation hubs to schools of poetry.

INDEX

accountability, 80–82, 83
aesthetic economy, 144–52
affirmation of the self, 167
Albert the Great, 201, 208–13
alcohol use, 51n23
Anselm, 192
anxiety, 103–4
apophatic rule, 213n17
Apple, 11–12, 98
Applebee's Boy, 1–3, 21–22, 61–64, 141–42, 205
Aquinas, Thomas, 201, 208–13
Arnoul of Orleans, 189–90
art, 24–25, 29–30
attention deficiency syndrome, 150n13
attention economy, 124–25
audience, 151n14, 152–54, 154n19
Augustine, 193–94, 210
authenticity, 13–17, 49, 85, 119–20, 229

baby boomer generation, 50–53
balance of power, 42
Balthasar, Hans Urs von, 156n21
basic, being, 160–61, 166
Bearded Brown Turtleneck, 22, 35, 61–64, 75, 87–88, 141–42, 204
Beat Generation, 50n21

beauty, 24–25, 28, 29–30
Bell, Daniel, 49n19, 50, 50n20, 53
belonging, 132–33, 167
Bernard of Clairvaux, 69–71, 70nn19–20
Bonaparte, Napoleon, 228–29
bravery, 167–68
Bröckling, Ulrich, 104n16, 114n3, 152n15
Brown, Brené, 125, 168
Brown, Tim, 147n8
Buddhism, 216n23
bullying, 14

Calvinist Protestantism, and capitalism, 76–78, 79n34
capitalism, 49n19, 50
    and the aesthetic economy, 144–45, 148–52
    contradictions of, 54–55, 63n3, 64–65, 76–82, 100–105
    as Darwinian calculation of human lives, 198n20
    durability of, 148
    emotional capitalism, 115–17
    entrepreneurship in, 57–60, 87
    flexibility and agility in, 59
    and growth rates, 53–60
    hoarding excesses of late, 74–75

origin of, 72–78
    and rise of counterculture, 50–53
cathedral crusade, 67–70
celebrity, 152
Challenger shuttle explosion, 89–90, 95–96
Chicago school of economics, 53n27, 58n40
child-centrism, 181n22
children, 233n12
church
    denominational standardization, 163–66
    falling behind the creativity dispositif, 143
    management and, 92–94
Churches and the Crisis of Decline (Root), 225
church growth movement, 93
Cistercian abbeys, 70nn19–20
clerical hierarchy, 28
Clinton, Bill, 153n18
Clinton, Hillary, 179
coaching, as management, 117
Cold Intimacies: The Making of Emotional Capitalism (Illouz), 115–16
Cold War, 47–50
competition, individual, 114, 133, 136
competition, market, 58n38

Congregation in a Secular Age, The (Root), 225, 233n12
consumer age, 47–48, 49–50
corporations
  culture of, 108
  duty to, 82–84
  protection of, 57–58
counterculture, 50–53, 74, 123
courage, 167–68
COVID-19 pandemic, 203–5
creativity
  creativity dispositif, 141–44
  epiphanic and mystical, 232–34
  etymology, 34n16
  as expressive act of the self, 109, 155–56
  God as source and end, 33–34
  and indispensability of the self, 169–71
  individual vs. communal, 38–39
  and mission, 39
  as principle of innovation, 8–13, 33–35
  as religion, 152n15
  and work, 29–30
crusades, 65–67, 67n13
Cultural Contradictions of Capitalism (Bell), 49n19, 50, 50n20
culture, corporate, 108
culture wars, 177–80

Dale, Gareth, 41n5
Dangerous Mystic: Meister Eckhart's Path to the God Within (Harrington), 220
Darwin, Charles, 42n8
debt, 199
denominational standardization, 163–66
depression, 104
design, 145–47
desire, 194
detachment, 219–24
difference. *See* singularity
differentiation, 161–62

Dionysus, 231
dispositif
  about, 139–41
  aesthetic economy, 144–52
  audience and the star system, 152–54
  creative dispositif, 141–44, 150n13
  design in, 145–47
divorce, innovation after, 7–8
Dominican order, 191, 194, 201
Doyle, Glennon, 8n3
Drucker, Peter, 90–91, 90n1
Durham Cathedral, 68–69
duty, 49, 80–84

Eat, Pray, Love (Gilbert), 7n2
Eckhart, Meister, 201–2, 206–7, 208–13, 215–16, 223, 231
Economic Consequences of the Peace, The (Keynes), 45n12
Edison, Thomas, 9–10
education, 118n9, 180–81
Ehrenberg, Alain, 104
emotional capitalism, 115–17, 148–49, 150
emotions, 109, 120–24
empathy, 147n8
Enlightenment, 66n9, 227–29
Entrepreneurial Self: Fabricating a New Type of Subject, The (Bröckling), 114n3
entrepreneurial selfhood, 104–10
entrepreneurship
  arrival of, 84–88
  innovation, and the secular, 63–65, 72
  rise of, 57–60
epiphanic aesthetic, 231–37
ethic of authenticity, 13n12, 14–15. *See also* authenticity
ethic of work, 75–78
European peace and prosperity, 40–46
evaluation, 182–85

exceptionality
  about, 171–72
  demand for, 180–82
  expectation of, 174–76
  God's love and, 176n14
  and the middle class, 177–80
  necessity of the social and, 176–77
  recognition and value in, 172–73
  See also self, the
Explaining Creativity (Sawyer), 33

faith, 81–82
faith formation, 158–60, 166
faithfulness, innovation and, 19–20
family, 167, 168
fascism, 56n34
feelings, 26–27
feminism, 51n23
Fiona (grant group), 136, 137–39, 156, 219, 222
flexibility, 128–30
Foucault, Michel, 114n2, 139
401(k), 86n45
Franciscan order, 191, 201
Francis I, 25
Francis of Assisi, 187–88
Franco-Prussian War, 40n2
freedom, 15n16
Freud, Sigmund, 120–24
Friedman, Milton, 53n27, 54–55
fundamentalism, 55n33
funding creativity, 8–13

Gates, Bill, 38
gender, and public-private domains, 118–19
gig economy, 58n39
Gilbert, Elizabeth, 7n2
Gillis, John R., 118n9
Gimpel, Jean, 67n13
God, the self encountering, 213–18
Godforsakenness, 210, 211

gold, 189, 196
gold standard, international,
    43–45, 54–55
Goodchild, Philip, 192, 193n9
gothic cathedrals, 67–70
Grand Evangelical Seminary,
    226
Great Transformation, The
    (Polanyi), 41–46
ground (*Grunt*), 212n15,
    219–24
growth, 204
    creativity and, 11–13
    economic, 47–50
    neoliberalism and, 54n30
growth rates, economic, 53–60
grunge, 113
guilds, 68n15
Gunthram, King, 189, 190

Hamann, Johann, 34n16
Han, Byung-Chul, 147n8
happy hour, 57n36, 101n9
Hayek, Friedrich, 53n27, 54–55
health care, 180–81
Hegel, Georg Wilhelm Fried-
    rich, 206n2, 227–29
hip-hop, 113
hoarding, 74–75
Hölderlin, Friedrich, 34n16,
    227–28, 229–32
home, sphere of, 118, 122–23
humanism, 26
humility, 233

IBM, 98
idealism, 229
identity, work and, 106–10
identity formation, 167–68, 223
Illouz, Eva, 115–16, 118, 119,
    120n12
imago Dei, 212n15
incarnation, 232
indispensability, 169–71
individual freedom, 43–44
industrial revolution, 30–33
inequality, economic and so-
    cial, 56n34

inflation, 58n37
innovation
    after divorce, 7–8
    arrival of, 84–88
    built on waste, 9–10
    creativity and, 4, 33–35
    detachment and, 221
    entrepreneurship, the secular
        and, 63–65
    evaluation and cancer of,
        182–85
    faithfulness and, 19–20
    flexibility and, 128–30
    management of permanent,
        97–100
    in Middle Ages, 20n20
    and mission, 6–7, 9, 17–18
    permanent and continual,
        97–99, 101–5, 174–75
    in post-industrial societies,
        32–33
    young adults and, 112–15
    See also exceptionality
*Innovation and Entrepreneur-
    ship* (Drucker), 90–91
Inside Bill's Brain (docuseries),
    37–38, 61
internet, 113
Invention of Creativity, The
    (Reckwitz), 102, 106n19,
    141

James, LeBron, 142n4
James, William, 118n8
Jennings, Willie James, 9n5
Jobs, Steve, 171n8
Jordan, Michael, 142n4
judgment, 16–17, 182–85
justice, 62
justification, 27, 78, 82

Kant, Immanuel, 227
Kanter, Rosabeth Moss, 129–30
*Karl Polanyi: A Life on the
    Left* (Dale), 41n5
kenosis of Christ, 217n24
Keynes, John Maynard, 45–46,
    45nn12–13, 48n17

Keynesianism, 58n37, 162
Kierkegaard, Søren, 227n2

laity, medieval, 66n11
Leave It to Beaver (TV show),
    92–93, 123
Leonardo da Vinci, 25
letting go (detachment), 219–24
liberal state, 43, 45–46
liberty, 15n16
Lilly Endowment, 31
Little, Lester, 189
Little Women (Alcott), 120, 121
loyalty, 82n41. *See also* duty
Lucas, William, 96
Luhmann, Niklas, 24nn2–3
Luther, Martin, 26, 27n8, 29,
    31–32

machine and factory, 30–32
Malthus, Thomas Robert, 42,
    42n8
management
    Challenger explosion and,
        95–96
    counterculture and, 84
    emotional capitalism, 115–17
    of the entrepreneurial self,
        104–10
    flexibility, 128–30
    innovation and the self,
        126–36
    innovation and workers,
        99–100
    midlevel, 108n24
    permanent innovation and,
        97–99
    rise of, 90–95
    team, 132–36
    team projects, 130–32
Marcuse, Herbert, 53n27
market, self-regulating, 42–43,
    54–57
Markkula, Mike, 11
Marksteen, 225–26, 234–37
Marx, Karl, 148
Marxism, 73n24
Mary (mother of Jesus), 232–33